The Three Stigmata of Friedrich Nietzsche

The Three Stigmata of Friedrich Nietzsche

Political Physiology in the Age of Nihilism

Nandita Biswas Mellamphy
University of Western Ontario, Canada

palgrave
macmillan

First published 2011 by
PALGRAVE MACMILLAN

Palgrave Macmillan in the UK is an imprint of Macmillan Publishers Limited, registered in England, company number 785998, of Houndmills, Basingstoke, Hampshire RG21 6XS.

Palgrave Macmillan in the US is a division of St Martin's Press LLC, 175 Fifth Avenue, New York, NY 10010.

Palgrave Macmillan is the global academic imprint of the above companies and has companies and representatives throughout the world.

ISBN 978–0–230–28255–1 hardback

This book is printed on paper suitable for recycling and made from fully managed and sustained forest sources. Logging, pulping and manufacturing processes are expected to conform to the environmental regulations of the country of origin.

A catalogue record for this book is available from the British Library.

Library of Congress Cataloging-in-Publication Data

Biswas Mellamphy, Nandita, author.
The Three Stigmata of Friedrich Nietzsche : Political Physiology in the Age of Nihilism / Nandita Biswas Mellamphy.
p. cm
Includes bibliographical references and index.
ISBN 978–0–230–28255–1 (hardback)
1. Nietzsche, Friedrich Wilhelm, 1844–1900. 2. Political science—Philosophy. 3. Nihilism. I. Title.
B3317.B575 2011
193—dc22 2010042397

10 9 8 7 6 5 4 3 2 1
20 19 18 17 16 15 14 13 12 11

Printed and bound in Great Britain by
CPI Antony Rowe, Chippenham and Eastbourne

for Dan
for ever

In Hindu mythology [...]
The entire cycle of human evolution is figured [...] in the form of a cow,
symbolizing *Virtue,*
each of whose four feet rests on one of the sectors
representing the four ages of the world.
In the first age,
corresponding to the Greek age of gold and called the *Creda Yuga* or age of innocence,
Virtue is firmly established on earth: the cow stands squarely on four legs.
In the *Treda Yuga,* or second age,
corresponding to the age of silver, it is weakened and stands only on three legs.
During the *Dwapara Yuga,* or third age,
which is the age of bronze, it is reduced to two legs.
Finally, in the age of iron, our own age,
the cyclical cow or human virtue reaches the utmost degree of feebleness and senility:
it is scarcely able to stand,
balancing only on one leg.
It is the fourth and last age, the *Kali Yuga,*
the age of misery, misfortune and decrepitude.
The age of iron has no other seal than that of Death.
Its hieroglyph is the skeleton bearing [...] the empty hourglass,
symbol of time run out, and the scythe, reproduced in the figure seven,
which is the number of transformation, of destruction, and of annihilation.
The Gospel of this fatal age is the one written under the inspiration of Saint Matthew.
Matthaeus, the Greek *Ματϑαίος,* comes from *Μάϑημα* and *Μάϑηματος,*
which means Science. [...]
It is the Gospel according to Science,
the last of all but for us the first,
because it teaches us that,
save for a small number of the élite,
we must all perish.

Fulcanelli, *Le mystère des cathédrales*

Contents

Acknowledgements

This book would not have been possible without the love and support of my husband, Dan, of my parents in Winnipeg and London, of my sister and her family in Ottawa, of my extended family in Toronto, of my dear friends (with special thanks to Scott Bakker and Sharron O'Brien) and of my canine sidekick 'El Moserino' (Moses Mellamphy).

My deepest thanks go to John Protevi, Keith Ansell-Pearson, Debra Bergoffen, Peter Sedgwick and the inimitable Horst Hutter for their generous comments on various drafts of this manuscript and the inspiration which their work has given me over the years. My appreciation and admiration also go out to Babette Babitch, Gary Shapiro, Heike Schotten, Vanessa Lemm, Don Dombowsky, Tracy Strong and Rainer Hanshe for their kind and constructive feedback at conferences where I presented portions of this work. I am also grateful to Bernard Stiegler and Barbara Stiegler for wonderful and productive interchanges that have directly contributed to the content of this book. I would also like to thank Francine Prévost at the *Maison Gai Saber*, Verónica Schild and Tony Calcagno at the *Centre for the Study of Theory and Criticism* and Nick Srnicek at *The Accursed Share/Speculative Heresy*, for their ongoing support of *The Nietzsche Workshop @ Western* and for providing me with venues to develop and present ideas from this work.

The University of Western Ontario's *Department of Political Science* and *Faculty of Social Science*, along with the *Social Science and Humanities Research Council of Canada* (SSHRCC), have provided both time and funding for portions of this work. Students who participated in my Nietzsche Seminars and in the annual *Nietzsche Workshop @ Western* have helped me develop many of the ideas in this book. Terence McKenna and Norberto Crenucci have been exemplars for me of Nietzschean 'philosophers of the future'. My thanks go to all of the above, to M. Bhuvanaraj, Melanie Blair and Priyanka Gibbons at Palgrave Macmillan, to The Brotherhood of Life publishing house for permission to use as epigraph an extract from Mary Sworder's translation of *Le mystère des cathédrales*, and to you, my dear reader, wherever and whoever you are.

Preface: The Three Stigmata

> I am still waiting for a philosophical physician in the exceptional sense of that word – one who has to pursue the problem of the total health of a people, time, race or of humanity – to muster the courage to push my suspicion to its limits and to risk the proposition: what was at stake in all philosophizing hitherto was not at all 'truth' but something else – let us say, health, future, growth, power, life.
>
> *GS* Preface: §2

> You ought to be the one that knows; you remember what you saw. All three stigmata: the dead, artificial hand, the [slits for] eyes, and the radically deranged jaw. Symbols of its inhabitation, he thought. In our midst. But not asked for. Not intentionally summoned. And we have no mediating sacraments through which to protect ourselves; we can't compel it, by our careful, time-honored, clever, painstaking rituals, to confine itself to specific elements such as bread and water or bread and wine. It is out in the open, ranging in every direction. It looks into our eyes, and it looks out of our eyes.
>
> Philip K. Dick, *The Three Stigmata of Palmer Eldritch* (1964)

The stigmatics of political physiology

In the following study, I examine three concepts found in the thought of Friedrich Nietzsche, but which are not usually treated together in the secondary scholarship: first, in the domain of his political thought, Nietzsche's concept of 'great politics'; second, in the phenomenological domain, his concept of 'eternal recurrence'; and finally, set against the backdrop of his materialist theory of the self-overcoming subject, the concept of 'the philosopher of the future'. None of these concepts are given explicit or systematic definition in Nietzsche's work, and yet arguably each one is *crucial*, and collectively they are the *crux* of Nietzsche's thought.

Why do I call these three central but ephemeral Nietzschean notions 'stigmata'? On one level, I invoke them as physiological symptoms, as bodily marks that resemble or mimic an*other* condition and as that which enables the dia*gnosis* of that condition. From this perspective, the three concepts under scrutiny are signs or symptoms of a larger vital process conceived as an entire living 'theatre' of contesting individuations.

But stigmata are also 'wounds', understood not in the sense of mere after-effects but as virulent loci of active and actual suffering (*pathos*).[1] In the end, there are three fundamental and fundamentally interrelated reasons for my use of the term 'stigmata': first, just as on the body of the Crucified, reference to *one* of the wounds or stigmata implies in turn the whole *set* of stigmata, so in this study the concepts of 'great politics', 'eternal recurrence' and 'the philosopher of the future' are seen as always co-extensive and mutually implicated. Like the stigmata, even when *one* of these notions appears ('eternal recurrence', for instance), our burden as interpreters of Nietzsche's thought is to bring these *other* notions ('great politics' and 'the philosopher of the future') to bear on it. The co-extensive, mutually implicative and manifold structure of the stigmata will thus serve to highlight the interrelation between these three crucial Nietzschean notions. Second, as is also the case with the crucified, the stigmata are afflictions at once physical and metaphysical which also lacerate the very notions of the 'physical' and the 'metaphysical', affirming them while also cutting through them or across them and in this way going beyond them (*Überwindung*); the three stigmata of Nietzsche's thought are thus at once *physical, metaphysical* and *beyond* the 'physical'/'metaphysical'. Finally, the burden of thinking the three stigmata together (these difficult but necessary, and necessarily difficult, notions), conjoining in so doing the physical and the metaphysical and their mutual overcoming, is a terrible one: it is a thought fraught with terrible tensions, ready to tear itself and its thinker apart, on the verge (in other words) of even further lacerations, of further stigmata. The task of political physiology and of the philosopher-physician is thus to contend with a thought that 'wounds' its thinker, and in this respect Nietzsche's thought could be characterized as one that is quite rightfully 'stigmatized' – one that rightly should *not* be thought (a 'transgression' as the Nietzschean Georges Bataille said).

The perspective of political physiology: Pathology and symptomatology

A major aim of this book is to bring Nietzsche's 'physiological perspective' to the question and discussion of the 'political', the 'anti-political' and the 'over-political' in Nietzsche's work.[2] When considering the latter, we can – and perhaps more forcefully we *should* – also read these three terms as stigmata that mark all of his late thought. It is not a matter of deciding which of the three positions we find more compelling but a question instead of discerning their perpetual presence – their mutual complicity. When seen as stigmata, these three conjoined positions reveal a pathological condition that Nietzsche had already diagnosed in his own age: the illness known as nihilism. Contextualized in terms of Nietzsche's diagnosis of the pervasive condition of nihilism, in the following pages I outline what I consider to be a theory of political physiology in Nietzsche's thought.[3]

The 'political', the 'anti-political' and the 'über-political' are the three generic standpoints that continue to circulate in the economy of Nietzsche studies today. In the recent volume, *Nietzsche, Power and Politics: Rethinking Nietzsche's Legacy for Political Thought*, the aim of which is to give a snapshot of the current interpretive landscape on this issue in the English-speaking world, these three terms are taken as *mutually exclusive* positions:

> Is Nietzsche a political thinker at all – or an anti-political philosopher of values and culture? Is he an aristocratic political thinker who damns democracy as an expression of herd mentality – or can his thought, especially his thought of the Greek *agon*, be fruitfully appropriated for democratic theory ... Is Nietzsche a political philosopher at all, or rather an anti-political – even a supra-political – thinker?[4]

Briefly, the 'political' standpoint claims that Nietzsche was either a proponent of a certain type of political perspective (be it 'democratic' or 'aristocratic', often connectable to a position that supports the goal of human 'perfectionism', as we see for example in Daniel Conway's argument); the 'anti-political' points to Nietzsche's explicit statement about being the 'last anti-political German' and a critic of the German Reich in favour of the superiority of the German cultural spirit; finally, the 'supra-political' view points to the many instances in which Nietzsche's philosophy aims beyond any form of co-existence, insofar as it dissolves any kind of human relationship between distinct entities.

Now, anyone who has read Nietzsche with these questions in mind faces the dilemma of finding all three positions in perhaps unholy (*unheilig*) but definitely unhomely (*unheimlich*) co-existence in Nietzsche's published and unpublished works (and this is one reason that this study will turn to both published and unpublished works despite the exegetical consequences). They are all *there*, and consequently, no one of them can finally dispense with the others without some form of interpretive reasoning or manoeuvring. They appear, sometimes less obviously sometimes more so, always together. From the perspective of a political physiologist, one could say that the three concepts, as stigmata, form a 'pathology of effects'. This work will attempt to think these three – the *political, anti-political* and *über-political* – as mutually *implicative* rather than mutually *exclusive* positions. This, however, is not merely an interpretive short-cut but more a kind of interpretive strategy that works with the inherent virulence of Nietzsche's thought. As Nietzsche himself acknowledged, in the historical condition of nihilism (a condition in which Nietzsche found himself and in which we find ourselves today), health and illness are not so easy to distinguish and may lead to many misunderstandings:

> Health and sickness are not essentially different [...] In fact, there are only differences in degree between these two kinds of existence: the exaggeration, the disproportion, the nonharmony of the normal phenomena constitute the pathological state (Claude Bernard). Just as *'evil'* can be considered as exaggeration, disharmony, disproportion, *'the good'* may be a *protective diet* against the danger of exaggeration, disharmony, and disproportion.[5]

The politico-physiological perspective is attentive to the problem of 'health' and 'illness', psycho-physiological states that are problematic for Nietzsche because 'health and sickness are not essentially different'. Although the concepts of 'great politics', 'eternal recurrence' and 'the philosopher of the future' are ill-defined in Nietzsche's thought and therefore can be said to be complicit with the very illnesses that Nietzsche sought to name, they are also 'signs of health' (*BGE* 154) that are meant to be part of the curatives characteristic of 'great health' (*GS* 382). Because the difference between 'health' and 'illness' is *intensive* not *substantial* – that is to say, 'health' is not a different substance forming a qualitatively different state than 'illness'; rather 'health' and 'illness' are only 'differences in degree' (*WP* 47). The symptoms of health and illness can only be distinguished by their toxicological effects on the organism in question (and in this passage, Nietzsche juxtaposes two symptomatic states that Deleuze would later strongly develop: 'strong/active' and 'weak/reactive').

The three stigmata thus form a pathology, the politico-physiological force of which can be interpreted within the terms of 'symptomatology', as Nietzsche himself notes in the preface to *The Gay Science* and as Deleuze reiterates in the introduction to *Nietzsche and Philosophy*. Following Nietzsche's declaration of the task of the philosopher-physician as interpretation of the 'hints and symptoms of the body' (*GS* Preface 2), Deleuze develops the critical force of Nietzsche's political physiology by emphasizing that this bodily symptomatology proceeds by way of a conceptualization of the relation between 'active' and 'reactive' forces that cannot avoid encountering a fundamental difficulty or confusion: if active forces 'by nature ... escape consciousness' and 'consciousness is essentially reactive', then 'it is inevitable that consciousness sees the organism from its own point of view ... that is to say, reactively'. 'The real problem is the discovery of active forces without which the reactions themselves would not be forces'.[6] As Deleuze rightly shows, when the 'whole of philosophy' is interpreted as a 'symptomatology', the pathology of effects forces the political physiologist to confront the untenability of maintaining the strict metaphysical opposition between 'appearance' and 'essence', as well as the scientific opposition between 'cause' and 'effect'.

> A phenomenon is not an appearance or even an apparition but a sign, a symptom which finds its meaning in an existing force. The whole of philosophy is a symptomatology, and a semeiology. The sciences are a symptomatological and semeiological system. Nietzsche substitutes the correlation between sense and phenomenon for the metaphysical duality of appearance and essence and for the scientific relation of cause and effect.[7]

The mutual implication of 'health' and 'illness', the 'active' and the 'reactive', the 'conscious' and the 'unconscious' is the pathology of effects most pertinent to the politico-physiological perspective because it directly confronts and exposes these two central misunderstandings or 'prejudices' of metaphysical and scientific knowledge: 'appearance' and 'essence', as well as 'cause' and 'effect' – what Nietzsche calls in *Beyond Good and Evil* 2 the 'belief in antitheses of values'. When viewed toxicologically, the relation between health and illness is not an issue regarding the qualitative and substantial properties of antithetical states, but rather it is a vital relation connecting a dynamic organizational network. The challenge of such a toxicological perspective would be to understand health not chiefly as the synthetic interplay of negativity or negation, but negativity itself as a poison that is necessarily part of the vital engine of an ongoing meta-stable process of becoming (in this sense, negativity becomes part of an experimental art/science in administering dosages of poisons).

Political physiology as pharmatechnics

From a literary perspective, my reference to 'three stigmata' also alludes to Philip K. Dick's 1964 science fiction classic, *The Three Stigmata of Palmer Eldritch*. The novel is evocative of not only our contemporary cultural situation but also of the critical applicability of a *Nietzschean* perspective – the perspective of political physiology within the modern context of nihilism I would argue – for a diagnosis of our present.

Dick's story is set in the near future wherein the scarcity of resources on Earth no longer makes it possible to support the terrestrial population, and so a lottery draft sends colonists to Mars to live in bleak underground hovels. The colonists can no longer *feel* authentically (let us say in a 'phenomenological' sense) and so they must *manufacture* affects by literally *ingesting* them. The colonists survive psychologically by taking the drug Can-D, which allows them to communicate with each other in a simulated but *shared* virtual reality (and we later find out that the drug itself is a communication technology linked to information hubs that relay messages to manufacturers and marketers of Can-D). Dick describes the psycho-technological effect of Can-D clearly in both political and psychological terms: colonists collectively project their consciousness onto miniature dolls; women undergo 'translation' as 'Perky Pat' and men become 'Walt'. The drug is primarily used in couples or in groups whereby all the women are projected into 'Perky Pat' and the men into 'Walt'. Based on the desire of the majority, the drug operates via a kind of collective mechanics whereby if two out of three people occupying Perky Pat want to go golfing, then Pat goes golfing.

Consumption of this drug induces and eventually functions as a kind of prosthetic 'self', one that permits the consumer to live a simulated existence, but one that nonetheless preserves the essential properties of modern subjectivity: despite its hallucinogenic properties, the users are reminded by the makers of Can-D that they are in an illusory world, and thus they retain the essence of their real individual identities at all times. This is a very important detail: it is crucial in the narrative unfolding that the users of Can-D can distinguish when they are and when they are *not* within the simulated world of Perky Pat and Walt. The demand for Can-D on Mars depends on creating desire in the inhabitants to continuously return to the Perky Pat world. The distinction, in other words, between a 'real' and an 'illusory' world is precisely established by the presence of a 'self' that travels between two bodily states. But while the essential self toggles between these two worlds, the narrative makes clear that the virtual promise of the Can-D world and the bleak reality of everyday life on Mars are part of the *same* apparatus of production: 'based in laws of conservation and corresponding systemic inequalities', the high standard of living on Earth requires the continuation of deprivation on Mars; in this way, the draft that forces some people to move to Mars clears up surplus population on Earth while assuring a strong market for commodities such as Can-D on Mars.[8] The *continuity* of the self is guaranteed by the necessary *gap* between the ideal – the dream of the Perky Pat world – and the dreary reality of everyday life on Mars. As Nietzsche remarked (particularly in *Beyond Good and Evil* and *Twilight of the Idols*), this 'faith in opposites' – in this case the ontological distinction between the 'illusory' and the 'true' worlds – is a necessary ingredient for the continued production of a subject endowed with and exercising agency.

Enter Palmer Eldritch. Eldritch, an elusive tycoon, introduces a new rival drug on the Martian market – Chew-Z. No one really knows who Palmer Eldritch is; all that is known about him is that, due to his dangerous dealings with traders outside the galaxy, parts of his body have become replaced by three prostheses by which he can be identified: a robotic arm, an implanted set of eyes and a distended metal jaw. Despite the rumours that Palmer Eldritch has gone mad, the Martian population welcomes the opportunity given by the inter-stellar market to try a new drug, which is cheaper and claims to last longer. What users discover, however, is that Chew-Z differs from Can-D in a major way: in the subjective experience produced by the ingestion of the drug, the user can no longer distinguish between 'inside' and 'outside' the drug experience; one can no longer know for sure when one is *in* the 'illusory' world or *in* the 'real' world. The only indications, as the protagonist Barney Mayerson discovers, *are the three stigmata of Palmer Eldritch*. Just when users think that everything is normal, that they are back in their everyday reality, they begin to see the three stigmata appear on others and sometimes even on their own bodies: the robotic arm, the prosthetic eyes and the metal jaw characteristic of Palmer Eldritch:

> Palmer Eldritch had once more thought rings around him, demonstrated his power over everyone who used Chew-Z; Eldritch had done something and he could not even tell what, but anyhow it was not what he had said. Not what had been promised. ... He heard, then, a laugh. It was Palmer Eldritch's laugh, but it was emerging

> from – Himself. Looking down at his hands, he distinguished the left one, pink, pale, made of flesh, covered with skin and tiny, almost invisible hair, and then the right one, bright, glowing, spotless in its mechanical perfection, a hand infinitely superior to the original one, long since gone. Now he knew what had been done to him. A great translation – from his standpoint anyhow – had been accomplished and possibly everything up to now had worked with this end in mind ... Now *I* am Palmer Eldritch.[9]

As Dick's book unfolds, the ontological stability that depends on the congruence of subjective experience and sequential time can no longer be sustained. Which world is authentic, which world is a simulation? The consequences of the infiltration of Palmer Eldritch's stigmata into Barney's world stands in stark contrast to the narrative's earlier clean division between 'ideal' and 'real' worlds (the worlds produced by the use of Can-D), appearance' and 'reality'. What we are left with by the end is an ontological destabilization that enacts a complete breakdown of the distinctions that enabled the 'ideal but illusory' domain and 'everyday reality' to be experienced and conceptualized as distinct domains.

What happens to the subject when this faith in the metaphysical opposition between 'appearance' and 'reality' cannot be sustained? The breakdown itself reveals what Nietzsche had hypothesized towards the end of his life: that the subject is a 'fiction':

> 'The subject' is a fiction that many similar states in us are the effect of one substratum: but it is we who first created the 'similarity' of these states; our adjusting them and making them similar is the fact, not their similarity (which ought rather to be denied).[10]

What Philip K. Dick's story shows is the 'individual' is not an inviolable substratum but an artificial extension or *prosthesis* governed by unknown forces, forces that have generative powers but that cannot be recuperated or represented within the constructed apparati of human volition. Nietzsche had already speculated about these forces, and he hypothesized that they formed a wider organic process in which 'consciousness' and 'unconscious' elements emerge corporeally as 'body':

> Perhaps the entire evolution of the spirit is a question of the body; it is the *history* of the development of *a higher body* that emerges into our *sensibility*. The organic is rising to yet higher levels. Our lust for

> knowledge of nature is a means through which the body desires to perfect itself. Or rather: hundreds of thousands of experiments are made to change the nourishment, the mode of living and the dwelling of the body, all kinds of pleasure and displeasure, are *signs of these changes and experiments*.[11]

What happens to thought when the body itself becomes a prosthesis of communication between aleatory and unknown interlocutors? After the 'death of God', the body can no longer be the guarantor of identity, a 'natural' physical presence inhabited by an essential self within. Nietzsche had already intuited this, perhaps because of the phantasms he had experienced as a result of his own illness. The breakdown of secure ontological divisions between 'real' and 'illusory' worlds produces the untenability of a stable body-self. Of all the published interpreters of Nietzsche, no one has developed the political implications of this idea better than Pierre Klossowski in his monumental work *Nietzsche et le Cercle Vicieux*. As Klossowski argues, Nietzsche was besieged by a double preoccupation:

> first, to find a mode of behaviour, in the organic and inorganic world, that was analogous to his own valetudinary state; and second, based on this mode of behaviour, to find the arguments and resources that would allow him to re-create himself, beyond his own self. Physiology, as he understood it, would thus provide him with the premises of a liberatory conception of the forces that lay subjacent not only to his own condition, but also to the various situations he was living through in the context of his epoch.[12]

Like the eventual infiltration of Barney Mayerson by Palmer Eldritch's stigmata in Dick's story, Klossowski shows how Nietzsche's thought becomes preoccupied with the problem of production *in which the 'self' that produces* is indistinguishable from *the 'self' that is produced*. All of Nietzsche's researches into aesthetics, geography, politics, physiology and biology stem from this problematic of subjective production.

Political physiology and the pathology of nihilism

The perspective of political physiology developed in the present study focuses on the pathology of a nihilistic subject (a subject who seeks and finds its own annihilating force), or perhaps more precisely, a subject in the throes of annihilation. It is, therefore, in Nietzsche's analysis of nihilism that we can start to chart the pathology of this dissolving subject. Nietzsche's analysis occurs relatively late in his thought; he sets it out most fully in 1887 and 1888, in the last years before his complete mental breakdown, but he had already begun to think about it as early as in 1883 (interestingly enough, also the year in which he coins the term *der wille zur macht* or 'the will to power' in the published works[13]). According to Nietzsche's own description in the unpublished works (namely Part One of Kaufmann's redaction entitled *Will to Power*), nihilism (the typology of which is tripartite: passive, active and theoretical) is a historical, epistemological and psycho-physiological condition in which the introduction of an externality into a system first functions to *fortify* it, but then triggers a cannibalistic response *against* it.

> In sum: morality was the great *antidote* against practical and theoretical nihilism.[14] [...] But among the forces cultivated by morality was *truthfulness:* this eventually turned against morality [...] – and now the recognition of this inveterate mendaciousness that one despairs of shedding becomes a stimulant [...] This antagonism [...] results in a process of dissolution.[15]

The pathology proceeds as follows: what is first introduced into a system as an antidote preserving the unity of a system turns against itself and results in the dissolution of that system (*WP* §4, §5[16]). (This is how modern immunology has characterized diseases of 'auto-immunity'). The effect and the affect of this process? Nietzsche says quite succinctly, 'The highest values devaluate themselves'.[17]

As *The Three Stigmata of Palmer Eldritch* palpably illustrates, in a society in which consumption becomes ubiquitous, nihilism consumes us, in all its voracity, until there is no way to distinguish 'it' from 'us'. What we either boast about or bemoan today – the destabilization of meaning, the triumph of secularism and the globalization of political systems and mass consumption culture – Nietzsche would characterize precisely as *nihilistic*: 'everything lacks meaning (the untenability of one interpretation of the world, upon which a tremendous amount of energy has been lavished, awakens the suspicion that *all* interpretations of the world are false)'.[18]

Political physiology as toxicology

The three stigmata of Friedrich Nietzsche – the pathology of the political, anti-political and over-political statements in the late works – are the *symptoms* of a bodily thought that is both a *product of nihilism* and a theatre of production that seeks to *overcome nihilism* by *actively* thinking through nihilism:

> Nihilism represents a pathological transitional stage ...: whether the productive forces are not yet strong enough, or whether decadence still hesitates and has not yet invented its remedies. Presupposition of this hypothesis: that there is not truth, that there is no absolute nature of things nor a 'thing-in-itself'. This, too, is merely nihilism – even the most extreme nihilism. It places the value of things precisely in the lack of any reality corresponding to these values and in their being merely symptom of strength on the part of the value-positers, a simplification for the sake of life.[19]
>
> [...] 'Nihilism': an ideal of the highest degree of powerfulness of the spirit, the over-richest life – partly destructive, partly ironic.[20]

This vital, active power which is partly 'destructive' and partly 'ironic' is, I believe, the operative principle of Nietzsche's concept of 'great politics'. In *Beyond Good and Evil* 208, Nietzsche calls the *reactive* manifestation 'petty politics', which he equates with 'a sickness of the will', and a knee-jerk impulse to *preserve and institutionalize a certain configuration of forces* (this is why the Hobbesian origins of the liberal subject inevitably make it 'slavish' and 'impotent').

> In the new generation that, as it were, has inherited in its blood diverse standards and values, everything is unrest, disturbance, doubt, attempt; the best forces have an inhibiting effect, the very virtues do not allow each other to grow and become strong; balance, a center of gravity, and perpendicular poise are lacking in body and soul. But what becomes sickest is the *will* [...] Paralysis of the will [...] This disease enjoys the most beautiful pomp- and lie-costumes; and most of what today displays itself in the showcases, for example, as 'objectivity', 'being scientific', *'l'art pour l'art'*, 'pure knowledge, free of will', is merely skepticism and paralysis of the will: for this diagnosis of the European sickness I vouch.[21]

From a politico-physiological perspective, 'great politics' and 'great health' are not substantive opposites of 'petty politics' and 'illness'; rather they must be viewed as thresholds that form around vital sites of becoming (here we understand will to power as the ongoing formation of meta-stabilities). This is why for a Nietzschean political physiology, when understood as a vital theatre of contesting tensions *qua* transformations, negativity and pessimism can be forces that strengthen as well as weaken: 'Pessimism as strength – in what? In the energy of its logic, an anarchism and nihilism, as analytic. Pessimism as decline – in what? As growing effeteness, as a sort of cosmopolitan fingering, as 'tout comprendre' and historicism. The critical tension: the extremes appear and become predominant'.[22]

The cultivation of critical tensions is the affirmative work of opposing forces, of overcoming. Pessimism is the handmaid of affirmation in the sense that pessimism, as an 'analytic' of forces, can manifest both as *strength* and as *decline* – *actively* as well as *reactively* – and in the energy conducted by this 'critical tension' in which 'extremes appear and become predominant', the work of overcoming happens. Affirmation must first work through negativity, through 'negations' (*WP* §11), intensifying the process of devaluation that consists in 'the smashing of idols' by the 'hammer of philosophy' (*Twilight of the Idols*). But this tension is *productive* because it is a reticulation that may produce *active* effects. It is in this sense of the productive effect of pessimism that I interpret sections 55 and 56 of *Beyond Good and Evil*, in which Nietzsche describes how cultivation of cruelty by slave morality (our culture) – that is to say, how the intensification of nihilism – *may* nonetheless lead to its overcoming (and I quote at length):

> There is a great ladder of religious cruelty with many rungs; but three of them are the most important. At one time one sacrificed human beings to one's god, perhaps precisely those human beings one loved best – ... Then, in the moral epoch of mankind, one sacrificed to one's god the strongest instincts one possessed, one's 'nature'; the joy of thin festival glitters in the cruel glance of the ascetic ... Finally: what was left to be sacrificed? ... Did one not have to sacrifice God himself and out of cruelty against oneself worship stone, stupidity, gravity, fate, nothingness? To sacrifice God for nothingness – this paradoxical mystery of the ultimate act of cruelty was reserved for the generation which is even now arising: we all know something of it already.
>
> ... he who has really gazed with an Asiatic and more than Asiatic eye down into the most world – denying of all possible modes of thought – beyond good and evil and no longer, like Buddha and Schopenhauer, under the spell and illusion of morality – perhaps by that very act, and without really intending to, may have had his eyes opened to the opposite ideal: to the ideal of the most exuberant,

> most living and most world-affirming man, who has not only learned to get on and treat with all that was and is but who wants to have it again *as it was and is* to all eternity ...

This is the trickiest and most disturbing aspect of the question of politics in the pathological condition of nihilism: that *affirmation* arises from the affirmation of *nihilism*. This is precisely what Leo Strauss's influential interpretation of will to power and eternal recurrence *resists* and *denies*: 'Nietzsche does not mean to sacrifice God for the sake of the Nothing'. Rather, Strauss claims that Nietzsche 'had doubts whether there can be a world, any world whose center is not God. Nietzsche brings out the fact that in a manner the doctrine of the will to power is a vindication of God, if a decidedly non-theistic vindication of God'.[23] Contrary to Strauss's interpretation, I will argue that it is precisely from the willing of nothingness that the possibility of overcoming nothingness emerges because it is only at this point of *contraction* in which the last artefact of the human – the will – *dissolves* that nihilism can transform itself from being a product of reactivity or negation to becoming purely active and affirmative because it returns to its active state of becoming. On this point, Karl Löwith's interpretation of Nietzsche is superior to Strauss's because Löwith acknowledges that the completion of the project of nihilism requires the *self-annihilation* of the philosopher to the most extreme form of nihilism: 'The search for self-eternalization is in a perverse way at one with the temptation to self-destruction'.[24]

In the absence of *stasis*, the mechanisms of which impose *limitations* (I think this is precisely where Kant and Nietzsche part ways), the affirmation of nihilism becomes the curative force of the poison of nihilism. This is the operative difference between 'passive' and 'active' nihilism.

> Nihilism. It is *ambiguous:*
> A. Nihilism as a sign of increased power of the spirit: as *active* nihilism. B. Nihilism as decline and recession of the power of the spirit: as *passive* nihilism.[25]

The force of active nihilism can be nothing other than *polemos* ('war'), the destructive but transmutative force that is also the necessary catalyst for creation (the force that the medieval alchemists called *melanosis* or *putrefaction*, a *composting*[26] or *decomposition* which characterizes the *Kaliyuga*, or *age of destruction*, according to vedic wisdom): 'It reaches its maximum of relative strength as the violent force of destruction – as active nihilism'.[27]

Active nihilism is the force of destruction/creation *qua* transformation. If we recall that for Nietzsche, reactive nihilism is a situation in which a system begins to eat itself by turning itself against itself (the pathology of 'auto-immune' disorders), hanging onto itself in order to preserve even a minuteness of its discharge, then active nihilism becomes the *transformative* activity of force that no longer turns back onto itself. It is the force of *morphosis*, the 'plasticity'[28] characteristic of active force in which nothing is carried over. It affirms by dominating, by commanding a weaker force to obey (in this sense force is always hierarchical), but its domination proceeds by expenditure not by recuperation (this is why the overcoming of nihilism for Nietzsche cannot ultimately proceed by dialectics or by fascism). Nietzsche even has a name for this active process: the active and most extreme form of nihilism – the process in which existence is lived and expended without limitation or recuperation : 'Let us think this thought in its most terrible form: existence as it is, without sense or aim, but inevitably returning, without a finale in nothingness: "the eternal return"'.[29]

What kind of politics would be adequate to this? 'What is to be done' politically when nihilism has become a 'normal condition'? The political physiological perspective is ever vigilant in remembering that what is a cure can also be a poison, and what is a poison can be a cure. The boundary separating values – high/low, noble/base, good/evil, healthy/ill – can no longer be securely differentiated and Nietzsche himself points to this fact:

> It is the value of all morbid states that they show us under a magnifying glass certain states that are normal – but not easily visible when normal. Health and sickness are not essentially different, as the ancient physicians and some practitioners even today suppose. One must not make of them distinct principles or entities that fight over the living organism and turn it into their arena. ...[30]

As the French philosopher Bernard Stiegler has recently said, the philosopher today must be a *toxicologist*,[31] and this echoes something that I have recently also said in relation to Nietzsche's call for a philosopher that is also a physician: in the politics conditioned by nihilism but which seek to overcome nihilism by activating the potency of nihilism, the philosopher-physician must be a *homeopathic* toxicologist governed and guided by the principle of *like cures like* (*simili similibus curentor*), the administering of the poison as the curative force itself.[32] This kind of politics – is there, truly, any alternative to this? – is fraught with so many *moral* dilemmas precisely because its operative principle works without seeking to – without *having* to – ontologize the distinction between 'true' and 'false', 'good' and 'evil'. This is also why for Nietzsche, the question of power is *not merely nor even primarily* a question of property or territory and the negotiating of its representations, but rather, power is a question of production, of *morphosis* and its transformations, the process of formation that emerges as a result of a tension of forces, the process that imposes 'upon becoming the character of being'.[33] Following Bernard Stiegler, the question of the 'political' must necessarily proceed via a pharmacological perspective: we must look for the signs of health in the very illnesses of the human condition, as well as be able to recognize signs of illness in what may be considered by the majority as signs of 'health'.

It is against this backdrop that the three stigmata of Friedrich Nietzsche are evoked once again: each stigmata is a poison and a cure; all three must be interpreted as forces whose collision – speculative and material – are necessary to Nietzsche's account of the completion and overcoming of nihilism. We can start to see why the politics of nihilism are so confounding, but for Nietzsche, the secret to the renewed health of our ever-ailing species depends on playing nihilism out, intensifying its forces. Nietzsche's thought is thus the greatest example of nihilism – not the passive and thus incomplete nihilism of the forms of life he attacks, but the virulent and curative nihilism that unleashes those forces of life that will lead to the organism's self-destruction, only in order to make way for a new form of life. This theatre of vital dramatization remains the crux of Nietzsche's conception of the 'tragic':

> At this point nihilism is reached: all one has are the values that pass judgment – nothing else. Here the problem of strength and weakness originates:
>
> 1. The weak perish of it;
> 2. those who are stronger destroy what does not perish;
> 3. those who are strongest overcome the values that pass judgment.
>
> In sum, this constitutes the tragic age.[34]

Introduction: The Mnemotechnics of Nihilism and the Political Physiology of Eternal Recurrence

> [W]e must once again recognize the terrifying basic text of *homo natura*. In fact, to translate man back into nature, to master the many vain and effusive interpretations and connoted meanings which so far have been scribbled and painted over that eternal basic text of *homo natura*, to bring it about that in future man stands before man in the same way he, grown hard in the discipline of science, already stands these days before the rest of nature [...] – that may be a strange and insane task, but it is a task ...
>
> *BGE* §230

Nietzsche had conceived of *Beyond Good and Evil* as a 'prelude' to and anticipation of an impending civilizational and cultural 'spectacle' whose enactment was still being put into place, but whose destiny had already inevitably been cast. This spectacle 'of a hundred acts that will occupy Europe for the next two centuries'[1] is that of *nihilism*. Although the kind of nihilism he presaged had yet to reach its dramatic historical crescendo in his own age, Nietzsche identified its faint tonalities in his account of the genesis and pathologization of 'bad conscience' in *The Genealogy of Morals*. My main aim here is to highlight that for Nietzsche, the 'human' has from its very first emergence been constituted by mnemotechnics (the evolutionary development of a 'memory of the will') which is simultaneously also a process of detachment and abstraction, or what Nietzsche describes as a process of intensive 'spiritualization'. The 'human' first emerges as the relation between a religious subjective mode that operates by way of intensifications of 'spiritualization' and the mnemotechnical ensemble of artifices without which the 'human' could not be instrumentalized. This process of spiritualization results in the birth of the 'priestly type' and, according to Nietzsche, heralds the first dangerous movement towards the 'domestication' of the human animal.

The mnemotechnical genesis of the 'human'

According to Nietzsche's account in *The Genealogy*, all aristocratic systems of value are ones in which the spectrum of value judgments are directly reflective of the power of the highest in social rank. In section 6 of *GM*, Nietzsche contrasts the political aristocratic and the priestly aristocratic: the political aristocratic expresses his power by exercising his material animal instincts; his rule is legitimized by his political superiority. The 'priestly' type, on the other hand, does not exercise but controls his material nature through dietary restrictions, control of bodily processes and forbidding of intermixing with the 'impure'. The priestly type was forbidden from externalizing and discharging his instincts and regulated them through strict adherence to a whole panoply of bodily prohibitions. Nietzsche says that this spiritual type embodies a kind of walking psychological contradiction: on the one hand, he feels his superior spiritual power over others, but compared to the warrior type, he also feels his material/physical impotence. Although the priestly types tried to over-compensate for this impotence by highlighting their *spiritual* superiority, this intensified spirituality was in fact a direct effect of a feeling of impotence, and therefore slowly festered into feelings of 'arrogance, revenge ... love, lust to rule, virtue – but it is only fair to add that it was on the solid of this essentially dangerous form of human existence, the priestly form, that man first became an *interesting* animal'.[2]

This psychological separation between mental and physical power internalized by the priestly type actually had the effect of complexifying the consciousness of the human animal; this new human was less animal because he was able to repress his animality through intellectual controls, but this human was also less healthy, increasingly becoming 'alienated' from the physical material basis of its animal state. According to Nietzsche then, the effects and influence of this priestification is both the first great *spiritualization* of the human animal and the first great moment of 'domestication' of human animality.

Nietzsche's account of the emergence of 'bad conscience' is a psycho-physiological account of the political animal. In this argument, Nietzsche claims that the founding of the first political societies required a constitutive moment of alienation at the level of the psycho-physiological evolution of human beings, a kind of 'archi-nihilism'.[3] Historically then, nihilism was the catastrophic consequence generated by an 'archi-nihilism' that itself first gave birth to and transformed the not-yet-human animal into a potential social and political agent:

> I regard the bad conscience as the serious illness that man was bound to contract under the stress of the most fundamental change he ever experienced – that change which occurred when he found himself finally enclosed within the walls of society and of peace. The situation that faced sea animals when they were compelled to become land animals or perish was the same as that which faced these semi-animals, well adapted to the wilderness, to war, to prowling, to adventure: suddenly all their instincts were disvalued and 'suspended'.[4]

The constitution of the political life, Nietzsche here argues, develops via psychic and physiological modifications in the human animal. According to Nietzsche, the constitutive moment of the *human* as 'political' rather than merely 'animal' occurs precisely at the moment in which the animal instincts cease to become discharged and instead become 'internalized', sublimated and deployed *subliminally*. Nietzsche describes this process as the early psycho-physiological transformation of the 'hominid' into the 'human' configured and given signification through an economy in which the renunciation of desire is made productive and meaningful:

> All instincts that do not discharge themselves outwardly turn inward – this is what I call the internalization [*Verinnerlichung*] of man: thus it was that man first developed what was later called his 'soul'. The entire inner world, originally as thin as if it were stretched between two membranes, expanded and extended itself, acquired depth, breadth, and height, in the same measure as outward discharge was inhibited. Those fearful bulwarks with which the political organization protected itself against the old instincts of freedom – punishments belong among these bulwarks – brought about that all those instincts of wild, free, prowling man turned backward against man himself. Hostility, cruelty, joy in persecuting, in attacking, in change, in destruction – all this turned against the possessors of such instincts: that is the origin of the 'bad conscience'.[5]

This transformation is a process of bifurcation in which a process of intensifying alienation resulting from the growing disconnection between the instinctive and sublimative registers results in the *complexification* of the animal into a human technical (tool-making), principally *mnemotechnical* (memory-making) – and hence a moralizing – *political* subject. In the second essay of *GM*, Nietzsche characterizes the 'human' with the ability to make promises, which itself requires the ability to ritualize pain by inscribing it into cultural memory:[6]

> How can one create a memory for the human animal? How can one impress something upon this partly obtuse, partly flighty mind, attuned only to the passing moment, in such a way that it will stay there? One can well believe that the answers and methods for solving this primeval problem were not precisely gentle; perhaps indeed there was nothing more fearful and uncanny in the whole prehistory of man than his *mnemotechnics*. 'If something is to stay in the memory it must be burned in: only that which never ceases to *hurt* stays in the memory' – [...] Man could never do without blood, torture, and sacrifices when he felt the need to create a memory for himself; the most dreadful sacrifices and pledges (sacrifices of the first-born among them), the most repulsive mutilations (castration, for example), the cruelest rites of all the religious cults (and all religions are at the deepest level systems of cruelties) – all this has its origin in the instinct that realized that pain is the most powerful aid to mnemonics.[7]

Just as in Kafka's stark tale of corporeal inscription in *The Penal Colony*, the 'human' for Nietzsche is a mnemotechnical political animal. If the human animal can become political, it is because the arts of remembering, identifying, ritualizing and symbolizing become the technical motor for the further psycho-physiological evolution. For Nietzsche, the 'human' is, constitutionally and constitutively speaking, mnemotechnical: its subjective and objective development is fundamentally linked to memory. The human develops subjectively into the priestly bad conscience by concretizing memory in the form of mnemotechnical objects. When read alongside Nietzsche's speculation regarding the 'subject' as 'fiction', the political animal is revealed to be a *prosthetic* engendered in tandem with the technical arts of remembering and forgetting.

The political and historical problem of nihilism, as such, is also a problem of the psycho-physiological transmutation of the animal human. Specifically for Nietzsche, the archi-nihilism that founds the human and later develops into the monotheistic self-consciousness (the 'bad conscience') becomes intensified and reified in modernity as the problem of willing:

> We can no longer conceal from ourselves what is expressed by all that willing which has taken its direction from the ascetic ideal: this hatred of the human, and even more of the animal, and more still of the material, this horror of the senses, of reason itself, this fear of happiness and beauty, this longing to get away from all appearance, change, becoming, death, wishing, from longing itself – all this means – let us dare to grasp it – a will to nothingness, an aversion to life, a rebellion against the most fundamental presuppositions of life, but it is and remains a will! ... And, to repeat in conclusion what I said at the beginning: man would rather will nothingness than not will.[8]

'Willing' becomes the hallmark of the political human, in due course becoming a symptom of its decadence as well as the active battleground for its overcoming (i.e. the Overman or *Übermensch*). In the psycho-physiological development of the human then as told by Nietzsche in *GM*, the process of sublimation eventually makes possible the production of knowledge and becomes the historical motor for the large-scale cultural decadence and degeneration characteristic of modernity (the 'ascetic ideal').

Nietzsche's solution to the problem of nihilism is not, however, a declaration simply rejecting willing in favour of returning to the animal instinctual state (i.e. through the willing of an economy of drives); because willing is itself a product of sublimation, Nietzsche knows very well that a nostalgic yearning for a bygone psycho-physiological state is both undesirable and (what's more) impossible. Rather he will suggest, as I argue in the following study, that the overcoming of nihilism must involve the violent playing-out of nihilism to its end, that is an intensification of nihilism – one which will necessitate a politics of nihilism as a necessary corollary of a 'philosophy of the future'.

The present work offers an interpretation of the relationship between the two central thoughts of Nietzsche's work – the will to power and the eternal recurrence, specifically against the backdrop of the mnemotechnics of nihilism which, as I will argue, are forced to play out on the political and mnemotechnical battlefield of bodily, organic psycho-physiological 'life' (i.e. the materiality of the 'self', and its related placeholder the 'subject'). In order for Nietzschean political physiology to undertake the task of overcoming both the historical problem of nihilism and its constitutive foundations ('archi-nihilism'), the intensification of nihilism (a process of decadence and degeneration) will be forced to play out on the subjective plane (in terms of the deployment of 'instincts', what Nietzsche infamously termed 'will to power'). The overcoming of nihilism requires the affirmation of the most extreme form of nihilism itself, the overcoming of willing through the affirmation of non-willing. The eternal recurrence thus becomes not a return to some authentic or original state, but a dynamic and violent process of individuation in which the human animal literally undergoes a psycho-physiological mutation, a playing-out that leads to the death of one form of existence (the decadent form of human as described for example in *The Genealogy of Morality*) into what Nietzsche hopes is the genesis of a new psycho-physiological configuration of self-organization. When interpreted from the perspective of political physiology, the eternal recurrence becomes comprehensible as a process of *morphosis* in which both physical and metaphysical mechanisms of subjectivity are forced to organize and individuate anew. It is in this operative sense that the eternal recurrence is the transformative mechanism driving Nietzsche's political physiology.

The eternal recurrence, in the present work, is a vital capacity of will to power, which is deeply implicated in the dynamics of becoming. In Nietzsche's thought, we find not only that power – what would be associated with politics, morality and even science – is will to power (i.e. these values have a primarily psycho-physiological basis), but more radically that will to power is nothing more and nothing less than the engine of vital overcoming (*qua* individuation) which actively takes place within various organizing domains of life. In this view, the task of great politics would consist in harnessing this individuation or incorporation. This point lies at the heart of Nietzsche's political physiology.

The political physiology of eternal recurrence

There has been a concerted intellectual effort to re-articulate and re-theorize Nietzsche's thought explicitly within the phylogenesis of Western political thought. Scholars have begun to cross the interpretive boundaries separating the German, French and Anglo-American schools in an effort to bridge the gap between them. Peter Sedgwick classifies the history of Nietzschean interpretation within three principal traditions or regimes of reading: the 'German' tradition tends to locate Nietzsche within the context of modern aesthetics and social theory and includes the work of Marxists (i.e. Frankfurt School) and hermeneuticists (Heidegger and Gadamer); the 'French' tradition, which includes the interpretations of the existentialists, the post-modernists and the post-structuralists (e.g. Bataille, Klossowski, Deleuze, de Man, Foucault, Derrida and Kofman), emphasizes questions of language, style, rhetoric in the context of literary, social and psychoanalytic themes; finally, the 'Anglo-American' tradition epitomized by Danto, Kaufmann, Hollingdale and Rorty highlights 'more classically determined conceptions of truth, politics, and subjectivity' in the context of analytic philosophy (Sedgwick 1995, p. 2). It will become apparent through my choice of critical commentators that my own interpretation is informed and influenced by all three regimes: I take each to be emphasizing an already existing facet of Nietzsche's thought, and as such, I attempt to reconstruct Nietzsche's philosophy based on the general sociological, linguistic and political concerns expressed by the aforementioned interpretive strands.

It would not be an exaggeration to claim that 'the eternal recurrence' (*ewige Wiederkunft*) is the most hotly contested notion in Nietzschean scholarship. The vigour of the debate is largely a result of the ephemerality of the concept *itself, which only appears in gestation – hence only suggestively – in the Gay Science* §341, in which it is described as 'the greatest weight' (*das grösste Schwergewicht*): simultaneously a burden of Faustian proportions and the limit-test by which the value of human life can be measured. Although it also reappears in Nietzsche's unpublished works (*Nachlass*), it is primarily in *Thus Spoke Zarathustra* that Nietzsche develops his conceptualization of the notion of eternal recurrence through the experiential and experimental narrative of his fictive philosopher-prophet, Zarathustra.

I situate my own interpretation of eternal recurrence within the existent scholarship as both a continuation and a departure from the main interpretive strands in modern Nietzsche interpretation. The eternal recurrence has been interpreted in various ways: as an ethical doctrine or imperative, as a meta-ethics, as a meta-physics and as a philosophical cosmology. By and large, despite the vast diversity of interpretations, the eternal recurrence is most generally characterized under two broad interpretive regimes: cosmological and anthropological.[9]

The cosmological perspective advances an understanding of the eternal recurrence as a theory of the world, universe or cosmos. In this view, recombinative possibilities produce the recurrence of forms constituted out of a chaotic, non-linear and non-teleological multiplicity.[10] The idea of a universe in perpetual flux occurs in one of Nietzsche's earliest work entitled *Philosophy in the Tragic Age of the Greeks*, in which he takes up Heraclitus's assertion that the universe is an endless play of cosmic forces and devoid of moral, transcendental overtones.[11] Those who put forth the cosmological view[12] attempt to either refute or validate Nietzsche's idea of the eternal repetition of all states of being, two important examples being Georg Simmel's proof that a particular state need never mathematically recur[13] and Walter Kaufmann's claim that Nietzsche is a 'dialectical monist' who understands 'will' as a basic cosmic principle similar to Hegel's 'spirit'.[14] One of the dangers of the cosmological view of eternity, however, is that it devalues or dismisses Nietzsche's historical cultural project. This is partly what enables those such as Kaufmann to assert that Nietzsche was predominately an 'anti-political' thinker,[15] thus obfuscating Nietzsche's statements about the prescriptive task of the will to power to establish the foundation for a 'great politics' of the future.

The second main interpretive regime, the anthropological perspective, focuses on the eternal recurrence as a feature of historical experience, namely in light of the strength and vitality of the human will in the world. From this view, the eternal recurrence is an imperative or normative doctrine of the human will to create new values through the willing of the eternal recurrence of all things. The ability to affirm eternity is an expression of the human will's ability to affirm life and suffering (rather than seek solace in metaphysical and religious illusions) and therefore a reflection of the qualities that the highest specimen of humanity would have to possess. Schacht characterizes the eternal recurrence as a test[16] and suggests that although Nietzsche partly intended to understand eternal recurrence cosmologically in the *Nachlass*, his prime concern was with historical relations between human beings. Eternal recurrence is important not because it reveals something about the cosmos, but because it reveals something crucial about human life: the idea of 'everything recurring eternally' must be confined to its function as an account of a hypothetical state of affairs 'for the purpose of making a very different sort of experiment, where what is at stake is not the world's actual nature but rather something having to do with our human nature and the enhancement of human life'.[17] The cosmological interpretation of eternal recurrence, as such, must be restricted or subordinated to the primacy of the anthropological. Even Kaufmann, who elaborates the importance of Nietzsche's cosmology, agrees that the eternal recurrence must be understood primarily as an experience rather than a philosophical, conceptual or speculative 'idea'.[18] The danger of the type of anthropological view is it leads some commentators to ignore the eternal recurrence altogether. By interpreting 'eternity' as primarily historical (i.e. as a feature of the historical contingency of the human will), the status of the eternal itself disappears, thereby obliterating the only experience of pure Dionysian affirmation available to the philosopher. In thus eradicating the notion of eternity and thereby privileging the most radical historicism, this view sometimes only highlights one feature of Nietzsche's thought, namely the process by which the devaluation of current historical values occurs and through which man becomes 'master and owner of nature'.[19] In these circumstances, the focus centres on the overabundant strength of the will to negate current values and on the process of devaluation of historical values. The added problem is that this particular shortsightedness is a danger inherent in Nietzsche's definition of will to power itself. Hence, as Leo Strauss argues, 'the difficulty inherent in the philosophy of the will to power led after Nietzsche to the explicit renunciation of the very notion of eternity. Modern thought reaches its culmination, its highest self-consciousness, in the most radical historicisms, i.e., in explicitly condemning to oblivion the notion of eternity'.[20]

One of the consequences of subscribing to either one or the other perspectives begins to emerge: the cosmological perspective understands eternity as characteristic of the inherent Dionysian flux of cosmological nature. In this view, all human events and activities must ultimately be viewed as goalless, valueless and meaningless. The anthropological view, in contrast, privileges the capacity and imperative of the human will to negate decadent and nihilistic historical values, and thereby subordinates Nietzsche's view of 'eternity' to his view of the radical 'historicity' of will to power. This quandary, in many senses, goes to the heart of the debate concerning Nietzsche's status as a political or anti-political thinker. For example, Frederick Appel and Ruth Abbey, in an effort to contest the anti-political view of Nietzsche made popular by Kaufmann, argue that Nietzsche's political statements reflect an 'architectonic conception of politics' by which he 'envisages the formation of a social, cultural and political elite and hopes, through this writing, to galvanize this elite'.[21] Appel and Abbey justify their arguments with exclusive reliance on the notion of will to power without any mention of the eternal recurrence. Daniel Conway also suggests that Nietzsche's notion of will to power is sufficient to understand the political dimension of Nietzsche's thought. Interpreting Nietzsche's political vision through the Emersonian concept of 'moral perfectionism', Conway argues that for Nietzsche human life is justified as the possibility of the perfectibility of the species as a whole, 'as evidenced by the pioneering accomplishments of its highest exemplars'.[22] Consequently, perfectionism becomes the sole justification for the reversal of nihilism and for the urgency of a new philosophy of the future. Conway claims that the teaching of the eternal recurrence is not even available to us because it would require a degree of vitality 'that is absolutely unknown to modernity'.[23]

The attempt to demonstrate the nomothetic importance of politics in Nietzsche's thought need not bracket the concept of eternal recurrence. Following Heidegger's influential claim that the will to power and eternal recurrence are inextricably connected, Leo Strauss and Laurence Lampert argue for the mutual relationship between the notions of will to power and eternal recurrence. Strauss and Lampert interpret Nietzsche's conception of eternal recurrence to emerge naturally from the historical devaluation undertaken by the will to power.[24] Karl Löwith's interpretation creates a third avenue of enquiry, one that takes both the cosmological and anthropological readings to be true. Consequently, Löwith claims that the inherent meaninglessness of Nietzsche's cosmological view of eternal recurrence clashes with the imperative of will to power to create meaning in the world. Therefore, Löwith contends that a dualism emerges in Nietzsche's work, which poses the following quandary: how can (and why should) one will what must necessarily happen anyway? Löwith asserts that the question remains speculatively (and therefore logically) unanswerable, thus locating an irreconcilable paradox between Nietzsche's elaboration of the will to power and eternal recurrence, one that ultimately destroys any possible unity between the two concepts.

The brief exegesis above enables me to locate my interpretation of the eternal recurrence within the terms of 'political physiology' in which organic processes (both conscious and unconscious) are diagnosed as expressions of individualities, as well as expressions of collectivities (cultures, peoples, etc.). A political physiology of eternal recurrence thus focuses on reading the language of bodies[25] (their drives and impulses), in order to reconstruct the crucial role of 'translation back into nature' (*zurückübersetzen in die Natur*) that Nietzsche describes as a central task of the philosopher of the future (we shall come to this in some detail). Of the contemporary interpreters that acknowledge the centrality of the body to Nietzsche's thought, Robert Gooding-Williams clearly articulates the connection between the philosopher's ability to create new values and the crucial experience of Dionysian chaos: 'Through Zarathustra, Nietzsche conceptualizes values as esteemed passions and as features of the self and body. He conceptualizes new values as effects of bodily transformation and self-overcoming'.[26]

Pointing to Nietzsche's *Birth of Tragedy* and *Untimely Meditations,* Gooding-Williams argues that although Nietzsche had envisioned in these earlier works the possibility of a Dionysian renewal in modernity through various media, for example the German nation and the German people or body politic, the later philosophy confronts a contradiction between the identity-less, boundary-less ephemerality of the Dionysian experience as outlined in *The Birth of Tragedy* and the necessary national delineation of a German identity required to reclaim modern European culture (as developed in *Beyond Good and Evil* and later).[27] As a result, a shift takes place and Nietzsche comes to believe that new-values creation finds its origin in the bodily Dionysian experience of 'going-under' in *Zarathustra*. Cultural innovation in modernity – the path through which Dionysus can enter the modern world – is now rooted in the body that 'goes under' rather than in the German nation. Gooding-Williams notes that this turn to the discourse of the healthy human body 'both frees the idea of a Dionysian modernism from the contradictions that initially haunted it and expresses a conviction that the German nation has been corrupted by the forces of modernity'.[28]

Nietzsche's overcoming of Platonic-Christian thought hinges largely on dissolving the dichotomy between the true and apparent worlds (what Plato called the dichotomy between the world of *being* and the world of *becoming*). This dissolution is a pre-condition of Nietzsche's perspectivism, his view that all claims to truth – and especially moral truth – are but interpretations. When linked to a genealogy of the body, Gooding-Williams suggests that Zarathustra regards all values as narrative interpretations or 'parables' that record the history of bodily states of elevation;[29] in particular, Platonic-Christian values represent the bodily history of the ascetic ideal (the extirpation of passions).[30] Gooding-William's point is that the possibility of the creation of new values – and therefore the overcoming of Platonic-Christian values – will require the transformation of the states of the body: the creation of new values cannot be effected apart from self-overcoming as the creation of new selves, that is of new bodily states of elevation.[31] The paramount importance of *Zarathustra* emerges from this presumption: that the eternal recurrence becomes the crucible of all Nietzsche's hopes for genuine philosophy; more pointedly, the eternal recurrence holds the key to what Nietzsche considers to be the only possibility for creating (and thus redeeming) the future of humanity.

This reading opens onto another regime of interpretation based on another avenue of possibility that establishes a pathology linking 'political', 'anti-political' and 'over-political' positions: at one point in the trajectory to be examined, the experience of the eternal recurrence is the basis of the philosopher's affirmative experience of the boundless multiplicity of Dionysian existence, and is the engine driving all of the philosopher's activity and experimentation. The experience of the eternal recurrence is the psycho-physiological experience of eternity in which self-conscious identity (political, social and cultural) undergoes dissolution. If endured, and if made communicable, then the eternal recurrence also becomes the basis for the radical re-organization of the collective organism in the creation of new values. From the perspective of political physiology then, the eternal recurrence is the engine of novelty and self-organization (auto-morphosis) in organic forms of life.

Among French interpretations of Nietzsche, of which Michel Foucault's is perhaps the most cited, is the work of Pierre Klossowski, one of the least-mentioned interpreters of Nietzsche in the past few decades. It is in large part from Klossowski's theorization of the eternal recurrence (as well as that of Georges Bataille) that Foucault was able to articulate the centrality of the body in Nietzsche's thought.[32] It is Klossowski's interpretation of Nietzsche that forms the foundation for the theory of political physiology offered in the present work. Klossowski understands the body to be an inchoate and primal battleground of affective drives that are translated and communicated into thought within the cultural code of everyday signs:

> Le corps est the résultat du fortuit: il n'est rien que le lieu de rencontre d'un ensemble d'impulsions individuées pour cet intervalle que forme une vie humaine, lesquelles n'aspirent qu'à se désindividuer. [33]

The body is a production of chance; it is nothing other than the site of conjunction and conflict between a concrescence of individuated impulses which come together for that brief time span we call 'a human life', impulses which aspire only to de-individuate themselves. From this perspective, the eternal recurrence is twofold: on the one hand, it is an experience of the singular body, an ecstatic unveiling or revelation, a 'forgetting' (of all identities, laws and boundaries) into which all identity is absorbed and revealed in its inchoate multiplicity; on the other hand, the eternal recurrence must be made intelligible and infinitely repeatable: it must be a necessity that is willed and re-willed.[34] The tonalities of the soul or fluctuations of intensity[35] have no meaning in themselves but only acquire signification through a process of translation by which the affective intensity of impulses become culturally and linguistically coded as signs:

> This flux and this reflux become intermingled, fluctuation within fluctuation, and, just like the shapes that float at the crest of the

> waves only to leave froth, are the designations left by intensity. And this is what we call thought. But nonetheless, there is something sufficiently open in us – we other, apparently limited and closed natures – for Nietzsche to invoke the movement of waves. This is because signification exists by afflux; notwithstanding the sign in which the fluctuation of intensity culminates, signification is never absolutely disengaged from the moving chasms that it masks. Every signification, then, remains a function of the chaos out of which meaning is generated.[36]

Klossowski theorizes eternal recurrence as *kymatic*, in terms of wave phenomena that interrupt the normal inscription of memory necessary to sustain self-consciousness: all directed exertions of the will commingle and disappear in the multiple swells and surges of the impulses which entail and require a profound subjective amnesis. It is in this sense Nietzsche claims that language cannot capture the essence of 'becoming'; 'linguistic means of expression are useless for expressing "becoming"; it accords with our inevitable need to posit a crude world of stability, of "things," etc. ... There is no will: there are treaty drafts of will that are constantly increasing or losing power'.[37] In the interruption of self-consciousness (the dissolution of 'self' that is undergone in the experience of eternity), the subject as a stable entity becomes a fiction, the affirmation of which becomes the means for reconnecting with the joyful but terrible and potentially perilous forces of life. As an experience of the 'suspension' of self-consciousness (and the emergence of the unconscious drives and impulses), the eternal recurrence is not primarily a conscious reasoning, a thought-experiment or a doctrine, but instead, a mechanism of mutation that reorganizes forces within a system (the 'informational' operationality of any system).

The eternal recurrence becomes a teaching only when it itself becomes a sign – a cultural imperative of a collectivity. In other words, the feeling produced by the experience of eternal recurrence must be translated into thought so that it can be re-willed anew and transmitted by those abundant enough to endure it. If the teaching of eternal recurrence is understood to be a translation of the philosopher's experience of Dionysian multiplicity (and a transformation of bodily states), then the materialization of 'great politics' rests largely on the singular organism's ability to endure, incorporate and translate these various conflicting and overpowering drives, impulses and psychological states into the affirmative language of life which will enable the creation of new values.[38] Through the paradoxicality of thinking the eternal recurrence,

Klossowski identifies the aporia inherent in the creation of meaning: all instances of valuation occur through the imposition of meaning onto what is essentially meaningless. Thinking is therefore a profoundly paradoxical experience: value and meaning have their origin precisely in that which lacks value and meaning.

This is what the philosopher affirms: the creation of new values and the overcoming of nihilism rest on the subtlety of one's perspective – the strongest and therefore wisest morality is one that recognizes its own radical contingency and fundamental immorality, its own enduring inextricability to the 'moving chasm that it masks'. This suggests that for Nietzsche the wisest morality is one that acknowledges that its 'ground' or 'origin' is not immutable but volatile, and its transformative potential arises from its willingness to reveal its own precariousness. The breakdown and potential transformation of the mnemotechnical operations of self-consciousness constitute the revolutionary potential (to borrow a phrase from Walter Benjamin) of eternal recurrence. The highest type, the Overhuman, can be distinguished from all other types precisely in its capacity for this activity of morphosis and translation.

Mapping the argument

This book is an examination and exemplification of Nietzsche's political physiology. The initial problematic is partly motivated by my attempt at understanding and reconciling two different interpretive poles; one that argues that Nietzsche is decidedly a political thinker whose future philosopher is undoubtedly a political figure, and the other that countermands this claim to focus on the aesthetic, artistic and philosophical nature of the Nietzsche's future philosopher. The objective of this study is to show how both poles co-exist and are co-operators in Nietzsche's thought.

In this study, the critical link between will to power and eternal recurrence is found in Nietzsche's psycho-physiological theory of the body and its function in the structure of Nietzsche's whole corpus. In Chapter 1, I begin by laying the groundwork of the argument by suggesting that for Nietzsche, the nature of politics is not located in the nature of the polis but in the nature of the human organism, that is in light of the psycho-physiology materiality of bodily life. Nietzsche understands 'body' exclusively in terms of 'will to power', but will to power itself plays out at various levels in Nietzsche's thought, for instance at the sub-individual level of unconscious drives, at the level of the self-conscious individual/ego and at the collective level of the history of peoples, institutions and ideas. Nietzsche's 'political' statements, as well as his notion of eternal recurrence, must, as such, be construed in terms of an interpretation of the body.

Chapter 2 sets out to clarify Nietzsche's understanding of 'nature' and its relationship to the concepts of 'culture', 'life', 'history' and 'translation'. I show that the body is the confluence between Nietzsche's vision of history and his conception of nature, both of which fall under his understanding of life. Following Nietzsche's suggestion that nature is a 'bad economist' and that culture transfigures nature by giving it a sustainable goal (to establish the favourable conditions for the reproduction of the philosopher), I propose that for Nietzsche, the realm of culture provides an efficient economy – a productive and renewable structure – to nature, which assures that the highest forms of life are produced and collectively deployed.

The nomothetic Dionysian task of the philosopher, as such, would involve the cultivation and institution of laws designed to imitate nature. I develop this Nietzschean idea based on Georges Bataille's terminology of general and restricted economies: in the former, unconditional expenditure is completely unlimited and unrestricted by the objectives of social utility, conservation and productivity; meanwhile the latter only involves the expenditure of social energy based on the principle of utility, conservation and production which is practically required by any social activity. Therefore, the future philosopher's task involves a relationship both to the restricted economy of the nomothetic pyramid of great politics and to the general economy of eternal recurrence, which is attributable to the Dionysian. Both economies are necessary to instantiate the task of translation: the restricted nomothetic economy contains and directs social and cultural energies within the goals set forth by 'great politics', while the general economy ensures the limitless creativity and continuation of the activity of self-overcoming of the highest types. From this point, I interpret the goal of 'great politics': in order for the philosopher to be free to experiment and overcome limitlessly, a restricted economy would have to be set up to establish the favourable social conditions under which the philosopher's experience of unrestricted expenditure could be made socially valuable.

At this juncture, a philosophical and political dilemma emerges. For Nietzsche, every form of morality places restrictions and constraints on a culture insofar as the cultivation of a new perspective of life requires an organized and organizing system of behaviour. Essential to the task of legislating, then, is the imposition and usurpation of one perspective over others, which necessarily involves selection and exclusion.

If, however, all perspectives are selections that necessarily include and exclude material, then how can we understand Nietzsche's claim that the highest type is one who says 'Yes' to all things? The problematic to emerge from the presentation of Nietzsche's notion of perspectivism concerns the seeming antithesis between the equally important projects of critical or negative philosophy ('nay-saying') and of affirmative philosophy ('yes-saying').

From the point of view of the general concern of this study, this implication forms the cornerstone of the argument that unfolds in Chapters 3, 4 and 5. The key to uncovering the relationship between will to power and eternal recurrence, from this point forward, revolves around making the correspondence between negation and affirmation, and more importantly in defining how the highest type engages in both 'nay-saying' and 'yes-saying'.

In Chapter 3, I turn to Wolfgang Müller-Lauter's observation concerning the tension between Nietzsche's philosophies of negation and affirmation. According to Müller-Lauter, Nietzsche's description of the most extreme form of nihilism contains two incompatible goals and thus reflects two incompatible human natures, leading to two distinctly separate lines of development for the highest type: on the one hand, greatness consists in 'philosophizing with a hammer' which is constituted primarily by the absolutization of one's perspective against all other ideals. On the other hand, greatness consists in the unrestricted acceptance of all ideals; far from requiring negation (i.e. selection and exclusion), this affirmation necessitates the unmitigated recognition of all perspectives. The tension between both visions of the Overman is expressly characterized as the antithesis between the strong and wise types. The former, in its preoccupation with achieving and maintaining strength, wants not to acknowledge ideals different from its own; the latter, in its ability to assimilate all counter-ideals, does not resist any knowledge. I use Müller-Lauter's exposition to argue that if the task of 'translation' requires both the affirmation of all ideals and a nomothetic project, then the Overhuman must somehow engage both in negation and in affirmation. The Overman's task thus seems to necessitate a radical transformation from negation to affirmation, and my argument sets out to give an account of this transformation in which the strong type necessarily becomes the wise. The task of the Overhuman, therefore, must encompass both the absolutization of ideals through negation and, at a certain historical point, also the affirmative and eternal acceptance of all ideals. How does this occur?

In Chapter 4, I consider Leo Strauss's account of how affirmation emerges spontaneously out of the demands set forth by negative philosophy itself. Strauss's interpretation of the relationship between will to power and eternal recurrence proves to be incisive insofar as Strauss avers that the affirmation of eternity – the 'unbounded Yes to everything that was and is' – emerges from out of the most profound denial of life. Strauss's insight here is crucial to the unfolding of my argument because he was able to see that Nietzsche intended the most incompatible philosophical exigencies (i.e. the exigency to criticize the values of one's time and the exigency to affirm everything) to be ultimately reconcilable over the course of a peculiar experiential process. But ultimately, Strauss resorts to a metaphysical (eliding the physical) argument and cannot fully explain the psycho-physiological mechanism that transforms negation into affirmation.

Here I turn to Karl Löwith's interpretation of eternal recurrence, which enables me to articulate the lacuna (or perhaps ambiguity) in Strauss's reading. I use Löwith's explanation of the eternal recurrence as both 'the most extreme form of nihilism' and the 'self-overcoming of nihilism' to show the crucial function of 'self-destruction' in the mechanics of nihilism in Nietzsche's thought. The completion of nihilism leads to the overcoming of nihilism insofar as the project of negation demands the negation of the last historical artefact that remains, the will itself. This is consistent with Nietzsche's claim and with Löwith's account that the very act of succumbing to nihilism may effect the overcoming of nihilism. The task of the 'strong type' within the project of negative philosophy is to complete the task of negation by finally completing the trajectory inaugurated by the Christian will to truth. The end of Christian morality is, paradoxically, the death of the will itself. Completing the course of nihilism must necessarily lead to a transformation in the history of human morality (see Part 5 of *Beyond Good and Evil* for Nietzsche's account). I re-articulate Löwith's understanding of the 'teaching of the Overman' into a proposition: at the peak of strength, the 'strong' type must affirm the dissolution of its will; that is, it must affirm non-willing (it must affirm affirmation itself). This would be the last step that would both complete the project of negative philosophy (No-saying) as well as demarcate the moment of transformation of negation into affirmation (the eternal Yes to all that is and will be). It is, however, precisely at the moment in which the highest type makes the most fundamental existential commitment to negate its 'self' that an antinomy surfaces: the affirmation of the dissolution of the will itself requires negation. The consequence of the antinomy is a profound destabilization that is also meant to be a psycho-physiological transmutation in the human. The experience of this antinomy, I argue, is the experience of eternal recurrence. I describe this antinomic moment, following Georges Bataille, as the experience of an extreme limit in which the metaphysical comfort promised by self-sacrifice turns into its opposite, the profound recognition of the absence of salvation. The experience of the eternal recurrence, as psycho-physiological modification, is felt by the organism that undergoes it as a crisis of will, the emblematic exemplar of this experience being the agonized words of Jesus on the Cross: My God, my God, why hast thou forsaken me? Through a reading of the figure of 'the Crucified', I want to suggest that the experience of eternal recurrence would be something as profoundly world-shattering as that moment in which Jesus believes that he is forsaken by the divine. Certainly, this interpretation of Jesus's words is thoroughly Nietzschean rather than consistent with any canonical understanding, but it is precisely my intention to try to explain the eternal recurrence as an experience that purifies Christian morality from out of the very conditions presupposed by Christian nihilism.

In the moment where Jesus, for the first time, experiences life without God, he experiences existence in its barest, most naked and exposed actuality. Nietzsche might say that in this moment, Jesus is the transformation of the 'human-all-too-human' into the 'Overhuman'. Abandoned by the divine and yet still existing as the brute occurrence of life itself, as both a mere moment in the course of eternity and therefore one with eternity itself, he is no longer a nihilistic man, but Overman, the one who is lightning. What is revealed in this antinomic crisis of will (simultaneously negation and the negation of negation) is that life is inexhaustible; it exists, persists. What is felt by the one who undergoes the eternal recurrence is a translation back into life. For Nietzsche, the love of eternity arises from this: life wills man and in so doing, life affirms man. It is in this sense that I understand the eternal recurrence as both the negation and affirmation (the negation of negation) of willing – both a denial of life and a love for life. Because the experience of the eternal recurrence shatters the mnemotechnics of self-consciousness, thus giving way to the multiplicity of the unconscious impulses, it consists primarily in the feeling of being willed (by life which is will to power) rather than in willing.

The experience of the eternal recurrence can now more clearly be seen in its function as a catalyst for a radical psycho-physiological modification that is intended to transform the human into the Overhuman. I connect Nietzsche's denouncement of the 'self-conscious subject' with the experience of eternal recurrence in order to understand how the 'individual' could be, at once, a 'fiction' that 'wills'. Following

Klossowski's lead, I suggest that in the eternal recurrence is experienced the dissolution of self-identity behind which lies 'the total discontinuity of our state'.[39]

In the final chapter, in which three figures are analysed at length (Socrates, Jesus and Odysseus), I consider the dynamics of translation as 'transmutation', the plastic or polytropic function of bodily transformation, or morphogenesis, that becomes the operative perspective through which Nietzsche's typology of 'high', 'higher' and the 'highest' can be interpreted as of various intensities, or intensive configurations of will to power (from most reactive to most active). 'Great politics' is the name for the cultivation of the Overhuman functionality of will to power within present configurations of existence. In this way, the Overhuman is the material expression of the 'eternal law of transformation'.

The experience of eternal recurrence is therefore not conceptual but affective; it is not a potentiality that must be actualized (to use Hegelian language), but a functionality that must be catalysed, the effects of which may transform the structural configuration of a system across various ontological scales (e.g. the 'individual', the 'collective'), thus 'translating' the human 'back' into its aleatory activity as the most active will to power. To be consistent with Nietzsche's rejection of reality as 'substance' oriented towards stability and equilibrium, the Overman cannot be conceptualized in terms of the model of the 'individual' or 'thing', and thus the teaching of the eternal recurrence cannot be understood within the framework of a doctrine or dogma. It is, instead, a self-organizing functionality, rather than a messianic 'self', the most active configuration that can take form in existence.

1
The Displaced 'Origin' of Political Physiology

> [O]ften I have asked myself whether, taking a large view, philosophy has not been merely an interpretation of the body and a misunderstanding of the body. [...] All those bold insanities of metaphysics, especially answers to the question about the value of existence, may always be considered first of all as the symptoms of certain bodies. And if such world affirmations or world negations – lock, stock and barrel – lack any grain of significance when measured scientifically, they are the more valuable for the historian and psychologist as hints or symptoms of the body, of its success or failure, its plenitude, power, and autocracy in history, or of its frustrations, weariness, impoverishment, its premonitions of the end, its will to the end.
>
> *GS* Preface: §2

> The question, and at the same time the task, is approaching without hesitation, terrible as Fate, but nevertheless inevitable: how shall the earth as a whole be ruled?
>
> *WP* 957

Nietzsche's place in the canon of political thought is often contested. Although Nietzsche's criticism of modernity is valuable when considering the competing claims between politics (the pursuit of power) and philosophy (the pursuit of wisdom), his prescriptive statements about how to overcome the malaise of modernity are at the very least resistant (some would say opposed) to articulation in wholly political terms.

The critique of the modern state is a leitmotif found in Nietzsche's early and later works which he articulates as an explicit rejection of 'politics' or 'petty politics' in favour of 'culture' or 'great politics'.[1] Nonetheless most commentators accurately point to Nietzsche's praise of the ancient Greek state that, he argues, provided the conditions necessary to breed the qualities required to create and sustain a strong and vital culture of heroic types.[2] Generally, the debate in contemporary Nietzsche studies between the 'political' and 'anti-political' readings of Nietzsche[3] continues to consider whether politics is central to Nietzsche's thought. What is it about Nietzsche's thought that tells us something unequivocally important about political existence? What is it that Nietzsche points to that still remains unthought in the history of political thought? And why does Nietzsche's thought resist interpretations that are based strictly on the terms and concepts provided by the history of political thought?

The psycho-physiological basis of will to power

Despite the effort to qualify or substantiate Nietzsche's 'political' philosophy, Nietzsche is still difficult to place among the pantheon of political thinkers because his concern with the polis, with a collective ordering of political existence, is subordinate to his preoccupation with the general phenomenon of life. If for Aristotle the necessities of biological life remained distinct from political and ethical life in the city, then for Nietzsche all life, from the most basic biological functions to the most complex intersubjective civic forms, emanates from the same dynamic principle that permits any form of life to exist. The origin of and key to political life, as such, is located not in the polis itself but in the impulses of organic existence that either allow life to grow and expand, or conversely to wither and dissipate. Political existence is, first and foremost, only a particular characteristic of all organic existence. Even the soul is an invention of the body, says Nietzsche's visionary prophet Zarathustra; Zarathustra knows that he is no more and no less than his body. Will to power is above all a self-organizing organic activity that is lived experientially and affectively in humans.[4] In *Beyond Good and Evil*, Nietzsche declares the 'soul' to be mortal, a 'subjective multiplicity' and a 'social structure of drives and affects'.[5] The 'soul' is a correlate and particular expression of the multiple drives and affects.[6]

Nietzsche advances a peculiar view of the body vis-à-vis political theory, but one that is not unknown to the Western history of ideas. His conception of the body picks up on Spinoza's contention that 'nature is always the same, and everywhere one and same in her efficacy and power of action'.[7] For Spinoza, both intellect and emotion, mind and body 'are one and the same thing ... [C]onsequently the order of states of activity and passivity in our body is simultaneous in nature with the order of states of activity and passivity in the mind'.[8] The centrality of the body in Nietzsche's thought follows this Spinozan innovation to the extent that he asserts that knowledge itself finds its basis and origin in the physiological movement of nature.

This idea grounds Nietzsche's argument concerning the role of 'consciousness' in the history of philosophy and morality, and also prefigures Freud's revaluation of the nature and function of consciousness and unconsciousness:

> It is essential that one should not make a mistake over the role of 'consciousness': it is our relation with the 'outer world' that evolved it. On the other hand, the direction or protection and care in respect of the co-ordination of the bodily functions does not enter our consciousness.[9]

Nietzsche's idea of an invisible and unknown threshold underlying 'consciousness' structures his entire vision of eternal recurrence and its relation to future philosophy. Nietzsche's view of the history of philosophy as 'an interpretation of the body'[10] revolves around his claim that 'that which becomes conscious is involved in causal relations which are entirely withheld from us'; consciousness is therefore not 'the directing agent' but an 'organ of the directing agent'.[11]

On the one hand, the body is the corporeal flesh of human life that is born, ages, declines and finally passes away. The body is the sensorial organs, the nervous system, cerebral activity, and the phenomenal experience of pain. In Nietzsche's many correspondences, he writes of his bodily ailments and sufferings, his migraines, hallucinations, his moments of suffering and joy.[12] On the other hand, Nietzsche speaks of the body as self,[13] the complex configuration of conscious and unconscious drives that reside in the midst of the senses and expresses itself through the effects and affects of the body. The Nietzschean notion of 'body' is both physiological and psychological. Body is only partially an image of consciousness, and the physical body may itself be an effect of an ongoing intensive modification. Nietzsche makes clear that philosophy as the interpretation of the body is, and always has been, a reflection of the particular, concrete and historical conflict between various wills to power. Not only does all 'will to knowledge' emerge from a physiological need of a particular organism and group of organisms, but the body of the organism is itself a social structure made up of multiple forces, and provisionally and temporarily fixed within certain configurations that, through language, are identified as a totality or 'self'.

Nietzsche assumes that the body (in its myriad effects) is both visible and invisible. This point is confirmed by Daniel Conway who writes that 'decadence is predicated not of the visible corporeal body, but of the 'invisible' instinctual body, the subsystem of drives and impulses that propagates the native vitality of the animal organism'.[14] Indeed, Lou Salomé, commenting on her correspondence with Nietzsche, remarks on this tension between the visible and invisible body: 'it was when he felt most healthy and most robust, in complete control of his creative powers, that he came closest to his illness: and it was the forced rest and idleness that would again allow him to recover and to keep the catastrophe in suspense'.[15] Nietzsche's understanding of 'body' concerns the body's apprehension of visible or immediate forces, and invisible or 'hidden' ones. Human history is no longer the history of consciousness or self-consciousness as understood traditionally; rather, Nietzsche attempts to locate the 'origin' of human existence in the interstice between 'conscious' and 'unconscious' forces. The 'individual' is a fluctuating concrescence and 'symptom of much more internal and more fundamental events', an expression of the 'entire process in its entire course'.[16] As Klossowski notes, Nietzsche's task is to attempt 'to specify the relationship between the "conscious" agent and the so-called "unconscious" activity of the impulses in relation to this agent' in order to demonstrate that self-identity is an arbitrary set of linkages (understood as a 'unity') that conceals 'the total discontinuity of our state'.[17]

The significance of this idea cannot be underestimated: not only does Nietzsche claim that all morality originates in the material conditions of the body, but more importantly, the language of the body replaces the language of the polis such that the experience of the drives and impulses of the body will become the originary site for all of Nietzsche's thoughts on society, culture and politics:

> If the body concerns our most immediate forces as those which, in terms of their origin, are the most distant, then everything the body says – its well-being as well as its diseases – gives us the best information about our destiny. Nietzsche therefore wanted to go back toward what, in himself, was most distant to comprehend the most immediate.[18]

The irony of this aetiology (the orientation of what is 'most immediate' towards what is 'most distant') is that the Nietzschean search for lucidity regarding the health and 'destiny' of any particular body necessarily entails delving into what is most obscure and conventionally unavailable to the intellect. If the degeneration of the physical body can signal nonetheless a deep-seated regeneration of the instinctual impulsional body, then Nietzsche's 'philosopher of the future' (*BGE* §211) would bear very little resemblance to what would normally be designated as 'philosopher'. Moreover, given that it is the hidden body that ultimately reflects health and vitality, this future philosopher would have to view all the customary markers of contemporary culture – institutions, civic forms of engagement, art, religion – with suspicion and even paranoia. And indeed, this is precisely what I take Nietzsche's message to be indicating: the philosopher of the future is as yet unknown,[19] perhaps because he is hard to recognize. The philosopher of the future is necessarily *untimely*; he is out of joint with his times, and this has a double political effect: one the one hand, this untimeliness almost pushes the philosopher to the margins of society and condemns him to marginality; on the other hand, this untimeliness compels the philosopher to resist this marginality precisely by *cultivating* it. Strategically therefore, the philosopher of the future must always be *contra-tiempo* (against the times), cultivating the art of rebellion. 'The philosopher as a *necessary* man of tomorrow and the day after tomorrow, has always found himself, and always had to find himself, in opposition to his today: the ideal of the day was always his enemy' (*BGE* 212).

We could say that Nietzsche's conception of the body reflects two major premises he holds. First, the body, like all features and elements of life, is an effect of the contest between the quanta of force that make up the will to power. This is a basis for Nietzsche's refutation of the metaphysical dualism between 'body' and 'soul'. And second, as a result of this, the body is a complex of events of which the historical conflict between various states of will to power are configurations and dramatizations. As Wolfgang Müller-Lauter writes:

> The resulting conflict of the drives or forces is thus the condition of all events. This conflict can never come to a standstill, 'for every drive also incites its counterdrive' ... Each of these drives feels itself impeded or promoted, flattered, with regard to every other one; each has its own law of development (its rise and decline, its tempo, etc.) ... In their 'For or Against' (*WP* §481), in 'the competition between affects' (*WP* §618), alliances form and break apart again; rulers replace one another; the subject-point leaps around.[20]

The body is a theatre of war, as well as a 'social structure' (*BGE* 19). As such, Nietzsche suggests that the body's activities consist of contestation and codification: the body is a battlespace of conflict between impulses that impose themselves on other impulses, out of which emerges a feeling of the 'self' that becomes conscious and then codified and communicated in and through language. Nietzsche makes literal the notion of 'body politic'; it is the material through which self-organizing organic processes are expressed. The body politic is the organization of the differing intensities of drives, and their multiform translation in cultural, social, historical values and institutions. For instance, multiple bodily impulses come into conflict with each other, and as one impulse gains mastery over another, the ordering which emerges is translated and communicated into language (signification) and designated as value – for example, in the language of 'high or low', 'healthy or ill', 'strong or weak'. This implies not only that all 'morality' and social valuation is at bottom an expression and interpretation of bodily states but also that the 'self-conscious' agent is nothing other than this fluctuating, temporary concretion of instincts. 'The subject', as Nietzsche insists, 'is a multiplicity'[21] and 'a fiction' (*WP* §485).

As I will argue in this examination, Nietzsche's conception of 'great politics' is grounded in the pre-eminence of his conception of body in which the superiority of the 'philosophy of the future' will lie in directly measuring and justifying the 'health' and vitality of the species in terms of the 'health' and vitality of the philosopher's innermost physiological and psychological workings. Thus, all life is begotten by the alchemy of the body: 'in the philosopher, conversely, there is nothing whatever that is impersonal; and above all, his morality bears decided and decisive witness to who he is – that is, in what order of rank the innermost drives of his nature stand in relation to each other'.[22]

Political ontology and the pre-Platonic physiologists

For Nietzsche, another tremendously important source for elucidating his formulation of 'will to power' as a 'physiological process' (e.g. *BGE* 242), as a 'pathology' and a 'sign of health' (*BGE* 154) lies in the thought of the early pre-Socratic Greek physiologists or *physiologoi*. Although Nietzsche coined the term *der Wille zur Macht* or 'the will to power' only in *Thus Spoke Zarathustra* (1883), the seed of the conception dates back to his earliest study of Thales, Anaximander, Pythagoras and Heraclitus.[23] Throughout his exploration of these *physiologoi* (physiologists qua natural philosophers), Nietzsche was profoundly struck not just by the speculative achievement of the pre-classical Greek materialists, but more so by the fact that their activity of thinking through the most mundane and elemental aspects of existence could be recognized by their whole civilization as a mark of both individual and collective greatness.[24]

Originally intended as a lecture series for philology students at the University of Basel, the collection of short essays was published over a century later as *The Pre-Platonic Philosophers*. Having been influenced in his early exploration of the 'organic' by the historical materialism of Friedrich Lange and the critical idealism of Arthur Schopenhauer,[25] what Nietzsche intuits right from his earliest study of the Greeks is that a rigorous investigation of the concept of the 'organic' would require an espousal of materialist principles, as well as a confrontation with the limits of materialism. Nietzsche's materialism could thus be interpreted as an 'experimental ontology', 'a transvaluation of [the] two great orientations of philosophical modernity, materialism and critique'.[26] Inspired by the vision of the Greek philosopher-physiologists, Nietzsche's brand of materialism would try to avoid the illusion of reductionism and mechanistic causality by reading or deciphering the materiality of the organic world in terms of its hidden or encrypted signatures. In this sense, his materialism is 'a paradoxical materialism without matter'.[27]

In his study of the pre-Platonics, Nietzsche brings together his thoughts on the organic problem of individuation and his philosophical and philological study of the Greeks. His interpretation centres on 'the riddle of defining the philosopher', which he explores in terms of a psycho-physiological spectrum of typologies. We see Nietzsche's fascination for the idea that in the ancient Greek-speaking world prior to Plato, there appear archetypal figures who pursue self-investigation ceaselessly, and who, in so doing, create their very persona or character (*ethos*) precisely in accordance with what is discovered as the vital principles of the natural world. 'The *human beings* themselves who became pre-Platonic philosophers are formal incarnations of Philosophia and *her various forms*'.[28] For Nietzsche, the philosopher is the physiological process and generative formation of an unprecedented kind of being, a being that, like all manifestations of *physis*[29] ('growth' or 'nature'), is subject to the formative forces of emergence.

In terms of the trajectory from philology to the 'philosophy of the future', we find in these lecture notes evidence not only of Nietzsche's lifelong preoccupation with the investigation of *physis* ('nature' understood here as 'becoming', or the emergent property of *logos*) but also with the psycho-physiological formation (what Nietzsche calls 'type') that corresponds to this conception of nature. Throughout his whole thinking life which was preoccupied with 'the riddle of defining the philosopher',[30] Nietzsche sought to name, and therefore legislate, the psycho-physiological configuration whose subjective and somatic organization best corresponded to the reality of 'becoming', as evinced in the material processes of organic life. In *Thus Spoke Zarathustra*, perhaps the most 'Dionysian' of Nietzsche's writings, this subjective formation is called 'Zarathustra', depicted as a childlike wanderer and as 'lightning'. In *Beyond Good and Evil*, this psycho-physiological configuration is called upon variously, as 'the philosopher of the future' and as 'homo natura', whose defining characteristics are 'ordering and ranking' and 'commanding and legislating', but whose such nomothetic activity is, nonetheless, fundamentally consonant with what Nietzsche called the 'eternal law of transformation'.[31]

In *The Pre-Platonic Philosophers*, Nietzsche analyses the course of materialism from Thales to Socrates that – he argued – generated the Western cultural prototype of the 'philosopher' as distinct from the 'wise man'. These early philosopher-physiologists had, generally speaking, rejected the mythological (Homeric and Hesiodic) account of the origin of *anthropos* (the human) as an artifice of the divine. Rather, the philosopher-physiologists explained the origin of humanity as arising from the same natural principles of ontological transformation that governed formation and differentiation in all existence (*kosmêsis* or 'ordering'; the coining of the word 'kosmos' is attributed to Pythagoras of Samos[32]).

Pre-Platonic materialism, as such, brought about a conceptual innovation that created a radical shift in the human being's awareness of itself. Apparently for the first time in the recorded history of Western societies, the 'two great scientific-philosophical questions of What and How' were posed, namely 'What is the primary stuff of which the world is constituted?' and 'How do the changes take place that bring about its manifold appearances?'[33]

These early physiologists, unlike their modern variants, did not seek to speculate merely about the fixable or quantifiable physical properties of nature because they intuited that the primal matter of which the world was made could only be understood in its manifestation, namely as a process or play of appearing (and passing). Without having to resort to metaphysical dualisms (e.g. 'real' as distinct from 'apparent', 'subjective' as distinct from 'objective'), early natural science hypothesized that 'qualities are in the main what they appear to be; they are properties of things primarily, of minds secondarily; and the distinction between the thing beheld and the mind beholding it was loose and fluctuating'.[34] Accordingly, thinking as an act(ivity) must correspond to the ever-fluctuating character of the world it seeks to know.

To these early investigators, however, the formal qualities of nature did not present themselves transparently as clear properties. Rather, the emergence of nature (*physis*) was cloaked, requiring decipherment. 'Nature loves to hide' (*phusis kruptesthai philei*[35]), making it necessary for the observer of nature to be able to discern nature's presentations. Henceforth, the *physiologoi* would seek to investigate the principles of nature by speculating about what had up to that point been considered the hidden aspects of the natural world.

The pursuit of this kind of knowledge would require a specific kind of human attribute – wisdom (*sophia*) – Nietzsche understands this term neither as divine foresight nor as a rational 'faculty', but rather as a selective proclivity or 'taste' for what would 'normally be termed out of the ordinary, miraculous, difficult, but useless' because 'it [has] nothing to do with humane goods'.[36] To think of 'wisdom' as a taste for the useless implied a peculiar conception of the *hodos philosophos,* the philosophical way of inquiry involving something beyond even what the man of science must know: 'the wise man must not only be able to know how conclusions follow from principles, but he must know even this as well: which branch of knowledge contains those principles most worthy of knowledge [...] Thus [pre-Platonic] sophia receives the character of the useless', says Nietzsche. 'In its service an excess of intellect is necessary'.[37] For the early philosopher-physicians, the 'first step' of wisdom thus involved describing 'each thing not as we think we know it to be, but as it directly appears to an actively percipient mind'.[38] (But not 'mind' as abstracted from the 'body'; rather the 'mind' being simply a correlate of or emergent activity of incorporating existence).

Generally speaking, the genius of the early pre-Platonic physiologists lay in the coalescing of the goals of cosmological and anthropological investigation (the principle of *anthropokosmêsis*[39]), the result of which was the invention of a materialist ontology that fused the science of nature with experiential knowledge (i.e. the search for the generative principles governing human experience).[40] In the homology between macrocosm and microcosm,[41] the Pythagoreans based their whole system of political theory on the principle of *harmonia,* which was based on the mixture and ranking of elements in nature, including a well-developed theory of the division of the soul into parts and its relations of proportion.[42] The same ordering principle that presented itself in the formation of nature also presented itself in the formation of the human, as clearly expressed in opposition of two intensities (limited/unlimited or definite/indefinite), as laid out in Pythagorean number philosophy (this philosophy of the relation between two opposing forces can also be seen in Heraclitean thought). For the Pythagoreans specifically (but also found in Anaximander's theories and the Milesian tradition; see Minar, 1942), all form (and harmony) was a result of recombination, the interaction of two forces in which one force (the 'noble' force destined to 'rule') subordinates another weaker force (thus subordinate but still necessary for *kosmêsis* or ordering). The anthropocosmic notion that 'the cosmos, the state and the individual are all governed by the same principles'[43] could be expressed as the harmonious but differential relation between ruling and ruled forces. For Nietzsche, the human is a theatre of ordering or *kosmêsis*,

From Pythagoras to Heraclitus and finding its culmination in the late mathematical school of the neo-Pythagoreans,[44] materialist ontology would require the first-hand investigation of 'inward nature' in order to discover cosmic principles (perhaps best captured in Heraclitus's fragment *edisesamen emeouton*, 'I have searched myself'[45]). Although Plato later adopted the microcosm/macrocosm analogy ('city' and 'soul') as part of the rationale for advancing the Socratic project of moral reform, Nietzsche also reminds us that with Socrates the investigation of nature becomes an epistemic pursuit. 'Knowledge [episteme] as the path to virtue differentiates his philosophical character: dialectic as the single path, induction (*epagogikoi logoi*) and definition (*horizesthai*)'.[46] The degeneration of Western thought begins with the Socratic view which 'dispenses entirely with physics' (*PP*, 143).

In this manner, the *physiologoi* were the inventors of natural science and philosophy, which Nietzsche proclaims to be the 'art that presents an image of universal existence in concepts'.[47] The philosopher, according to Nietzsche's definition, is the wise practitioner of this art, who himself is 'hewn from one stone',[48] who takes himself to be synonymous with all other matter in the universe and is therefore subject to the same laws of individuation. This activity of wise 'self-fashioning' according to the principles of material transformation is the type 'philosopher', and it is against the backdrop of 'this riddle of defining philosopher' that we can interpret Nietzsche's lifelong interest in 'physiology' and his self-identification with 'we physiologists' (or 'we physicists' referring to those such as Friedrich Ueberweg, Friedrich Lange and Hermann von Helmholtz).[49]

From this interpretive context, the formulation of 'will to power' can be seen as an expression of Nietzsche's interest in the 'becoming' or generation and formation of the philosopher as 'homo natura',[50] the embodied concrescence (*anthropos*) of universal ordering (*kosmêsis*), which is the 'subject' of pre-Platonic *physis*, as well as the 'subject-formation' that would best correspond to the 'philosophy of the future':

> We desire to establish first of all that the Greeks were driven from within themselves toward philosophy and to ask, 'To what end? Second, we want to observe how 'the philosopher' appeared among the Greeks, not just how philosophy appeared among them. To become acquainted with the Greeks, it proves extremely noteworthy that several among them came to conscious reflection about themselves: perhaps even more important than this conscious reflection is their personality, their behavior. The Greeks produced archetypal philosophers.[51]

What distinguishes the pre-Platonic thinkers from both their predecessors and their inheritors? 'Becoming', 'purpose' and 'knowledge' – the pillars of pre-Platonic thought identified by Nietzsche in these lectures[52] – belong to a matrix of emergence that the pre-Platonics called *physis*, conceptualized as the 'birth, growth, activity, and the unforeseen emergence of new qualities'.[53] The pre-Platonics set themselves apart from their Homeric predecessors by successfully 'overcoming' the mythological worldview, first by 'thinking conceptually'; second by 'systematizing'; and third by 'creating one [unified] view of the world'.[54] According to Nietzsche, the *physiologoi* sought a single unified theory of nature and 'had to find the path from myth to laws of nature, from image to concept, from religion to science'.[55] They accomplished this by speculatively and culturally integrating the domains of natural science (the investigation of the qualitative character of *physis*) and of philosophy (the pursuit of wisdom) in order to structure political law or *nomos* (nomothetic ordering) which always fundamentally concerns the issue of 'the relation of the philosopher to nonphilosophers, to the people [Volk]'.[56]

The pre-Platonic physiologists also distinguished themselves radically from their 'classical' heirs insofar as their ontological speculations broadly regarded *nomos* (law or convention) as the 'lawful' manifestation of *physis*, 'the world of nature as it can be experienced'.[57] Much more than merely a philosophy of education, a school of thinking, or a philosopheme, these Greeks had cultivated a historically unprecedented type of human being (*anthropos*) capable of regarding itself as homologous with nature. Pre-Platonic *nomos* (laws), in reality, is synonymous with *physis* (growth), especially in the thought of Heraclitus, who Nietzsche admits is the one who came closest to Dionysian philosophy.

The nomothetic framework in which the pre-Platonic physiologists arose is of particular interest to Nietzsche, who noticed that these societies ranked the philosophical type highly and honoured rather than persecuted the philosopher. The *physiologoi* were driven to think by their compulsion to know how *physis* works both 'inwardly' and 'outwardly'.[58] Nietzsche finds it remarkable that this philosophical compulsion was not deemed to be at odds with the greatest needs and aspirations of the larger collectivity in which it arose:

> Each one of those [pre-Platonic] men is entirely hewn from one stone; between their thought and their character lies rigorous necessity [...] Each is the first-born son of philosophy [...] It has been rightfully said that a time is characterized not so much by its great men but by how it recognizes and honors them. That constitutes the most noteworthy thing about the Greeks, that their needs and their talents coincided.[59]

Beginning with the reaction of Platonic political philosophy to Sophism, the 'talents' of the philosophical type – so much in demand in pre-classical Greek societies – are considered contrary to (and even inconsequential for) the cultural development of the polis.

While it is certainly true that Nietzsche looked to the world of Homeric and Hesiodic culture to find content for his articulation of the 'noble type', and that Nietzsche praises the Homeric Greeks and their political culture in such early texts as *The Greek State* and *Homer's Contest* (both written in 1872), it is in relation to the thought that arises within the time frame between Thales and Democritus (or Socrates if we adopt Nietzsche's chronology) wherein lies the key to elucidating Nietzsche's formulation of 'will to power' as a physiological process. The pre-Platonic 'philosopher' that arises out of the 'preliminary forms' of the hero-prince, the bardic poets and the ceremonial priest (*PP*, 18) is the embodiment of homo logos (or 'homo natura' as Nietzsche calls it in *BGE* §230).[60] 'Thales', as such, is not only the name of the first philosopher (physician). 'Thales' is itself the physiological process and generative formation of an unprecedented kind of being, a being that, like all manifestations of *physis*, is structured within the eternal law of 'becoming'.

Of these novel types of subjective dispositions, it is perhaps in the 'Heraclitus' type that we find the closest precursor for Nietzsche's conception of 'will to power' as a materialist theory of subject formation and as a physiological process. If for Nietzsche the generative catalyst and subsequent hallmark of Hellenic natural philosophy was the 'turning inward of thought',[61] then it becomes more clear why Nietzsche calls Heraclitus the Dionysian philosopher par excellence (despite Heraclitus's criticisms of the Dionysian cults of his own day). For it is in Heraclitus, more than in any other thinker in the speculative history of the pre-Platonics (including Pythagoras and Socrates), that the activity of 'inward turning' becomes the *arche* or principle of physical reality as well as the impetus for ethical activity. For Heraclitus, the principle of 'inward turning' was both the expression of the dynamic tension of opposites in nature (*palintropos harmonia*[62]) and the foundation for the self-reflective activity of the philosopher's quest(ioning).[63] Nietzsche clearly recognizes this principle of 'inward turning' or *palintropos harmonia* at work in Heraclitean thought when he says, 'Nature is just as infinite inwardly as it is outwardly: we have succeeded up to the cell and to parts of the cell, yet there are no limits where we could say here is the last divisible point. Becoming never ceases at the indefinitely small. Yet at the greatest [level] nothing absolutely unalterable exists'.[64]

Within the law of universal flux (which in later years Nietzsche calls 'Dionysian nature'[65]), all manifestation (differentiation and formation) is made possible by the tense harmonization of two opposing forces (which for Heraclitus is symbolized in the principle of 'fire'[66]). 'Change is an alteration [of quality] from opposite to opposite'.[67] In 'the knock-down battle between two ontological opposites',[68] the truth of reality is that it is necessarily both *one* and *many*[69]; without this tense harmony of opposites, nothing would appear.

> Thus, the one overall Becoming is itself law; that it becomes and how it becomes is its work. Heraclitus thus sees only the One, but in the sense opposite to Parmenides. All qualities of things, all laws, all generation and destruction, are the continual revelation of the existence of One: multiplicity, which is a deception of the sense according to Parmenides, is for Heraclitus the cloth, the form of appearance, of the One, and in no way a deception, for otherwise, the One does not appear at all.[70]

The necessary condition for all manifestation (given the permanence of change in the universe) is *polemos* (war or strife). It is in this sense alone that *polemos pantôn men patêr esti*, 'strife is the father of all'.[71] Strife, therefore, is a necessary condition for the emergence (*physis*) of the universal Logos. Physically, physiologically and metaphysically, *palintropos harmonia*, the 'back-stretched connection' of opposing forces in flux, is the dynamics of the law of becoming, which is also the law of formation (a tense and intensive harmony), the back and forth movement of which Heraclitus expresses as *polemos*. Moreover, the universal dynamic of strife manifests itself both in outward and inward nature in Heraclitean thought. The implication here is that self-knowledge is not the search for a fixed or stable identity but rather the search to uncover the hidden play of strife (of opposing forces), the interaction of which gives rise to character (ethos) or subjective disposition.

The political physiology of power: Hobbes vs. Nietzsche

Although Nietzsche is not the first to posit a connection between the body (or soul) and social structure (Plato's analogy between the city and soul being the most influential), he departs from this tradition in order to posit that the 'body' is first and foremost a historical phenomenon, not based on any a priori understanding of the dualism between 'body' and 'soul'. Nietzsche understands 'body' exclusively in terms of 'will to power', both in terms of the visible manifestations of the conflict of will to power in human history (as they appear, for example, in the history of peoples, institutions and ideas) and the invisible conflict of impulsional drives.

In the history of modern philosophy, Nietzsche is again not the first to envision this connection between 'body' and 'power'. Hobbes also understood human nature in terms of bodily passions and the pursuit of power. The Galilean Revolution in physics formed the foundation of Hobbes's view of the body as a purely mechanistic system: the body including all features of human psychology and physiology is as much a function of the scientific principles of motion as are astral and other planetary bodies. All human behavior including feeling, sensation and thought could be reduced to its essential physical and natural principle as an object in motion. Unlike Nietzsche's vision of the body as a living personality (the union of soma and psyche), Hobbes's body is a machine that comes into contact and collides with other bodies in motion; every body wants the 'power to move' (Book II, Chapter 21 of *Leviathan*) and therefore seeks self-preservation (the preservation of the ability to move) against others. Thus, 'freedom' for the Hobbesian body is the fact of being unhindered by another body from doing (i.e. moving towards or away from) what it wills to do (see, for example, Hobbes's definition of 'freeman' in Book II, Chapter 21 of *Leviathan*).

I want to highlight two main similarities and differences between the Hobbesian and Nietzschean bodies. First, Hobbes's mechanistic model of motion (of which the body is another instantiation) superficially resembles Nietzsche's view of body-as-will-to-power: in both views, the sensorial strata of the body is the source of human motivation and valuation; value is measured in terms of the degree to which the body's vitality is increased or decreased. The difference, however, is that for Hobbes the physiological principle behind self-preservation is defined simply as the continuation of biological existence. Hobbes's view of the body that continually seeks the 'power to move' is based on the presupposition that desire for power is instrumental to the struggle for existence, and so the fundamental need of all human existence is the desire for security.

For Nietzsche, the body is the nexus between biological/material and psychological/spiritual existence, described in terms of 'the development of a higher body that emerges into our sensibility'.[72] Body is thus both conscious senses and sensibility as well as unconscious and hidden instincts that merge into the senses. The feeling of heightened corporeal vitality for Nietzsche is not identical with the brute continuation of biological life – the necessary principle underlying the Nietzschean body is experimentation with the various tonalities and timbres of the physiological/psychological body in order to experience the possibilities of bodily existence. Concern with self-preservation is thus anathema to the concern with experiencing and overcoming the limits of the living self (this is how we can interpret what Nietzsche calls the 'longing for freedom' in *BGE* §260).

Second, for Hobbes, the means of continuing biological existence is the restless desire for and pursuit of power after power, which ceases only in death (*Leviathan*, Chapter 11). For Hobbes, as for Nietzsche, power is the motor of life, the capacity through which the vitality of existence is sought. But for Nietzsche the vitality of the individual body can be a reflection of the vitality of many bodies, understood collectively as 'culture': thus Nietzsche can speak of the health or illness of the body as a mark of the health or illness of a particular culture that espouses a particular set of moral beliefs. Hobbes's view of the body, however, is strictly individualistic; unlike Nietzsche's view of culture as a mode of species or collective breeding, Hobbesian bodies can only be brought together by mutual interest in pursuing individual self-preservation. Society is therefore only a means to the end of pursuing individual security, and culture is simply the sum of each individual's self-interest in self-preservation. The social contract requires a utilitarian calculation: since the right to self-preservation is the motive of all human behavior, we give up our natural liberty to do whatever we like in the state of nature in order to set up an 'artificial body' – the Sovereign – which is nothing other than a coercive power that is supposed to guarantee the continuation of the conditions by which each individual can pursue the means of acquiring continual self-preservation. All civilization and culture for Hobbes is thus a result of the limitation (considered to be mutually beneficial) put on the expression of most of the natural human instincts (except that of self-preservation).

Hobbesian power differs from the Nietzschean articulation because for Hobbes power is a representation of the individual's unilateral pursuit of self-preservation/security; power can be both tangible, as in wealth, reputation, honour, and intangible, what Hobbes refers to as 'glory'. Hobbesian power is the 'means' of acquiring an object of desire, and felicity or happiness consists in continual success in obtaining those things that man desires. In contrast to this, Nietzsche understands 'power' to be an act of overpowering, which may only incidentally permit the means of acquiring objects of desire. Unlike Hobbes, Nietzsche understands power to be, not primarily a means or an instrument, but the very impetus of motion in nature (in this regard, Nietzsche understands by 'will to power' what Hobbes understands by 'motion'). Will to power is a *pathos* (in terms of its Greek connotations as 'occasion, event, suffering, destiny), the elemental condition of existence that permits the possibility of Hobbesian motion:

> Mechanistic theory formulates consecutive appearances and it does so semeiotically, in terms of the senses and of psychology (that all effect is motion; that where there is motion something is moved); it does not touch upon the causal force. The mechanistic world is imagined as only sight and touch imagine a world (as 'moved') – so as to be calculable – ... If we eliminate these additions, no things remain but only dynamic quanta, in a relation of tension to all other dynamic quanta ... The will to power not a being, not a becoming, but a pathos – the most elemental fact from which a becoming and effecting first emerge.[73]

Hobbesian motion is therefore a sign or symptom of the dynamism of will to power. Power, for Nietzsche, is not a 'means' that is capitalized upon by human nature; will to power is the entirety of all organic processes (human is a piece of nature in this regard, cf. *BGE* §9). Will to power, as such, is the subject of life (power wills), as well as the object of any and all human action (power wills power). Nietzsche thus equates 'power' with 'willing', power as the fundamental (f)act of 'willing-something'. Deleuze suggests that to Hobbes 'man in the state of nature wants to see his superiority represented and recognized by others',[74] whereas for Nietzsche, will to power is an active exertion – power as emanating from and producing an effect on the emotions – rather than a recognition or representation. Following Deleuze, Paul Patton notes,

> for Nietzsche, it is only the slave who understands power in terms of representation since this is a mediocre and base interpretation of power. Any such representational concept of power is prone to implicit conformism, since it implies that an individual will only be recognized as powerful in accordance with accepted values.[75]

Hobbesian power, understood as self-preservation, is thus considered a reactive rather than active conception of power; 'it is the manner in which power is typically exercised from a position of weakness'.[76] This is a reactive vision of power that effectively renders the body 'sick' because it devalues by spiritualizing it in relation to abstract concepts. The 'healthy' body, as such, is always earthly. Zarathustra speaks from the position of the 'healthy body', that body which affirms itself as the 'meaning of the earth'. The overcoming of nihilism must reunite the body with the earth concretely rather than abstractly. Zarathustra equates the body with the earth; those who despise body also despise the earth.[77] The reuniting of body with the earth is referred to in aphorism 230 of *Beyond Good and Evil* as the 'strange and insane task' of future philosophy: 'to translate man back into nature'. Hence, 'translation' operatively will reunite human being(s) understood as embodied nature.[78] This study will undertake to demonstrate that the incorporation of the body into a new conception of political existence is the central task of future philosophy and the philosopher of the future.

The nomothetic activity of political physiology

As mentioned earlier, the body is the primary, primal and primordial repository of feeling (qua *pathos*) produced by different quanta and fluctuations of force and affective intensities. The aim of Nietzsche's elaboration of will to power is to show that all human endeavour is fundamentally affective. The experience of the eternal recurrence is an experience of feeling, the effects of which Zarathustra experiences as longing, fear, nausea, physical convalescence and finally joy. This is why Nietzsche insists that the fate of human existence rests on the philosopher's experience of the eternal recurrence, that singular 'going-under' of the body in which the self-directed will feels its Dionysian multiplicity precisely as a lack of identity (in *The Birth of Tragedy*, Nietzsche contrasts this Dionysian principle with the principle of Apollo, the ancient Greek god of the city).

Zarathustra, like Jesus, speaks in parables. The poetic nature of Zarathustra's language is an expression of his ability to be a creator. The affective drives of the body which Zarathustra describes as the experience of 'going-under' are translated into and represented as the creative multiplicity of poetic language. As a *poiêsis* emerging from the body, poetic language is a purely creative activity of the healthy body that is primarily affective; its task is to communicate through integration the essential chaotic multiplicity of the body. This ability to endure and integrate the chaotic multiplicity of the body is the mark of the 'genuine philosopher' (*BGE* §211), and also determines the hierarchy of types from slave, to master and finally to the Overman (Nietzsche also refers to this hierarchy as the distinction between the weak types, the free spirits and the very free spirits). Nietzsche's own definition of 'political' reflects this: 'political (the art of enduring the tremendous tension between differing degrees of power)'.[79]

The art of politics is thus associated with the activity of organizing bodily contestation, the effect of which is the feeling of enjoyment produced by the 'art of enduring' that Nietzsche calls the 'freedom of the will'.[80] Here 'freedom of will' is synonymous with what Nietzsche elsewhere calls the 'freedom of spirit'. This freedom is fundamentally a feeling of commanding and obeying the body, rather than a feature of thinking. Commanding consists largely in the will's ordering of the impulses that produces an effect or action which the ego feels as the exercise of volition. It is an 'expression for the complex state of delight of the person exercising volition, who commands and at the same time identifies with the executor of the order'.[81] In tandem with commanding, obedience consists in obeying the 'tyranny' of the 'capricious laws' of the impulses (will to power as flux) out of which will to power is ordered and directed.[82] Thus, Nietzsche associates obedience not only with obeying the impulsional substructure of organic processes (the means to 'spiritual freedom' of the highest types) but also with the political and social obedience characteristic of the 'spiritual unfreedom' of lesser types. Even this last type of obedience has its cultivating effect on the will:

> The long unfreedom of the spirit ... the discipline thinkers imposed on themselves to think within the directions laid down by a church or court, or under Aristotelian presuppositions, the long spiritual will to interpret all events under a Christian schema ... all this, however forced, capricious, hard, gruesome, and anti-rational, has shown itself to be the means through which the European spirit has been trained to strength, ruthless curiosity, and subtle mobility, though admittedly in the process an irreplaceable amount of strength and spirit had to be crushed, stifled, and ruined.
>
> (*BGE* §188)

Nietzsche recognizes that this unfreedom of the spirit has nonetheless educated the spirit; as such the degree to which a spirit is enslaved both politically and spiritually is still 'the indispensable means of spiritual discipline and cultivation'. Nonetheless, Nietzsche suggests that the degree of 'mastery' (and spiritual freedom) coincides directly with the extent to which one commands and obeys the impulses. For the highest, most spiritual type, the ability to impose order from out of the chaotic and incoherent multiplicity of corporeal impulses is the process by which the active will to power seeks to integrate and express its intensity, which Nietzsche calls 'commanding-legislating' (*BGE* §211). The 'political', I suggest, is the art of enduring and ordering the chaotic and impulsional intensities of the body. If the impulse-driven states of the body inform Nietzsche's understanding of the 'body politic', then it is in one's singular capacity to integrate, order and rank, and ultimately creatively sublimate and transform – hence 'cultivate'– the chaotic drives that the highest types are distinguished from the lower types.

More importantly, however, this idea suggests that all of Nietzsche's statements concerning politics and culture, as well as nature and history, must be taken as forces that act and are interpreted through the singularity of this corporeal experience. Will to power and eternal recurrence, the twin cornerstones of Nietzsche's thought, must therefore be understood primarily in terms of successful or unsuccessful (or rather active or reactive) experiences of the body's attempt to endure, order and eventually unify the conflicting instincts and drives of the body. The consequence of Nietzsche's revaluation of the body politic is to transform the sacred origin of political existence from the polis to the body. Nietzsche offers the body as the new sacred site for the emergence of a new philosophy of the future, and with it, the formation of a new sense of political existence. The use of the term 'sacred' (as well as 'religion' and 'spiritual'), as such, does not imply or necessitate any theistic faith in or beliefs about God or gods on the part of the philosopher. As I will make clear during the course of the present study, my reading of Nietzsche's 'Dionysian religion' rests on the philosopher's refutation of belief in theism or faith in metaphysical divinity.

Recall that as the teacher of eternal recurrence, Zarathustra's task is to redraw 'sacred' boundaries (*TSZ III*: On Old and New Tablets, §19). It is important to remember that the form that the integration of drives takes does not and cannot annul the originary chaotic multiplicity and corporeal fundament of all existence. Rather, among the conditions for the 'Dionysian task' of the philosopher of the future is the giving-form to the inchoate impulses; once ordered, the decisive mark of the 'Dionysian nature' (*EH: Thus Spoke Zarathustra*, §8) is revealed in a creative language that celebrates its fluctual nature by giving form without devaluing the originary sacred multiplicity of the body.

Nietzsche understands religion to be a breeding agent and species-building tool specifically for those types that are incapable of self-integration and self-direction. His hierarchy of types is laid out explicitly in *The Antichrist*, §57: the spiritual, executive and professional types are stratified within the pyramid of culture according to their capacity for self-mastery and ability to endure experimentation. The highest types live in accordance with a noble master morality (and therefore are considered 'master' types), while the lower types live according to slave morality.[83] Nietzsche's numerous discussions of 'master', 'slave' and 'free spirits' further suggest that 'mastery' and 'slavery', as expressions of spiritual capacity (e.g. unconditional spiritual freedom), are a matter of degree: thus, the rarest and highest types are completely 'commanders and legislators', and as lawgivers, they have the ability to master themselves and create values for the rest of society.[84] The second in rank – the higher types – are the executive arms of the most spiritual type;[85] while they have the ability to command authority socially, politically and economically, they are still more slavish than their superiors regarding self-direction and the ability to endure experimentation.[86] All other types below this are distinguished primarily by their lack of self-mastery and are considered to be 'slavish' because of a fundamental deficiency of spiritual freedom.[87]

It is for all types except the most spiritual (but especially for the lowest professional types) that religion – that is, revelation and tradition[88] – becomes necessary. Nietzsche suggests that religion (as the religious 'essence' or 'instinct') is the yoking of the spirit to a system of rules and beliefs (including prohibitions and restrictions) and the spiritual absence of the longing for freedom.[89] The freer the spirit, the more this spirit desires freedom and emancipation from all conditions, yokes and beliefs (*BGE* §46). The religious instinct is characteristic of the moral period of human history, here perceived as 'the unconscious aftereffect of the rule of aristocratic values'.[90] The religious instinct, as such, can indicate a certain loftiness of spirit; hence, Nietzsche points to the historical reverence of the saint by powerful men who sensed behind the ascetic's ragged exterior 'the superior force that sought to test itself in such a conquest, the strength of the will in which they recognized and honored their own strength and delight in dominion: they honored something in themselves when they honored the saint'.[91] Ancient Greek religiosity was noble because it upheld and privileged the life-affirming and spirit-freeing experience of 'a very noble type of man'.[92] The nobility of ancient Greek religions results from the fact that the value placed on nature (as life) was guaranteed and supported by the placing of the higher types (e.g. the oracles and the Greek 'hero') at the peak of the social pyramid. The religion of the Greeks thus oriented all types towards affirming life and serving the higher types through sacrifices, rituals, theatre and festivals. Nietzsche's preference for ancient Greek religiosity is reflected most clearly in *The Birth of Tragedy*, in which he praises the intimacy between Greek religion and Greek art: 'the cultured Greek felt himself absorbed into the satyr chorus, and in the next development of Greek tragedy state and society, in fact all that separated man from man, gave way before an overwhelming sense of unity which led back into the heart of nature'.[93]

Nonetheless Nietzsche makes clear that the freer the spirit, the less necessary the belief in religion becomes; as such, the highest types use religion as a tool of cultivation for and orientation of those types that need a system of rules and beliefs for a sense of meaning and self-worth.[94] The philosopher does not need religion for its own process of self-experimentation – the philosopher wants, above all, unconditional freedom, and the value s/he will place on the eternal celebration of life (experienced as the eternal recurrence) is not a religious belief but rather an expression of the unconditional freedom of nature (note: this might explain why Nietzsche, despite his praise of the Brahmanic stratification of caste, criticizes the ancient Vedic lawgiver Manu, who was mistaken in thinking that the hierarchy of types was a result of the truth of his belief in vedic cosmology, rather than the expression of the rule of unconditional freedom in and of nature, see *AC* §57).

What then is the relationship between 'religion' and the 'sacred'? Hierarchy is the common ground understood by all types, from the highest to the lowest. I use the term 'sacred' here with reference to its Greek translation as *hieros*; as such, 'sacred' as 'hieros' is consistent both with Nietzsche's mention of the 'sacred' task of Zarathustra in *Thus Spoke Zarathustra* as well as with his discussion of hierarchical ordering in *Beyond Good and Evil*. Based on Nietzsche's references to the freedom of the spirit characteristic of the philosopher, 'sacred' as 'hieros' connotes nature's expression of the rank and order of types independent of any particular system of religious belief, faith and institutional rules. Nature orders human types hierarchically so that the experience of unconditional freedom can be experienced by those who can endure it; in tandem, the experience of unconditional freedom becomes the highest, most hallowed, spiritual goal of the philosopher. But 'sacred' also refers to the experience of all lower types who may not be able to endure experience unconditional freedom: they can nonetheless experience Dionysian nature within their particular capacity and thereby feel its intimacy. For all types other than the philosopher, the 'sacred' as 'hieros' (defined as the intimacy with Dionysian nature) is expressed in the language and system of beliefs provided by a future Dionysian religion. Religion, as such, while being a reflection of the spiritual unfreedom characteristic of base types, nonetheless performs an important function for the philosophy of the future: on the one hand, for the lowest types, religion provides the means of cultivating the spirit through revelation and tradition; on the other hand, for the philosopher, religion provides the necessary conditions for legislating and commanding (i.e. lawgiving).

The experience of the eternal recurrence becomes central to the task of establishing 'great politics' through the creation of a new Dionysian religion. Dionysus, the ancient Greek deity of 'wine and intoxicated ecstasy',[95] is the emblem of the total affirmation of life. If the task of future philosophy is to permit the emergence of a new Dionysian culture, then its religion would be one that would affirm rather than deny life. Because Nietzsche believes the eternal recurrence to encompass and represent the total affirmation of earthly corporeal life, the new philosophers would erect this experience as the core mythic Dionysian symbol of this new culture. Although few could actually experience the eternal recurrence, it would nevertheless have to be given the highest value (i.e. become 'sacred') within the social pyramid. Sacred as 'hieros' is thus the total expression of nature's nomothetic order: it provides the experience of unconditional freedom to those capable of experiencing and enduring it (the experience of eternal recurrence), and also to those lesser types, the sacred provides limited access to the experience of unconditional freedom via mythic emblems and social practices (the symbol of the eternal recurrence as expressed by a Dionysian religion).

I attempted to establish the critical role that the psycho-physiological body plays in Nietzsche's theorization of human life within the context of the pathological condition of nihilism, as well as in terms of the 'philosophy of the future'. From the beginning of *Beyond Good and Evil*, in which he anticipates the 'new philosophers', Nietzsche re-articulates philosophy as an effect and affect of bodily processes. The body, however, is not an instrument onto which conflicting drives are projected, but is itself a 'social structure' staging the effect of the affects. On this basis, Nietzsche makes the link between the individual body and the collective body: all feelings of power, whether in the 'complex state of delight of the person exercising volition' or in the 'governing class' of a commonwealth, emanate from the affect of command produced through the body.[96] Morality becomes the expression of the 'relations of supremacy under which the phenomenon of 'life' comes to be' (*BGE* §19), more specifically, the body becomes the stage upon which the history of morality can come to be discerned, read and rewritten.

2
The Economic Problem of Production: Nature, Culture, Life

> He who has recognized the unreason in the nature of his age, then, will have to think of means of rendering it a little assistance; his task however, will be to make the free spirits of his age and those who suffer profoundly from our age acquainted with Schopenhauer, assemble them together and through them to engender a current capable of overcoming the ineptitude with which nature employs the philosopher.
>
> —*UM* III, 7

The interpretation of bodily states is the nexus between Nietzsche's vision of history and his conception of nature, both of which fall under his understanding of life. Nietzsche's political physiology encompasses ongoing ranking and ordering (*Rangordnung*), as do all organic processes. Therefore, an examination of the relationship between 'nature', 'culture' and 'life' is crucial for understanding why the task of the highest type is to 'translate man back into nature'. Despite the fact that Nietzsche himself did not define 'great politics',[1] we must assume, at the minimum, that it must necessarily involve the philosopher-physiologist's diagnostic activity of symptomatology, namely, of reading the 'symptoms' of vitality or degeneration of organisms (of diagnosing values in terms of 'the physical constitution – of individuals or classes or even whole races'[2]). In *Nietzsche, Genealogy, History*, Michel Foucault points to the body as the originary scene of all historical phenomena. Foucault develops Nietzsche's genealogical project as a challenge to the philosophical pursuit of origin or *Ursprung*. Genealogy is concerned not with itself as the site of truth as 'the exact essence of things, their purest possibilities',[3] but rather with origin as *Herkunft*, the primal scene of the body as the 'inscribed surface of events (traced by language and dissolved by ideas), the locus of a dissociated Self (adopting the illusion of substantial unity), and a volume in perpetual disintegration'[4]. Foucault shows that for Nietzsche, the task of the philosophical and thus genealogical interpretation of history is to read the body as the primordial scene of conflict and emergence (*Entstehung*) of the repeated play of domination that makes up history.[5] He makes the implication of this idea more clear: as an 'emergence' rather than as an authentic ontological state, the body as an 'origin' is also described as a fiction, an 'invention' (*Erfindung*), 'a sleight-of-hand, an artifice (Kunststück), a secret formula, in the rituals of black magic, in the work of the Schwartzkünstler'[6] (or 'black magician'). To the political physiologist, like to the genealogist in Foucault's account, is revealed 'something altogether different': the secret that even the body is a prosthesis with 'no essence and that [its] essence was fabricated from alien forms'[7].

General economy and the genesis of the philosopher

In *Schopenhauer as Educator,* Nietzsche argues that although nature produces the philosopher, it only does so as a matter of accident, not deliberately or even productively. 'Nature seems bent on squandering ... and if nature were human it would never cease to be annoyed at itself and its ineptitude'.[8] Specifically with regard to the production of the artist and philosopher, he notes that 'nature is a bad economist'; its 'house-rule' leads to its ruin because it tends to spend more than it procures. The sustained (re)production of the 'genius' is marred by the fact that nature does not expend its energies efficiently and thus is predisposed to produce unfavourable circumstances for the flourishing of the genius. In history, the 'development of strange concepts and fanciful requirements', as well as the 'perversity' of the times, often results in the hampering and crushing of the philosopher-genius.[9] Nietzsche echoes this sentiment in his later works and links the political and cultural task of future philosophy with the cultivation of nature's predisposition for extravagant squandering: 'to teach man the future of man as his will, as dependent on a human will, and to prepare great ventures and overall attempters of discipline and cultivation by way of putting an end to that gruesome dominion of nonsense and accident that has so far been called "history"'.[10]

What is the importance of Nietzsche's early discussion of nature's inefficiency in the production of the philosopher for his later understanding of 'translation back into nature'? Perhaps it is to suggest that the relationship between nature and culture is symbiotic: the task of culture is to correct the foibles of nature not by transcending nature, but by imitating it with efficiency and purposiveness. This is Schopenhauer's lesson: the political/cultural task of the philosopher is thus to harness the inherent rich but wasteful economy of nature through the cultivation of laws: 'to acquire power so as to aid the evolution of Physis and to be for a while the corrector of its follies and ineptitudes'.[11] If nature is a bad economist then 'culture' is the philosopher's transfiguration of nature, the cultivation of a 'regulatory total picture' that directs nature by providing it with an 'exalted and transfiguring overall goal'. Hence, culture is a 'transfigured physis', and the philosopher is a lawgiver, one who engages in the task of cultivating the favourable conditions that 'nature' itself fails to achieve systematically for the sustained production of the genius and philosopher.[12]

In *Beyond Good and Evil,* Nietzsche links the inefficiency of nature's economy to its adverse effect on the higher types:

> The accidental, the law of absurdity in the whole economy of humankind, manifests itself most horribly in its destructive effect on the higher men whose complicated conditions of life can only be calculated with great subtlety and difficulty.[13]

The goal of the human should be to 'seek out and create the favourable conditions under which great redemptive men can come into existence'.[14]

As noted earlier, Nietzsche's political vision undergoes a shift from his early period to his mature works. In the earlier thought, Nietzsche finds promise in the potential of the German nation to culturally renew an ailing modernity, but by the Zarathustran works, the German nation becomes one of the critical problems of modernity and is no longer considered the conduit through which a Dionysian renewal can occur. The emphasis, as such, on what constitutes 'favourable conditions' for the flourishing of the philosopher also changes to the extent that in *Beyond Good and Evil* Nietzsche even claims that the philosopher is always 'untimely' and out of joint with current social conditions.[15] In other words, 'favourable conditions' would consist in those cultural forms that would allow the philosopher to be both the creator and the giver of values, while still being able to conduct its activities of experimentation. The realm of culture is meant to provide an efficient and sustainable economy – a productive and renewable structure – to nature, the goal of which is to assure that the highest forms of life are the least squandered.[16] 'It is the fundamental idea of culture, insofar as it sets for each one of us but one task: to promote the production of the philosopher, the artist, and the saint within us and without us and thereby to work at the perfecting of Nature'.[17]

In an essay on the relationship between 'life' and 'nature' in Nietzsche's works, Daniel Conway argues that the forces of Apollo and Dionysus in *The Birth of Tragedy* accommodates 'the transformation of aesthetic categories into economic principles'.[18] Conway employs Georges Bataille's two models of economy, which Bataille borrows from anthropologist Marcel Mauss (see *The Gift: The Form and Reason for Exchange in Archaic Societies*). A general economy is a field of unconditional expenditure unrestricted by the objectives of social utility, conservation and productivity. In contrast, a structural or restricted economy is governed by the principle of utility, conservation and production which are fundamentally required by any social activity.[19] Conway argues that just as Apollo is merely a 'moment' within the economy of Dionysus, 'so Life comprises a subsystem sheltered within the boundless economy of nature'. 'Life' as a transfigured *physis* (nature) is properly characterized as the *restricted* structural economy of culture. As Conway continues to explain, 'while nature partakes of the model of general economy, unrestricted by conditions governing its intake and expenditure, Life partakes of the model of restricted economy, conditioned by the peculiar needs of human existence'.[20]

From this Conway astutely concludes that Nietzsche's 'return to nature' hinges on an equivocation in the understanding of the term 'nature'. On the one hand, Nietzsche characterizes nature along the lines of a general economy, 'as a boundless force indifferent to human concerns'. On the other hand, nature is the 'affective ground of human agency', a normative standard that justifies and privileges some forms of life over others.[21] As in the case of Karl Löwith's argument, what emerges is a tension between the lawlessness, boundlessness and arbitrariness of the general economy of nature and the restricted nomothetic or normative task of the 'return to nature'. Conway makes a keen observation in demonstrating the tension between the requirements of a restricted economy and those of a general economy, but the conclusions he draws are disputable.

The crux of the argument here is not only that the philosopher is never dissociable from nature, but that nature itself is not dissociable from the embodiment of its highest specimens. This is why Nietzsche claims that the body is always a 'social structure' and an aristocracy (*WP* §660). For Nietzsche, Dionysian nature (flux) does not 'exist' properly speaking apart from its material manifestations (this is the crucial lesson that he had learned from his reading of the pre-Platonics, especially from Heraclitus). Existence can only be known in its formalities. In *Beyond Good and Evil*, Nietzsche merges nature and life as will to power: nature is a reflection of the self-tyrannical drive of philosophy, the tendency of will to power to always create 'the world in its own image ... the most spiritual will to power, to the "creation of the world," to the causa prima'.[22]

It is not a question of choosing between one or the other economic principle then: if nature cannot exist apart from its materiality, then 'life' must somehow consist of a specific relationship to both economies respectively. The philosopher's task involves both a relationship to a restricted economy of nomothetic organization (or 'great politics', which is the political teaching of eternal recurrence) and to a general economy (the singular experience of eternal recurrence). Both economies are necessary to the philosopher's task of 'translation': on the one hand, the restricted nomothetic economy, by necessarily limiting and containing social and cultural energies within the goals set forth by great politics, makes nature more efficient for philosophical activity. At the same time, if the philosopher's activity within the restricted economy – for example, the activity of self-overcoming – is necessarily limited, then the philosopher must also be able to access a boundless, limitless general economy which guarantees and regenerates the limitless continuation of its activity of self-overcoming beyond the requirements of utility or social preservation.[23] The nature of the restricted economy does not necessarily nullify or contradict that of the general economy. In terms of the present study, Bataille's terminology will prove useful insofar as I will argue that both economies are necessary to the task of translation: the restricted nomothetic economy directs the expenditure of energies through the nomothetic organization of types, while the general economy ensures the limitless access of the highest types to the unconditional freedom of nature. The sovereignty of the philosopher depends on a negotiation between ordering expenditure productively and on discharging expenditure non-productively.

Conway's conclusions, however, do not diminish the usefulness of understanding Nietzsche within the terms set forth by Bataille. For Bataille, the general and structural economies do not necessarily exclude each other; in fact, what is necessary is to somehow achieve a functional relation (a circuitry or 'feedback loop') between the two.[24] Conway, however, proposes to keep the two positions mutually exclusive: either nature serves as a standard for nomothetic legislation or as an amoral 'agency', but it cannot be both simultaneously. The general economy (the boundlessness of Dionysian nature) is accessible only to the one who embodies the reconciliation between nature and life which is the effect of the psycho-physiological transmutation that results from the experience of eternity. I therefore use Bataille's terminology to elucidate this relationship: the eternal recurrence provides the organism's experience of the general economy of nature (thus effecting its translation back into nature); if endured and made communicable, this transmuted organism (the philosopher) establishes the restricted economy of the social order so as to provide itself with favourable conditions under which s/he can continually access this limitless economy.

The structural economy of 'great politics'

In order to uphold the philosopher's experimentation (the activities that catalyse 'self-overcoming'), a restricted economy must be established which organizes the social hierarchy of types along the principles of conservation and utility (only then can culture truly be a 'transfigured physis' within the context of the overcoming of nihilism). The objective or end of this structural economy is ultimately to uphold and privilege the philosopher's experience of unrestricted expenditure, the general economy of Dionysian nature. This is why Nietzsche will claim in *Beyond Good and Evil* that 'society does not exist for society's sake but only as the foundation and scaffolding on which a choice type of being is able to raise itself to its higher task and to its higher state of being'.[25] This 'higher task' and 'higher state of being', I suggest, consists of the experience of unrestricted expenditure that leads to a profound morphosis in the organism that experiences it.

In *Beyond Good and Evil*, Nietzsche lays out his nomothetic vision for the future. The geometry of the pyramid can be used to represent and describe his political and cultural vision of aristocracy and inequality. I contend that the task of 'great politics' is the establishment of a hierarchy in and through which the designed production of the highest human types can occur. The link between *Beyond Good and Evil* and *Thus Spoke Zarathustra* reveals itself in Nietzsche's fundamental desire to erect the philosopher's singular and redemptive experience of the eternal recurrence as the core symbolic image and founding myth of future cultural, social and political existence. However, Nietzsche claims that only a rare few can truly experience and endure the sublime and terrifying experience of the eternal recurrence (even Zarathustra, in his stillest hour, is unwilling to look into the abyss). The problem becomes evident: while the experience and teaching of the eternal recurrence may achieve the translation back into nature of the highest type, they do not automatically translate all other types back. The philosophy of the future requires the transformation of the bodily states of all other types as well, each according to its own capacity.

Within the structural economy of 'great politics', the highest type is the philosopher in its capacity as lawgiver. This economy is governed by the 'law of placing' – the nomothetic[26] – and represents the scheme of social hierarchy through which the lawgiver can accomplish its goals of translation. Thus, the experimental art of self-creation is also the political and aesthetic art par excellence: politics is first and foremost a cultivation of the technique of giving form to chaos through the art of placing and ordering the plurality of instincts within the organism, as well as the ordering of organisms within the structure of society. If we connect the claim that 'every enhancement of the type "man" has so far been the work of an aristocratic society'[27] to the claim that society only exists for the development of its highest specimens,[28] then it can be argued that the lawgiver is both the creator (and 'cultivator') and the created (and 'cultivated') subject of 'great politics'.

In *Untimely Meditations, Beyond Good and Evil* and *The Antichrist*, Nietzsche defines the role and interest of nature in the production of the rarest and greatest individuals, and he links the task of culture to the task of politics and to a vision of the future. The future is not the impartial progression of evolutionary time; it is an event which will only come under certain circumstances – an event which man must invoke, which he must become:

> [W]hat type of man shall be bred, shall be willed, for being higher in value, worthier of life, more certain of a future. Even in the past this higher type has appeared often – but as a fortunate accident, as an exception, never as something willed.[29]

Although the 'translation back into nature' uses the pre-Platonic *physis* as a model as I have argued, Nietzsche does not intend the 'return' back to nature to be the result of a return to the past (like we see, for example, in Rousseau's discourse of the 'noble savage'). The erection of the nomothetic economy is entirely a response to the degradation and degeneration of the modern spirit (thus demanding a strictly modern response). As Rosen points out, the return to nature is artificial; if we can return to nature as Nietzsche desires, we cannot simply return as Greeks – we must return as moderns.[30] This observation underscores one of the main contentions of the present work: that it must be by way of art, artifice and the artificial (*technê*) that the translation back to nature proceeds.

Why is it that we cannot simply recreate the past in the present? As Nietzsche's analysis of the mnemotechnics of nihilism has revealed, it is because we have become organisms that – psychologically and physiologically, biologically and culturally – have forgotten the complex unity of life and thought: 'of this pre-Socratic unity we no longer have even the slightest idea'.[31] So we cannot simply remember the past, and in remembering it, live it anew. Conversely, why is it that we cannot interpret the 'future' as the 'not-yet' which, given the right state of affairs, ideas and political, social and cultural arrangements, will arrive and redeem humanity (the achievement of the Hegelian ideal from which can be proclaimed the end of history and of ideology)? Because the human is a product of nihilism, 'man is a reactive being who combines his forces with nihilism. The eternal recurrence repels and expels him. The transmutation involves an essential, radical conversion that is produced in man but that produces the Overman'.[32]

The theatre of the overhuman

This is the novel thought that Nietzsche introduces into modernity, a thought which makes a break with the history of Western thought, a thought that breaks history into two.[33] As Deleuze rightly claims, something completely new begins with Nietzsche: he does not 'set up a philosophical theatre'; he invents an 'incredible equivalent of theatre within philosophy, thereby founding simultaneously this theatre of the future and a new philosophy':[34]

> When Nietzsche says that the Overman resembles Borgia rather than Parsifal, or when he suggests that the Overman belongs at once to both the Jesuit Order and the Prussian officer corps, we can understand these texts only by taking them for what they are: remarks of a director indicating how the Overman should be 'played'.[35]

Although the Overman is produced in man, it is not produced by man.[36] *Physis* (nature/growth), *nomos* (laws) and *technê* (invention) form a complex unity that is dramatized within the nomothetic activity of organic life (both at the singular and collective levels). Through the art of placing, the general and restricted economies become theatres for the organic enactment of the future in the moment, effectively rendering future philosophy immanent in the 'here and now'. Therefore, the most abundant and powerful will to power is the active will that is a selection; the active will to power (as opposed to the reactive) is the organism's affirmation of a forgotten capacity to legislate 'the superior form of everything that is'.[37] Deleuze makes the point most succinctly:

> Nietzsche replaced the ideal of knowledge, the discovery of truth, with interpretation and evaluation [...] The interpreter is the physiologist or doctor, the one who sees phenomena as symptoms and speaks through aphorisms. The evaluator is the artist who considers and creates 'perspectives' and speaks through poetry. The philosopher of the future is both artist and doctor – in word, legislator. This image of the philosopher is also the oldest, the most ancient one. It is that of the pre-Socratic thinker, 'physiologist' and artist, interpreter and evaluator of the world.[38]

In the exertion of willing, value is created; thus, from the fundamental fact of human existence arises the most fundamental fact of living: that existence is not characterized by a radical sameness, but by a fundamental distinction or difference. Even within a Hobbesian framework in which all existence is matter in motion, the question of rule must arise because every movement 'towards' or 'away from' is an act of willing:

> just as sensations ... are to be recognized as ingredients of the will, so, secondly, should thinking also: in every act of the will there is a ruling thought – let us not imagine it possible to sever this thought from the 'willing' as if any will would then remain over![39]

This differential operation is inevitably sown within the seeds of all organic life. Even in the most basic states of living, an aristocracy exists: as the creation of value from inchoate multiplicity, the rule of one element over others will occur and the vital activity of the organism will depend on this differential functionality. Will to power is magnitude,[40] and it is in this sense that the creation of values is an effect of the aristocratic (that is, differential) activity of will to power. The fundamental fact of life then is the emergence of greatness, and Nietzsche links its achievement to the philosopher's nomothetic capacity to be as internally manifold as possible: 'Precisely this shall be called greatness: being capable of being as manifold as whole, as ample as full ... [T]o ask it once more: today – is greatness possible?'[41]

The answer to Zarathustra's question of how the earth shall be *directed* is the answer to the question of how the Overman should be *played*. Accordingly, 'greatness', which is one of the cardinal themes of *Beyond Good and Evil*, must be interpreted as the differential magnitude (the aristocratic pathos of distance) of will to power. It 'is above all an affect, and specifically the affect of command ... the affect of superiority in relation to him who must obey'.[42] Nietzsche's reference 'the Roman Caesar with Christ's soul',[43] when connected to his assertion that the philosopher is the 'complementary man',[44] establishes an important and necessary link between great politics, will to power (as magnitude), and the ability to be 'internally manifold'.

In a strange twist, then, it is not chiefly the Greeks that vindicate the art of nomothesis for Nietzsche, but rather the Romans:

> My sense of style, of the epigram as style ... One will recognize in my writings, even in my Zarathustra, as very serious ambition for Roman style, for the 'aera perennius' in style ... This mosaic of words in which every word, as sound, as locus, as concept, pours forth its power to left and right and over the whole, this minimum in the range and number of signs which achieves a maximum of energy of these signs – all this is Roman and, if one will believe me, noble par excellence.[45]
>
> I received absolutely no such strong impressions from the Greeks; and, not to mince words, they cannot be to us what the Romans are ... My recreation, my preference, my cure from all Platonism has always been Thucydides, and perhaps the Principe of Machiavelli, are related to me closely by their unconditional will not to deceive themselves and to see reason in reality – not in 'reason', still less in 'morality.'[46]

Nietzsche seems to use the term 'Roman' here as a catachresis, since neither Machiavelli nor Thucydides was Roman (Machiavelli was a Florentine and Thucydides an Athenian). The mistake provokes the hypothesis that 'Roman' in this context is an expression of 'commanding and legislating'. Greatness is thus demonstrated in the activeness (the differential magnitude) of will to power. Like Machiavelli's armed prophet, the use of force is made legitimate not first and foremost out of military or utilitarian necessity (what Machiavelli would call 'power', rather than 'glory'), but rather as a necessity and capacity for artistic passion: 'for that devotion to "form" for which the phrase l'art pour l'art has been invented' and for which France owes its cultural superiority over Germany.[47] The use of violence and cruelty therefore belies an even deeper and more profound cruelty to oneself – the cultivation of a tyranny of the spirit. This spiritual tyranny is precisely the quality necessary for the thriving of all aristocratic societies. When viewed within the nomothetic and structural economy of the pyramid, commanding and legislating are like Machiavelli's 'art of the possible', the art and technique practiced by the lawgiver that Nietzsche calls the sovereign art of 'giving style to one's character'.[48]

Nietzsche's 'immoralism' finds many points of convergence with Machiavelli's delimitation of the great founder who is so rare as to possess mythic qualities. The philosopher as *Versucher*, or 'attempter' (but also as a 'tempter'), requires the use of both virtue and vice; like all lawgivers, the philosopher must know how to use *nomos* in the service of a 'new and improved physis'. The most 'spiritual' will to power – and thus the most genuinely 'philosophical' of spirits – proves itself always to be also the most artful will to power. Every great lawgiver is like the mythic Hermes in this sense, who, as the intermediary and translator, articulates and manipulates the position between Dionysus and Apollo, nature and culture, chaos and law. For the Greeks, Hermes was the messenger, the great communicator – but also in the same instance a trickster, a being of exquisitely cunning intelligence, whose words were repetitions (eternal repetitions) and therefore not the *logos* from on high, but its translation into the worldly word as *mythos*, as mythical speech. The lawgiver, like Hermes, is a winged messenger: always in flight (always in motion), forever transgressing established boundaries and, as such, following the flow of *physis*, while in this very transgression affirming the margin and framework of culture. Every great lawgiver, every veritable act of nomothesis, must demonstrate this disposition towards myth-making, here understood also as myth-speaking and myth-giving.

The strongest morality is a function of both the will to truth and the will to deception: it is one that, in the imposition of its own perspective over others, nonetheless recognizes its own radical contingency and fundamental immorality. Like Machiavelli before him, Nietzsche demonstrates that behind the philosopher's 'virtue' lies a profound use of vice. The collapse of the dualism between reality and appearance announced in *Twilight of the Idols* ('How the "Real World" at last became a Myth: History of an Error') is prefigured in *Beyond Good and Evil* as the radical monism between all seemingly opposing values. Questioning the metaphysician's faith in opposite values,[49] Nietzsche does more than merely question the inviolability between the will to truth and the will to deception; instead, he destroys our ability to even tell the difference between the two by upholding the necessary continuity between the wills to truth and deception. Indeed, *Beyond Good and Evil* begins with the observation that without these 'fictions of logic', 'man could not live'.[50]

Alexander Nehamas – long considered to be a champion of the 'anti-political' view of Nietzsche –addresses the connection between Nietzsche's nomothetic project and his philosophical perspectivism-cum-monism. In an effort to rearticulate the relationship between the will to knowledge and the will to ignorance, Nehamas suggests that for Nietzsche every form of morality places restrictions and constraints on its practitioners and that 'an organized and organizing systems of behavior' is crucial to the creation of a new view of life. Nietzsche criticizes Christianity not because it has 'tyrannized' its followers or because it has led them towards a single direction, but instead, because he rejects the particular direction (and here, I suggest we take this in its theatrical sense) towards which Christianity has led, namely the devaluation and denial of life produced by the ascetic impulse. For Nehamas, perspectivism in the context of morality 'implies that in order to engage in any activity we must necessarily occupy ourselves with a selection of material and exclude much from our consideration. It does not imply that we see or know an appearance of the world instead of that world itself'.[51]

Nehamas's explanation, however, does not sufficiently solve the problem that arises in his account of Nietzsche's perspectivism. If, as he claims, all perspectives are a selection that necessarily includes and excludes material, then how can one understand Nietzsche's claim that the Dionysian philosopher is one who says 'Yes' to all things? How is the future philosopher to engage both in the critical project of 'nay-saying' or devaluation of historical values and in the affirmative 'yes-saying' to everything? Going back to the terms of the present study, what connection is there between Nietzsche's political and nomothetic vision, and his understanding of affirming inchoate multiplicity in the experience of the eternal recurrence?

Let us briefly consider this tension between Nietzsche's affirmative philosophy and his critical philosophy. For example, in *The Gay Science* 276, Nietzsche claims that

> I do not want to wage war against what is ugly. I do not want to accuse; I do not even want to accuse those who accuse. Looking away shall be my only negation. And all in all and on the whole: some day I wish to be only a Yes-sayer.

However, in *Ecce Homo*, in the first passage in which he reconsiders *Beyond Good and Evil*, Nietzsche asserts that

> the task for the years that followed now was indicated as clearly as possible. After the Yes-saying part of my task had been solved, the turn had come for the No-saying, No-doing part: the revaluation of our values so far, the great war – conjuring up a day of decision. This included the slow search for those related to me, those who, prompted by strength, would offer me their hands for destroying.

In his unpublished work, Nietzsche gives a clue as to how the philosopher is to negotiate between negation and affirmation: if read in relation to Nietzsche's account of the 'three metamorphoses' in *Thus Spoke Zarathustra*, Nietzsche suggests that there must be a necessary transversion or point of mutation (leading to transmutation) in the philosopher's activity of experimentation with negation and affirmation:

> Such an experimental philosophy as I live anticipates experimentally even the possibilities of the most fundamental nihilism; but this does not mean that it must halt at a negation, a No, a will to negation. It wants rather to cross over to the opposite of this – to a Dionysian affirmation of the world as it is, without subtraction, exception or selection – it wants the eternal circulation: – the same things, the same logic and illogic of entanglements. The highest state a philosopher can attain: to stand in a Dionysian relationship to existence – my formula for this is *amor fati*.[52]

In the aforementioned passage in *Ecce Homo*, 'yes-saying' (affirmative philosophy) precedes 'no-saying' (negative philosophy). In the passage from *Will to Power*, however, he suggests that affirmation may follow from a will to negation. What are we to make of this?

In relation to the philosopher's task of forging a Dionysian association with existence, the philosophy of the future must contain both a critical, or negative, dimension centred around the philosopher's devaluation of current historical values and an affirmative one which hinges on overcoming the nihilism that results from this devaluation. In other words, the task of translation occurs not only at the level of selection and cultivation of bodily states but also at the level of experiencing existence 'without subtraction, exception or selection'.[53] For the highest types, the manifestation of Dionysus in modernity will have to entail a metamorphosis of the organism, and consequently of the modes of valuation of the organism. This is the reason why the philosopher must be prepared to accept and engage in the will to truth as well as the will to deception: the metamorphosis of critical philosophy into affirmative philosophy (and vice versa) will necessitate the boundless experimentation with clarity,[54] honesty,[55] conscience and responsibility,[56] as well as perversity and multiplicity of character,[57] flexibility[58] and naivety.[59]

The conclusion we can draw here is that Nietzsche envisions future philosophy both in terms of the future philosopher's relation to a restricted economy in which collective societal and cultural energies are selected, cultivated, bred and directed, and in terms of the philosopher's relation to a general economy in which the philosopher's experimentation is unconstrained by considerations of selection, direction or utility. How can Nietzsche negotiate between restricted nay-saying and unrestricted yes-saying?

3
The Dynamics of Opposition and the Transformation of the Übermensch

> I stand before my final peak now and before that which has been saved for me the longest. Alas, now I must face my hardest path! ... But whoever is of my kind cannot escape such an hour – the hour which says to him: 'only now are you going your way to greatness! Peak and abyss – they are now joined together.'
>
> —*TSZ* III: The Wanderer

Yirmiyahu Yovel, commenting on a series of essays devoted to Nietzsche's philosophy of affirmation, makes an observation that most readers of Nietzsche viscerally encounter at some point or another: Nietzsche's affirmative philosophy, which celebrates the inherent impermanence of values, is challenged and even contradicted by 'the more noticeable blows of his critical hammer'.[1] The implicit view here is that the conditions and consequences of affirmation preclude those necessary for critical or negative philosophy. In terms of the argument set forth in the present study, we might reword this to suggest that the condition and consequences of the will to power's nomothetic task to establish a restricted economy come into conflict with the condition and consequences of self-overcoming in the general economy of the eternal recurrence. If 'great politics' necessitates 'no-saying' in terms of the virulent critique of all ideals and values, then how can Nietzsche also claim that the Dionysian philosopher is one who says an unbounded 'yes' to all things eternally? How is the future philosopher to engage in both? Both Wolfgang Müller-Lauter and Leo Strauss have articulated this same problematic but in distinct ways and using different terms. Let us first begin with Müller-Lauter's interpretation of the relationship between negation and affirmation.

Double vision: Contradictions in the concept of the overman

The usefulness of Müller-Lauter's argument for the present examination lies in his analysis of Nietzsche's notion of the Übermensch or Overman (interchangeable with my use of 'Overhuman'). Through a careful consideration of the critical and affirmative goals of will to power, Müller-Lauter uncovers two contradictory forms of Overman, thereby arguing that two incompatible forms of future philosophy develop in Nietzsche's thought. Using Müller-Lauter's observation, I will show that this incompatibility is, instead, a com-possibility that can be understood as a transmigration of one form of Overman into the other. Nietzsche reminds us in *Twilight of the Idols* that the philosopher's warrior spirit is enhanced by its musical ear: the 'hammer' of philosophy, as Nietzsche makes clear, is also necessarily a tuning fork. The task of future philosophy requires the use of negation and affirmation, that is posing 'questions with a hammer' as well as being prepared to 'receive for answer that famous hollow sound'. The philosopher is thus a 'pied piper', one who 'has ears behind his ears' and for whom 'that which would like to stay silent has to become audible'.[2]

The first important point made by Müller-Lauter concerns the nature of 'contradiction' in Nietzsche's corpus. While there are indeed significant contradictions in Nietzsche's work as a whole, these tensions relate to and reflect what Nietzsche believes is 'contradictory' in the modern experience of existence. So, for Müller-Lauter, 'contradiction' forms the leitmotif of Nietzsche's thought: as such, the interpretive task is not to demonstrate the overall coherence or incoherence of Nietzsche's philosophy, but to examine Nietzsche's 'philosophy of contradiction'.[3] He begins by fleshing out the tension between Nietzsche's philosophies of negation and affirmation with an examination of the notion of will to power. Nietzsche's emphasis on perspectivism as the basic condition of all life establishes that the will to power of all existence – not simply human existence – perceives the world from its own viewpoint: 'there is nothing beyond "the totality" of the differently construing power-centers'.[4] Once this perspectivism is connected to the idea that there are many kinds of truths, and consequently that there is no truth,[5] the history of morality turns against itself and leads to nihilism (while simultaneously discovering that nihilism was always the core aim of morality).

The result, contends Müller-Lauter, is that all values and ideals associated with morality are devaluated and ultimately destroyed. Thus the overcoming of nihilism and morality overturns the historical conquest of the weak and inaugurates the dominion of the strong individual.[6] The strong individual exerts its power as a 'breeding agent'; its will effects the 'strengthening of the strong', while simultaneously shows itself to be 'paralyzing and destructive for the world-weary'.[7] By living through the 'whole of nihilism to the end', the strong-willed individual – 'the perfect nihilist' – will leave nihilism behind, 'outside [it]self'.[8] Müller-Lauter thus points to Nietzsche's claim that the overcoming of nihilism will lead to the condition in which 'pleasure in saying No and doing No' will emanate from 'a tremendous strength and tension derived from saying Yes'.[9] From Müller-Lauter's perspective, however, Nietzsche's description of the most extreme form of nihilism contains two incompatible goals and reflects two incompatible human natures, leading to two distinctly separate lines of development for the future philosopher: accordingly, the Overman is either *strong* or *wise*:

> Neither the multiplicity of names intended to suggest that there are many forms of ascendant humanity, nor the unity of the goal aspired to of producing the Overman, can hide the fact that in Nietzsche's portrayals two different tendencies are locked in conflict, mirroring the incompatibility of their contradictory natures.[10]

On the one hand, the Overman's greatness consists in 'the absolutization of [its] perspective'[11] in which it imposes its 'ideal against the ideals of other men and remakes them in [its] own image'.[12] To philosophize with a hammer thus means that the commander-legislator must direct 'the will of millennia by giving direction to the highest natures'[13] and determine the frontier of possibilities within which its own ideals will exist and rule. On the other hand, the other form of greatness consists in the unrestricted acceptance of all that is and was; far from requiring negation, this affirmation necessitates the recognition of all other ideals.

Therefore, the problem gains clarity: will to power is either strong or wise. Will to power either confirms its own sense of power by repudiating and overcoming others, or it affirms other ideals and effectively loses the basis for claiming its own supremacy over others. The problem with the former case is that will to power must fix and absolutize in accordance with its own ideal, thereby limiting the amplitude of power it can pursue; in the latter case, by accepting all perspectives, will to power potentially opens itself up to being subjugated by another stronger will. The incompatibility between negation and affirmation is revealed in the incompatibility between the strong and wise embodiments of Overman: 'by absolutizing one perspective, the will to power is immobilized; by absolutizing "everything is permitted", it loses any effective form. In both cases, a self-damaging of the previously dominant power-will occurs and it will have to submit to a stronger will'.[14]

In the first vision of Overman, the highest type's strength of will is measured by the extent to which it resists: its greatness comes from the 'great cultivating idea' against which all 'other modes of thought will ultimately perish'.[15] In the second vision of Overman, the greatness of the highest type is measured to the extent that it ceases to resist and is 'richest in contradictions', thereby accomplishing a 'grand harmony' of opposites.[16]

Müller-Lauter further distinguishes the two types: the strongest type, who in its preoccupation with achieving and maintaining strength, wants above all not to know[17] or acknowledge ideals different from its own; and the wisest type, who in its ability to assimilate all counter-ideals, is one who does not resist or withdraw from any knowledge and embraces all perspectives. Thus, Müller-Lauter sums up the problematic relationship between these two conflicting doctrines of Nietzschean Overman: while both types are concerned with power, the wise type necessarily loses power the more it affirms and absorbs conflicting counter-ideals, rendering it 'terribly delicate and fragile'.[18] The more manifold one is, the more fragmented and precarious one's self-integration becomes.[19] The ramification of this tension for Nietzsche's vision of the Overman is that 'if one of the two modes of behavior overcomes the other, the result is either rigidity or the loss of self in the multiplicity of what could become real'.[20]

Although Müller-Lauter acknowledges that Nietzsche intends these two antithetical forms of greatness – which requires either the negation or affirmation of other ideals – to be present in the highest type, the question of exactly how both strength and wisdom can simultaneously lead to the increase of power remains unanswered. He therefore concludes that it is not possible to bring these two antithetical elements of will to power into successive historical sequence. 'The fact remains that the great man is strong or wise. Only alternation of the two types of greatness could perhaps be made plausible in this way, but not their approximation, not to mention their amalgamation'.[21] From this, he reasons that the doctrine of eternal recurrence cannot be obtained from the characteristics of the violent or strong Overman but rather follows logically from the manifoldness and 'radical self-understanding' of the synthesizing wise type.[22] In the final analysis, he acknowledges that although Nietzsche's belief is that when pushed to the extreme, both forms of Overman will converge into one, both remain irretrievably separate to the extent that the meaning of the eternal recurrence 'remains insurmountably split into a duality'.[23]

For the purposes of our argument, we can highlight an important point that Müller-Lauter's argument seems to indicate: if the eternal recurrence is the source experience for affirmation in Nietzsche's thought, then only the wise Overman can truly undergo and express affirmation; meanwhile only the strong Overman can really undergo and express negation. If, however, the 'translation back into nature' requires the future philosopher to affirm all that is and was, then the philosopher must experience the eternal recurrence in order to catalyse and accomplish its Dionysian task (the teaching of the eternal recurrence, which necessitates the nomothetic ordering conducted through 'great politics').

The twin functionality of negation and affirmation can be linked to the importance of the highest type's relation to both a restricted and a general economy. Negation, because it is essentially limited by the principles of efficiency and preservation, itself cannot lead to a 'translation back into nature;' self-overcoming is ultimately limited within the structural economy of the nomothetic political ordering of types (and therefore not 'self-overcoming' at all). Affirmation, however, cannot become a cultural symbol unless it is produced deliberately by a nomothetic organization of all types. Contrary to Müller-Lauter's assertion, both negation and affirmation – the strong and wise Overmen – can be operationalised beyond the logical requirements of the principle of non-contradiction. Indeed, when read in tandem with the 'Three Metamorphoses' in *Thus Spoke Zarathustra*, the Overman's task does seem to include both negation and affirmation, namely in terms of the metamorphosis from the stages of the *Thou shalt*, to the *I will* and finally to the *I am*.[24] The three metamorphoses refer to the three stages that must be crossed on the way to the Overman: the camel, the lion and, finally, the child.

Although the three metamorphoses will be carefully considered in the following chapter, suffice it to say that the camel represents the stage of asceticism in which the spirit is sufficiently free to be dissatisfied with the present conditions of the world. In the second stage, the lion represents the overcoming of the camel's dependence on moral values, but the lion, in its attempt to say 'I will', must still contend with the dragon 'Thou shalt', the moral law. The lion overcomes the camel not only by seeking freedom but also by creating a freedom of the spirit through the exercise of that scepticism which is necessary for the devaluation of all previous moral values (the sacred 'No'). The lion is not yet capable of transvaluation, and must himself be overcome by the third and final stage, the sacred 'Yes-saying' of the child. These psycho-physiological stages of the morphosis correlate with the seemingly antithetical tasks of negation and affirmation. We might understand this in terms of a twofold process: the philosopher must negate current ideals, which hastens the devaluation of all values (characteristic of nihilism). Negation involves the exercise of the nay-saying hammer by the strong and mighty type; therefore, to reach the final stage of affirmation (the sacred 'Yes'), the strong man must also become the wise man:

> The two incompatible factors rely on each other. The strong man can only remain strong and become stronger if he becomes the wise man who not only has the multifarious contradictions outside himself but assimilates them into himself. And the wise men will be lost in the perspectival contradictions and suffer losses in form and strength, if he does not commit himself to the exclusive guidance of the one ideal.[25]

Müller-Lauter admits that Nietzsche intends for this transformation to occur; he does not believe that the transformation required between these fundamentally different natures is possible. I not only contend that the success of this metamorphosis distinguishes the merely higher types from the highest type, but that the Dionysian task of future philosophy fundamentally depends on both. It is at this juncture that we turn to Leo Strauss's interpretation of how affirmation emerges out of the demands set forth by negative philosophy itself (in other words, how the wise man emerges naturally from out of the strong man).

The harmony of opposites: The 'complementary man'

With the proclamation of the 'death of god' first in *The Gay Science* and then in *Thus Spoke Zarathustra*, Nietzsche ensures the liberation of the will from faith precisely through the refutation of all supernatural or divine powers. The prescience of this divine death severs the relation between human and divine, will and redemption. Radical historicity replaces faith in divinity to the extent that human being's alienation from 'eternity' is the price s/he must pay for emancipation from the past. Strauss rewords this problematic in terms of the seeming inconsistency between the demands of will to power and those of eternal recurrence:

> The difficulty inherent in the philosophy of the will to power led after Nietzsche to the explicit renunciation of the very notion of eternity. Modern thought reaches its culmination, its highest self-consciousness, in the most radical historicism, i.e., in explicitly condemning to oblivion the notion of eternity. For oblivion of eternity, or in other words, estrangement from man's deepest desire and therewith from the primary issues, is the price which modern man had to pay, from the very beginning, for attempting to be absolutely sovereign, to become the master and owner of nature, to conquer chance.[26]

In the attempt to be autonomous from the morality of its time, the strong type applies the hammer of historicism to all ideals in order to exorcize all traces of the 'other-worldly' or transcendental from historical existence. Nietzsche's negative philosophy, as such, is the apotheosis of modern morality insofar as it completes the modern tendency to subjugate nature and being. Strauss here, following Heidegger, points to the fact that inherent in Nietzsche's doctrine of will to power is a radical historicism that negates and consigns all ontological concerns to the hammer of history. The problem for Nietzsche's philosophy is revealed as a dualism between the intrinsic historicism of will to power and the inherent ontological prerogative of eternal recurrence. We might reword this as the irreconcilability between the radical negation required of negative philosophy and the radical affirmation required of the affirmative philosophy. 'While Nietzsche's turn from the autonomous herd to the new philosophers is in perfect agreement with his doctrine of the will to power, it seems to be irreconcilable with his doctrine of eternal recurrence'.[27]

Strauss picks up on the contradiction many – including Müller-Lauter and Löwith – identify. One of the principal reasons Strauss claims that although Nietzsche's turn from the autonomous herd to the new philosophers accords with will to power but appears incompatible with eternal recurrence is that the task of negation leads to and demands the mastery of all elements of life, human and natural (which entails a forgetting of the question of being). The project of devaluation (philosophizing with a hammer) enables the philosopher to negate all opposing ideals, which requires the mastery and devaluation of nature. Even nature's inherent lack of ideals and valuelessness contradicts the philosopher's quest to unilaterally absolutize its own ideal. Negation is limited to the mastery of nature and, 'as the act of the highest form of man's will to power, the Vernatürlichung of man, is at the same time the peak of the anthropomorphization of the non-human, for the most spiritual will to power consists in prescribing to nature what or how it ought to be'.[28] In other words, the 'translation into nature' of the human thus coincides with the humanization of nature. Strauss describes the great responsibility of the 'complementary man' as unfolding on the 'summit' and the philosopher 'being the summit' of all existence.

> The philosopher's 'high spirituality', consists in the spiritualization of justice and of that kind of severity which knows that it is commissioned to maintain in the world the order of rank, even among the things and not only among men. Being the complementary man in whom the rest of existence is justified (*BGE* 207), standing on the summit, nay, being the summit, the philosopher has cosmic responsibility.[29]

By characterizing the philosopher as 'the summit', Strauss refers not only to the Aristotelian understanding of man's nature or end[30] but also to the philosopher's privileged position as the highest 'peak' of the social existence (a point established first by Pythagoras, Socrates and Plato). Most importantly in this passage, Strauss finds that it is in the embodied spirituality of the philosopher – the 'complementary man' – in whom the reconciliation between the negation and affirmation of nature occurs. As a culmination of the historical process, the philosopher is also revealed to be the one who integrates history and nature.[31] The term 'complementary' is borrowed from Nietzsche's characterization of the philosopher as distinct from the scientific type, the ideal scholar, the objective spirit in *BGE* 207. In this passage, Nietzsche discusses 'objectivity' and 'subjectivity' and suggests that the philosopher is one in whom 'objectivity' and 'subjectivity' coalesce and are harmonized.[32] On the one hand, like the 'selflessness' ('de-selfing') and 'disinterestedness' of the objective type, the philosopher looks away from its own self and knows itself to be a part of nature; on the other hand, like the subjective type who refers everything back to itself, the philosopher knows itself to be the one in whom 'the rest of existence is justified'.[33]

'Complementary' thus points to the philosopher's ability not just to be the 'master' but, more importantly, to be synthetic and manifold, a 'mobile pot for forms that still has to wait for some content and substance in order to "shape" itself accordingly ...'.[34] The 'complementary man' is the one in whom opposites are made congruent, in whom the radical scepticism of will to power and the affirmation of eternity is reconciled. As a culmination of the historical process, the nature of the philosopher is also revealed to be, in itself, an affirmation of eternal nature:

> Instead of explaining why it is necessary to affirm the eternal recurrence, Nietzsche indicates that the highest achievement, as all earlier achievements, is in the last analysis not the work of reason but of nature; in the last analysis all thought depends on something unteachable 'deep down'.[35]

Strauss's chief emphasis is on explaining the Nietzschean claim that 'noble nature replaces divine nature' (cf. *BGE* §188, 'Die vornehme Natur ersetzt die göttliche Natur)'. We might understand Strauss's point in the following manner: the ascent up the pyramid of social existence necessitates a complete abjection of all matters related to eternity in order for the strong type to free itself from all dogma. And yet, once the will has rid itself of all faith in dogmatic belief, in order not to fall back into a nihilism of the will (willing nothingness), the will must show its ultimate strength in an act of willing in the absence of all negation and negatives: willing as affirmation. In other words, the will for the first time wills actively rather than reactively (that is to say, against other counter-ideals).

> the *Vernatürlichung* of man presupposes and brings to its conclusion the whole historical process – a completion which is by no means necessary but requires a new, free creative act. Still, in this way history can be said to be integrated into nature.[36]

This affirmative moment is supposed to be at once the crucial refutation of morality as dogma and the liberation of the will from faith – what Nietzsche calls transition from the 'Thou shalt' and the 'I will' – and the first crucial emergence of the necessity of eternity as the fatum of man. Although Karl Löwith disagrees with Strauss's conclusions, in the following passage he aptly captures Strauss's point:

> At the peak of his freedom, however, the will to nothingness inverts itself into the willing of the eternal recurrence of the same. The dead Christian God, the man before the nothing, and the will to eternal recurrence characterize Nietzsche's system as a whole as a movement

> first from 'Thou shalt' to the birth of the 'I will' and then to the rebirth of the 'I am' as the 'first movement' of an eternally recurring existence amidst the naturelike world of all that is.[37]

Strauss argues that the notion of eternal recurrence emerges naturally from the doctrine of will to power. This is the most crucial point of his entire reading of *Beyond Good and Evil* and solves his earlier problem concerning the incompatibility between will to power and eternal recurrence. Strauss will show in his reading that if the entirety of *Beyond Good and Evil* was, as Nietzsche stated, a grand project of 'nay-saying', then in the final moment, as man stands at and embodies the peak of the pyramid, he will have to finally say 'Yes' – an 'unbounded Yes to everything that was and is, i.e. the affirmation of eternal recurrence'.[38] The 'complementary' nature of the philosopher reflects Strauss's conclusion that it is in the philosopher's willing of the eternal recurrence that the rift between philosophy and religion is healed. Therefore, according to Strauss, Nietzsche rightly reveals that in the person of the philosopher, the complementary man, 'philosophy and religion, it seems belong together – belong more closely than philosophy and the city'.[39]

For Strauss, how can the philosophy of the future rise from a philosophy that is still a product of nihilism? In other words, from out of the most 'world-denying' pessimism, how can the most profound affirmation emerge? By bringing together Nietzsche and *Plato* (or rather by Platonizing Nietzsche), Strauss suggests that at the peak, affirmation emerges naturally from out of negation through the philosopher's love for eternity (qua the eternal recurrence). At the beginning of his essay, Strauss conjures two images for the reader: Dionysus as a super-Socrates and the lonely man at the peak who nevertheless carries an Atlassian burden. These suggestive images compel us to wonder how, once at the summit, negation can be eventually overcome by affirmation. And how does the ultimate affirmation finally free philosophy from nihilism once and for all, without carelessly shirking the great weight of responsibility which characterizes the philosopher?

The key to affirmation lies in Strauss's claim that the religion of the future must necessarily emerge from the philosophy of the future. He begins by distinguishing between the past, the present and the future: the 'virtues' of the free spirits of *Beyond Good and Evil* are still those of 'precursors and heralds' of the future. In other words, within the restricted nomothetic economy of hierarchy, the philosopher who applies the hammer to current historical values is still implicated in the decadence of its times. Negative philosophy involves the smashing of counter-ideals, but also the employment (through the process of accumulation, preservation and sublimation) of those ideals. In this regard, Strauss understands negation as wholly as *dialectical*.[40] Here, the important implication is that all philosophical activity that occurs as a result of negative philosophy (such as self-overcoming) is necessarily teleologically directed, productively expended and finite. As yet, '"our virtues" are not those of the future'.[41] Strauss discloses that the philosophy and virtues the philosopher uses to attain the peak are not those that characterize the philosophy of the future. It thus becomes necessary to make a break with the past and present, in order to finally usher in a new philosophy of the future.

The greatest virtue of the 'heralds and precursors' thus far has been their historical sense; as a defect of modernity, it will nonetheless open up a new horizon and point 'to a way of thinking and living that transcends historicism, to a peak higher than all earlier peaks'.[42] While the negation of current historical values has proceeded by way of a subjugation and mastery of nature that has necessitated a radical historicism (thus consigning the eternal verity of nature to oblivion), the final creative act of the will to power can only be brought about through a final unbounded affirmation of nature. Hence Strauss avers that the task for the future requires a 'return' to nature,[43] that is an affirmation of the entirety of life itself. This purely Dionysian moment justifies the denial of those forms of life:

> Hitherto suffering and inequality have been taken for granted, as 'given', as imposed on man. Henceforth, they must be willed ... While paving the way for the complementary man, one must at the same time say unbounded Yes to the fragments and cripples. Nature, the eternity of nature, owes its being to a postulation, to an act of the will to power on the part of the highest nature.[44]

For Strauss then, the source out of which affirmation necessarily arises is the love for eternity found in the innermost depths of the philosopher's soul. Love vindicates negation and again becomes the guiding light of philosophy: the negation of life that was a by-product of critical philosophy is ultimately vindicated by the philosopher's most profound love for philosophy, as the 'love for truth'. This is what ultimately brings Plato and Nietzsche together for Strauss. Thus, as Laurence Lampert claims in his reading of Strauss,

> eternal recurrence belongs to Nietzsche's as its affirmative culmination: life is lovable as it is. Strauss's little essay depicts that inner

> logic of love in his own chosen sobriety, with constant reference to philosophy's other great erotic, Plato. Is Nietzsche's thought a relapse into Platonism? Philosophy cannot avoid such a relapse. Philosophy is a lover's passion for the greatest of beloveds.[45]

In the end, Strauss believes that what prompted Plato is the very same thing that prompted Nietzsche, and this is one reason that Dionysus is a 'super-Socrates' who perhaps reveals, even to Plato himself, that 'the gods also philosophize' (contrary to Diotima's conclusion).[46] Thus, the atheistic denial of eternity required by negative philosophy is only a transitional phase for the philosopher of the future. The image that concludes Plato's *Symposium*, of Socrates wearing the wreath of Dionysus, comes to mind at this point: the eternal recurrence emerges as a reconciliation of the fundamental and traditional antagonism between philosophy and religion.[47]

> The circle of eternal recurrence is the circle denoted religiously by dying and rising Dionysus. The new religion celebrates life as the highest. In this way, the religion of the future grows naturally out of the philosophy of the future as an earthly religion that affirms life.[48]

Strauss and Lampert offer a Platonic rationale for the metamorphosis between negation and affirmation: from the core of the philosopher's soul, the love of eternity and life is reborn from its opposite, the denial of eternity and life. The circle emerges out of the pyramid to reveal that the pyramid is ultimately only a vindication of the circle. Love, Platonic love as a force of the idea, saves the philosopher from perishing at the hands of nihilism. Platonic love redeems Nietzschean nihilism, for as Strauss states: 'Nietzsche does not mean to sacrifice God for the sake of the Nothing'.[49] Rather, Nietzsche 'had doubts whether there can be a world, any world whose center is not God. Nietzsche brings out the fact that in a manner the doctrine of the will to power is a vindication of God, if a decidedly non-theistic vindication of God'.[50]

The Straussian account ultimately fails; it circumvents but does not tackle the dangerous implication of reconciling negation and affirmation, will to power and eternal recurrence: that affirmation arises from the affirmation of nihilism – from the willing of nothingness emerges the possibility of overcoming nothingness. Affirmation, to be consistent with Nietzsche's thought, must affirm the very nihilism that negation sought to overcome. What Strauss misses, according to Karl Löwith's interpretation, is the crucial and necessary role of self-sacrifice in the transformation of negation (the most 'world-denying way of thinking') into the eternal celebration of life.

The sacrificial teaching of the overman

Löwith's account provides the reader with an understanding of the process by which the affirmation of life emerges from its denial through an examination of the essential predicament posed by nihilism. In terms of the sequential development of *Beyond Good and Evil*, the appearance of the only mention of the eternal recurrence occurs in the chapter on religion, namely as the unintended or accidental result of the experiment of thinking 'pessimism through to its depths'.[51] But what triggers this inversion?

We have already acknowledged, following Müller-Lauter, that Nietzsche intended for negation to lead to the most profound affirmation, but what is the mechanism of this transformation through which one 'may just thereby ... have opened his eyes to the opposite ideal?'[52] The thought of the eternal recurrence that arises from thinking pessimism to its depths leads to the most life-denying possibility thus envisaged by the philosopher: the temptation to self-destruction. From this point, I show, borrowing from Löwith, the dynamics that enable the capitulation to nihilism to become the overcoming of nihilism. 'The search for self-eternalization is in a perverse way at one with the temptation to self-destruction'.[53] The completion of the project of nihilism requires the self-sacrifice of the philosopher to the most extreme form of nihilism.

The critical point in the transformation of negation into affirmation is the total existential commitment made by the philosopher, a species of 'freedom' towards death through which 'the truly liberated spirit transforms the last result of "logical world-denial" into a metaphysics of eternally recurring world-affirmation'.[54] Löwith contends that it is the sacrificial core of the teaching of the Overman that catalyses the transformation between nihilism and the redemption of life. 'What Zarathustra "knows" but cannot will is that one can voluntarily destroy one's existence; whereas later, in the sight of life, he knows that life recurs precisely in sacrifice'.[55] According to Löwith, this sacrificial core (resonant not only of the life of Zarathustra but also that of Socrates and Jesus) ultimately confines Nietzsche's conception of the will to the very Christian source he wishes to eliminate. It is critical to grasp that Nietzsche intends to sacrifice God 'for the sake' of nothing: the death of God does and must lead logically to the state of Godlessness understood as nothingness if the teaching of the eternal recurrence is intended to recognize the inherent multiplicity of nature that Löwith describes as 'the meaninglessness of an existence that recurs without any goal'.[56] The teaching of the eternal recurrence is therefore both 'the most extreme form of nihilism' and the 'self-overcoming of nihilism': 'the "redeeming man of the future" is not only the conqueror of god but also the conqueror of the nothing, for this nothing is itself the logical expression for the success of godlessness'.[57]

With the death of god, the philosopher's quest to critically apply the hammer to the present and past leads to the most extreme form of nihilism which can only be overcome by succumbing to this most extreme form of nihilism itself. Within the restricted economy of negative philosophy, the devaluation of current historical values will lead the philosopher to a historical impasse: a moment will come in which the task of negation will require the philosopher to negate even itself and its own ideals. By completing the project of negation through self-sacrifice, the philosopher simultaneously affirms nihilism and overcomes it. Löwith's claim that this encapsulates Nietzsche's 'teaching of the Overman' is therefore instructive for us here: it explains the reasoning and process by which negation becomes affirmation. Nihilism has an inevitable and crucial interim position, between the death of God and the rebirth of the tragic Dionysian world.[58]

Within the restricted economy, the rule of chance (nature) is recuperated within the economy of culture through the strong type's mastery of nature and the imposition of its ideals over and against all counter-ideals. But this dominion and abolition of chance is still only a manifestation of negative philosophy. Recall that Müller-Lauter denied that the strong type was able to become the wise type without contradicting its nature, thereby making the transformation from negation to affirmation unrealizable:

> [H]ow this readiness can follow from this behavior remains incomprehensible. Whoever has imposed his ideal against others cannot open himself to the multiple contents of other ideals without giving that prerogative. Such surrender would be self-surrender of the 'iron man' in favor of the sublime. It can be understood not as a transition, but only as a qualitative leap.[59]

Here perhaps unintentionally, Müller-Lauter foreshadows the very argument that Löwith uses, that the overcoming of the most extreme form of nihilism – the transformation of negation into affirmation – necessitates the self-surrender or sacrifice of the strong type to the sublime experience of the eternal recurrence. At the peak of the pyramid, the philosopher's transmutation from strong to wise necessitates that s/he leap off the peak, at which point peak and abyss become one. This is the philosopher's sacrifice (for Bataille, the general economy is precisely an expression of the non-productive expenditure characteristic of sacrificial practices). This is consistent with Zarathustra's explanation that in order to climb upwards, the philosopher must necessarily experience 'going under':

> I love those who do not first seek behind the stars for a reason to go under and be a sacrifice, but who sacrifice themselves for the earth, that the earth may some day become the Overman's.[60]

During his ascent, Zarathustra realizes that in the end, one experiences only oneself:

> I stand before my final peak now and before that which has been saved for me the longest. Alas, now I must face my hardest path! ... But whoever is of my kind cannot escape such an hour – the hour which says to him: 'only now are you going your way to greatness! Peak and abyss – they are now joined together' ... 'And if you now lack all ladders, then you must know how to climb on your own head' ... 'Before my highest mountain I stand and before my longest wandering; to that end I must first go down deeper than ever I descended'.[61]

For Nietzsche unbounded affirmation only occurs in the experience of the eternal recurrence, which, as I argue, occurs at the peak of the pyramid, the point at which the strong type justifies its whole existence and that of the world by finally becoming wise. Between the philosopher's quest and the greatest peak of eternity, however, lies the great abyss of nihilism; as such, the sacrificial core of the teaching of the Overman must be a precondition for 'great politics' (what I argue is 'the teaching of eternal recurrence') for as Löwith remarks, 'only the man who has overcome himself can also will the eternal recurrence of all that is'.[62] If for Strauss, 'noble nature replaces divine nature', then an account must be given of the genesis of this new nobility, given that he admits that 'our virtues' are not those of the philosopher of the future.

In the following chapter, we will examine closely the process by which the transformation between negation and affirmation occurs through the teaching of the Overman and the experience of the eternal. In relation to the three stages of metamorphoses in *Thus Spoke Zarathustra*, I argue that the final metamorphosis will require the philosopher to face the most difficult transformation yet: the logical conclusion of the project of negation requires the strong type to negate even its own values which are as yet, not 'new', but still a function of the nihilistic values left in the wake of the death of God. So the creation of new values, at this juncture, depends on the philosopher's final act of negating the very values that brought it to the summit of the social pyramid in the first place. Nietzsche will later name this stage 'the eternal recurrence', but in order to reach this stage, Zarathustra must understand the crucial transition from the lion to the child in the teaching of the Overman. Therefore, through Löwith's account of the sacrifice of the Overman, I will attempt to show not only that the affirmation of eternal recurrence emerges from the exigencies set forth by negative philosophy, but also how this transformation occurs.

4
Self-Annihilation and the Metamorphosis of Nihilism

> [P]olitical: the art of enduring the tremendous tension between differing degrees of power.
>
> *WP*, 719

The critical moment – the moment of metamorphosis of critical (negative) philosophy – is now at hand. The last chapter posed the initial problem of the relationship between negative and affirmative philosophies by demonstrating two essential points: first that the negation of current historical values is a necessary precondition for the tasks of affirmation and translation; and second, that the metamorphosis between negation and affirmation depends on the crucial role of nihilism. One objective of this chapter is to uncover the glitch in Löwith's logic in order to reveal that the problem is much more complicated than previously anticipated: if self-sacrifice is required to overcome nihilism, why is this necessarily the last act of negation (the last result of 'logical world-denial')? How is the sacrifice of the philosopher's will a negation of the will? And if 'freedom toward death' is of necessity the culmination of the strong type's project of 'philosophizing with a hammer', then on what basis can Zarathustra be distinguished from the two historical figures for whom self-sacrifice was pivotal, namely Socrates and Jesus? We shall first consider why and how the greatest expression of human will to power necessitates the disintegration of the very will to power in question.

The sacrifice of willing and the overcoming of Christian nihilism

Following Müller-Lauter's distinction between the 'strong' and the 'wise', Nietzsche portrays two different tendencies that 'are locked in conflict, mirroring the incompatibility of their contradictory natures'.[1] The 'strong' type measures itself according to the extent to which it resists and denies all ideals contrary to its own; the 'wise' type, in contrast, measures itself to the extent that it ceases to resist and accomplishes a 'grand harmony' of opposites.[2] At the peak of the summit, the 'strong' type's 'philosophizing with a hammer' reaches the critical point: having negated all of history, the logical completion of the project of negation calls for the negation of all current historical values, including the ideals s/he has espoused to date – without this step, no new values free from nihilism and decadence are possible. Müller-Lauter illustrates this point when he contends that

> Just as the radical nihilist rejects reality totally [insofar as he denies life], the Overman's affirmative openness must be equally total. His Yes must extend to the whole world, after the nihilist has condemned this whole. If the Overman's affirmation were only partial, the nihilist would be right with regard to the excluded part. Since the sole world comprises a seamless complex, a 'half-Yes' would be just as inconsistent as a 'half-No'. Whoever says 'Yes' to one fact must affirm all facts, if his Yes is to be a genuine Yes. For the affirmed fact exists only with all others, through all others ... The Overman must, then affirm even the nihilistic condemnations that he himself condemns.[3]

Between the philosopher's pursuit and the highest apex of eternity exists the great chasm of nihilism; the project of negation demands the negation of the last historical artefact that remains, the will itself. This very act of succumbing to nihilism, following Löwith's explanation of the teaching of the Overman, is supposed to effect the overcoming of nihilism.

Recall that Nietzsche defined nihilism as the condition in which 'the highest values devaluate themselves'.[4] The Platonic-Christian will to truth has turned against itself to reveal that the consequence of moral valuation is the most profound and radical nihilism, the belief in valueless or 'the conviction of an absolute untenability of existence when it comes to the highest values one recognizes'.[5] In conjunction with Löwith's argument then, we see that in order to begin the task of creating new values, the philosopher who wants to 'reach for the future'[6] must overcome the nihilistic past once and for all; this requires the completion of the project of devaluation or negation, the transformation of 'logical world-denial' into 'world-affirmation'.[7]

Nietzsche tells us that nihilism is implicated in the false dualism between the noumenal and phenomenal worlds.[8] The nihilist, according to Nietzsche, is one who 'judges the world as it is that it ought not to be, and of the world as it ought to be that it does not exist ... Will to truth as the impotence of the will to create'.[9] In other words, nihilism is a crisis of material existence that results when the will to power posits a false dichotomy between reality and appearance (or truth and falsity). It is experienced as an impotence, and the will has no other alternative but to devalue and deny itself. Decadence, therefore, in correspondence with nihilism, is the 'rendering secondary' or devaluation of the only creative force of human existence, the will to power.

If for Nietzsche nihilism is a situation in which the will is at its most decadent (the 'unhealthy' body according to Zarathustra) and thereby unable to interpretively and sensuously orient or relate itself to the world, it is also the situation in which the will renders its ability to experience the world impotent by projecting its hopes into a 'beyond' that cannot materially be experienced. One of the most nihilistic features of Christian morality is the erroneous belief that 'death' (tied to the belief in the resurrection of the body) can be experienced and therefore can redeem life. This metaphysical abstraction strips the will of its raison d'être and deprives the active will from fulfilling its function of integrating the various drives that make up bodily health. By placing all its hope in an abstract existence of life after death (the eternal life promised by the Christian god) which cannot possibly be an expression of will to power, the Christian will deprives itself of the very essence of existence, that is the will to power as growth, as immanent worldly activity:

> If one shifts the centre of gravity of life out of life into the 'Beyond' – into nothingness – one has deprived life as such of its centre of gravity. The great lie of personal immortality destroys all rationality, all naturalness of instinct – all that is salutary, all that is life-furthering, all that holds a guarantee of the future ... So to live that there is no longer any meaning in living: that now becomes the 'meaning' of life.[10]

Thus the Platonic-Christian will, the paradigmatic example of nihilism, is self-defeating: it 'would rather will nothingness than not will'[11] at all; here nothingness is understood as the condition or symptom of willing that negates the primacy of willing in constituting material existence. As Mark Warren points out, nihilism cannot be understood apart from its historical materializations: 'there are no nihilistic consequences of ideas taken in themselves, divorced from the historical world of which they are a part'.[12] This is significant for our purposes: to understand Löwith's account of the overcoming of the most extreme form of nihilism requires understanding how for Nietzsche, the history of nihilism itself leads to the possibility of its own overcoming.

Nietzsche explains that the basic and general feature of all 'higher culture' has been the imposition of dominion and rank onto the masses, which he names the 'spiritualization [qua sublimation] of cruelty'.[13] The overcoming of modern (European) nihilism is thus primarily a political predicament.[14]

Nietzsche notes that one advantage of the Christian moral world view is that it was an antidote to and means of preservation against the 'practical' nihilism that resulted from the ancient hierarchy between master and slave, and also concurrently against the 'theoretical' nihilism of meaningless suffering. The history of nihilism thus begins, ironically, in tandem with the most natural expression and exertion of the strongest will to 'command and legislate' in the founding of the first political societies. The origin of nihilism develops simultaneously with the origin of the 'bad conscience', that 'illness' which man was bound to suffer with the first stirring of civic life:

> I regard the bad conscience as the serious illness that man was bound to contract under the stress of the most fundamental change he ever experienced – that change which occurred when he found himself finally enclosed within the walls of society and of peace ... Among the presuppositions of this hypothesis concerning the origin of the bad conscience is, first, that the change referred to was not a gradual or voluntary one and did not represent an organic adaptation to new conditions but a break, a leap, a compulsion, an ineluctable disaster which precluded all struggle and even all ressentiment. Secondly, however, that the welding of a hitherto unchecked and shapeless populace into a firm form was not only instituted by an act of violence but also carried to its conclusion by nothing but acts of violence – that the oldest 'state' thus appeared as a fearful tyranny, as an oppressive and remorseless machine, and went on working until this raw material of people and semi-animals was at last not only thoroughly kneaded and pliant but also formed.[15]

Recall that we have already defined nihilism as 'the will's inability to create meaning in the world without devaluing itself'. In the passage above, Nietzsche indicates that this kind of cleavage between will and its creative capacity occurred historically at a time of fundamental change, at a historical juncture in which the posited values of a culture conflicted with individuals' actual relation to and experience of living. Moreover, this process of 'civilization' by which political identity is formed, like Freud's account in *Civilization and Its Discontents*, is a violent one that demands the 'taming' of the natural instincts.[16] Nihilism in its European manifestation not only signals the impotence of the will erected by Christian morality, but also marks that moment in which the disparity between the values posited by morality (what Freud would call the 'reality principle') and the actual experience of natural instincts (the 'pleasure principle') is so great as to lead to another threshold of 'fundamental change' and enactment of 'tyranny'. 'The democratization of Europe is at the same time an involuntary arrangement for the cultivation of tyrants – taking that word in every sense, including the most spiritual'.[17] The development and intensification of nihilism – because of its inherent contradictoriness – increases the tension between the values it puts forth and lived experience.

Thus, Christian truthfulness turns against the values it posits (*WP*, §5[18]). If we understand the 'will to truth' as the impotence of the 'will to create' as Nietzsche did[19] then we must also understand that it is precisely out of the will to truth – that is out of the tension of opposites – that the will to create is made possible. As Nietzsche indicates at the end of *The Genealogy of Morality*,

> Unconditional honest atheism [...] is not the antithesis of [the ascetic] ideal, as it appears to be; it is rather only one of the latest phases of its evolution, one of its terminal forms and inner consequences – it is the awe-inspiring catastrophe of two thousand years of training in truthfulness that finally forbids the lie involved in the belief in God [...] What meaning would our whole being possess if it were not this, that in us the will to truth becomes conscious of itself as a problem? As the will to truth thus gains self-consciousness – there can be no doubt of that – morality will gradually perish now: this is the great spectacle in a hundred acts reserved for the next two centuries in Europe – the most terrible, most questionable, and perhaps the most hopeful of all spectacles.[20]

The nihilism of Christianity, when played to its logical conclusion – and as a direct consequence of the rigorous application of its own value of truthfulness – leads to a situation in which it betrays and turns against itself. More importantly, I take Nietzsche to be suggesting here that the most spiritual types of this age – those 'higher' types – will engage in the project of exposing the contradictions of nihilism precisely by carrying out the very impulses of nihilism to its conclusion. Nietzsche here hints at the important connection between the development of nihilism, its overcoming and the project of negation taken on by those individuals of rare spiritual strength. The strong type who engages in and perhaps even strives to complete the project of negative philosophy is still complicit with nihilism. Negation is still nihilistic and the strong type is still a nihilist, to use Müller-Lauter's term. But this imbrication with nihilism does not lessen the great task of the strongest type who must, in a real sense, complete the task of negative philosophy by finally completing the trajectory inaugurated by the Christian will to truth. The ramification is that the will to truth of Christian morality leads not only to the murder of God, but also necessitates the murder of the will itself. For Nietzsche, this is precisely what the Christian, who would rather will nothingness than not will at all, is unable to will.

> What ... is to be condemned in the sternest terms is the ambiguous and cowardly compromise of a religion such as Christianity: more precisely, such as the church: which, instead of encouraging death and self-destruction, protects everything ill-considered and sick and makes it propagate itself –
>
> Problem: with what means could one attain to a severe form of really contagious nihilism: such as teaches and practices voluntary death with scientific conscientiousness (– and not a feeble, vegetable existence in expectation of a false afterlife –)?
>
> One cannot sufficiently condemn Christianity for having devaluated the value of such a great purifying nihilistic movement, which was perhaps already being formed, through the idea of the immortal private person: likewise through the hope of resurrection: in short through the continual deterrence from the deed of nihilism, which is suicide –
>
> It substituted slow suicide: gradually a petty, poor, but durable life; gradually a quite ordinary, bourgeois, mediocre life, etc.[21]

The goal of Christian morality is, paradoxically, the death of the will itself, and Nietzsche says that 'one cannot sufficiently condemn Christianity for having devaluated the value of such a great purifying nihilistic movement'. Nietzsche recognizes that the death of the will, the most extreme conclusion of the nihilistic Christian will to truth, is also the moment of consummation and purgation of nihilism. Unless this be recognized as the fundamental contradiction of European nihilism (that the will to truth leads to the annihilation and purification of the will), no new values that are free from the effects of nihilism are possible. To 'philosophize with a hammer' is thus to risk the danger of completing the project of negative philosophy, the culmination of which is the simultaneous intensification and overcoming of nihilism.

Löwith's focus on the teaching of the Overman therefore centres on the pivotal role of voluntary death in the overcoming of nihilism. And in this respect, Zarathustra's trajectory as the strongest type reveals that the completion of the Christian will to truth inevitably necessitates an *imitatio Christi*, the self-sacrifice of life.

In several passages, Nietzsche extols the 'willing at the right time to die'; 'death. – One must convert the stupid physiological fact into a moral necessity. So to live that one can also will at the right time to die!'[22] Not every or just any act of willing self-annihilation is in accordance with the criteria necessary to overcome nihilism. The general intention to kill oneself is not what Nietzsche means by 'free death'. Freedom towards death as the necessary criteria for willing the overcoming of nihilism is only available to the one who has first travelled the path of negative philosophy, the one who has already destroyed all faith and belief in present human morality. Nietzsche thus suggests that the metamorphosis between negation and affirmation happens as an accident. The death of god is vindicated only by accident (chance), and this is perhaps what Nietzsche means in aphorism 56 of *BGE*, that one stumbles upon the world-affirming ideal (the counter-ideal of the most extreme form of nihilism) 'without really meaning to do so' and makes this accident necessary because one 'makes himself necessary'. One must therefore distinguish between 'willing to die at the right time' for those who lack the virtues of the future philosopher and the existential commitment or freedom towards death that characterizes the experience of the highest types in the eternal recurrence. In the former case, it is indeed a kind of wisdom to will death for those whose impotency is incurable. Like in the case of Socrates, death is indeed the only physician for some.[23] For the 'plebeian' types, dying is the mark of a certain level of courage, but one that is a result of resignation rather than of strength. For Nietzsche, Socrates is significant insofar as he is a negater of the values of his times. But because he raises morality above even himself, the impact of Socrates's actions provokes the degeneration of Greek culture: 'moral judgments are torn from their conditionality, in which they have grown and alone possess any meaning, from their

Greek and Greek-political ground and soil, to be denaturalized under the pretense of sublimation'.[24] As a negater although Socrates philosophizes with the 'dialectical' hammer,[25] he is only still an ascetic (a camel burdened by morality). His malice is barbed, both derisive and hidden,[26] unlike the Sophists who 'possess the courage of all strong spirits to know their own immorality'.[27] Socrates does not possess the 'leonine' courage to admit that he strives to master the world around him. His sacrifice is an act of martyrdom, the act of a saint rather than of an artist. His freely chosen death is a sign of his ressentiment and impotence rather than of his abundance and potency.[28]

On this basis, one might argue that the existential commitment made by Zarathustra is of a different nature; the courage of strong spirits is a freedom towards death that produces a transformation of identity. It is characterized first and foremost as an expenditure that is affirmative because it is unrestricted and aimless. Rather than a dialectical act of self-preservation through sublimation (what theologically speaking could be called a 'trans-substantiation'), Zarathustra's existential commitment relates to self-sacrifice as a squandering (which Bataille associates with the boundless or general economy of nature). 'Why sacrifice? I squander what is given to me, I – a squanderer with a thousand hands; how could I call that sacrificing? ...'.[29] It is perhaps this lack of distinction concerning 'dying at the right time' that has 'stumped interpreters', as Kaufmann suggests.[30]

In this manner, Jesus, who Nietzsche laments 'died too early', must also be differentiated from Socrates. Nietzsche's distinction between 'Jesus' and the 'Crucified' is critical to understanding his positive appraisal of Jesus as a representative of the psychological type of the redeemer.[31] In the passage 'On Free Death', Zarathustra suggests that freedom towards death (freely chosen death) belongs to the values of the highest types. At the same time, however, martyrdom – to sacrifice oneself for the sake of something – is rejected by Nietzsche as 'the inference of all idiots'.[32] Claudia Crawford suggests that 'if one becomes a martyr for a cause, gives up one's life for Christianity or any other external cause, one dies reactively'.[33] While this does explain Nietzsche's perspective on Socrates's death, it does not account for why Nietzsche believes that Jesus 'died too early'. It also does not explain the actions of Zarathustra, who while extolling the virtue of freely chosen death does not himself carry out this deed.

> Thus, I want to die myself that you, my friends, may love the earth more for my sake; and to earth I want to return that I may find rest in her who gave birth to me. Verily, Zarathustra had a goal; he threw

> his ball; now you, my friends, are the heirs of my goal; to you I throw my golden ball. More than anything, I like to see you, my friends, throwing the golden ball. And so I still linger a little on the earth: forgive me for that.[34]

Lampert suggests that Zarathustra's teaching here is intended to offer freely chosen death as an example and tool of inspiration for Zarathustra's audience.

> Death becomes glorious as done for them; it can serve their purposes by being the occasion for swearing earnest vows to also live sacrificial lives. Like Lykurgos's death, it can show the living what their lives are to serve – no longer Sparta or an order that already exists, but solely the coming of the superman. To those few like himself who measure all their actions in the pure light of the good, the act of death, can be a gift to the living. Such men seize death at the right moment, the singular moment in which their historical contribution to the historic good reaches completion, in which their gift has been given and heirs created.[35]

Here Lampert clearly seems to be making an argument for the desirability of martyrdom, but in this case death is chosen not for the sake of Christian values as in the case of Jesus, nor for the sake of philosophy, as in the case of Socrates, but solely for the coming of the Overman. According to Lampert, Zarathustra betrays his own teaching by depriving his disciples of such an exemplum of death and for this reason must seek their forgiveness. The weakness of this interpretation is that it contradicts Nietzsche's perspective on the undesirability of martyrdom and it cannot account for why, given that Nietzsche considers him superior to both Socrates and Jesus, Zarathustra does not choose death freely. Moreover, Lampert's explanation does not clarify how the death of the individual's will results in the affirmation of life: in other words, how does freely chosen death relate to the eternal celebration of existence? I am suggesting that Lampert conflates the doctrine of freely chosen death espoused by Zarathustra in the early part of the dramatic unfolding of *Thus Spoke Zarathustra* with the experiment of free death – the subjective condition of undergoing the experience of willing one's death. The distinction is significant for the argument here because for Nietzsche, freedom towards death is not a symbolic or sublimated 'thought' but a 'deed' that requires a total existential commitment by the one who finally accepts his 'most abysmal thought'.

We have already established that as a culmination of Christian truthfulness, the strong type who is still a nihilist attempts to complete the project of negation by negating the very virtues that have hitherto led it to the peak of its existence. This highest type believes that s/he has no other alternative but to succumb to nihilism in order to overcome nihilism. S/he proves to be superior to the Christian morality that has so far been negated. This type now intends to freely choose the dissolution of its own will. Zarathustra, from the beginning, teaches the virtue of sacrifice, which he equates with 'going under' and 'crossing over' for the sake of the earth:

> I love those who do not know how to live, except by going under, for they are those who cross over. 'I love those who do not first seek behind the stars for a reason to go under and be a sacrifice, but who sacrifice themselves for the earth, that the earth may some day become the Overman's.' 'I love him who makes his virtue his addiction and his catastrophe: for his virtue's sake he wants to live on and to live no longer'.[36]

What is not clear from Zarathustra's words is how self-sacrifice of the highest exemplar benefits the earthly philosophy to which Zarathustra clings. Death after all is a cessation of life; even as a display of martyrdom to inspire and stir the hearts of others, the death of the highest type has a limited impact on the celebration of life. Viewed in light of these queries, Löwith's claim that the overcoming of nihilism requires the sacrifice of the highest type is consistent with his claim that Nietzsche's teaching of the Overman is still mired in Christian valuation: with respect to the sacrificial core of the teaching of the Overman, the self-sacrifice of the highest man is indeed both the completion of Christian nihilism and an example of nihilism itself.

The salient question at this point is the following: if we take Löwith's assertion to be correct – and so far, it is consistent with the philosophy of negation that the completion of nihilism does require the self-sacrifice of the strongest type – then how does this process effect the transformation of negation into affirmation? If the strongest type's self-sacrifice is successful – of willing the dissolution of the will is successful – how does the overcoming of nihilism emerge? If willing the dissolution of the will is required to overcome nihilism, why is this necessarily the last act of negation, 'the last result of "logical world-denial"'?[37]

5

The Pathology of *Amor Fati*: *Eros* and *Eschaton*

> Eli Eli, lama sabachthani? My God, my God, why hast thou forsaken me?
>
> *Psalms* 22:1; *Matthew* 27:45

As we saw previously, Müller-Lauter rightly claimed that the heart of the problem of negation–affirmation centred on the (im)possible transformation of the strong nature into the wise: 'Whoever has imposed his ideal against others cannot open himself to the multiple contents of other ideals without giving up that prerogative. Such surrender would be self-surrender of the "iron man" in favor of the sublime. It can be understood not as a transition, but only as a qualitative leap'.[1] The significant point is that the completion of the project of negation requires the negation of all ideals including, in the final moment, one's own. That which Müller-Lauter identifies with the untenable and unrealizable 'transition' or 'qualitative leap' is identified by Löwith as the sacrificial core of 'the teaching of the Overman'. Referring to *Thus Spoke Zarathustra*, Löwith argues that in the wake of the revelation of the death of God, Zarathustra attempts to bring to the people the teaching of the Overman, but as Zarathustra's narrative shows, in order to become Overman, man must first overcome himself; only then can he apprehend the vision and solve the riddle of the eternal recurrence.

The teaching of the Overman is perceived as the sacrificial transformation of the 'strong' into the 'wise' and is expressed as the highest type's willingness to make a total existential commitment. This is the fundamental precondition for the affirmation of the eternal recurrence. If we were to encapsulate Löwith's understanding of the teaching of the Overman into a proposition, it might be the following: at the pinnacle of his strength, the 'strong' type would 'will the dissolution of its own will to power'. This would be the last step that would both complete the project of negative philosophy (No-saying) as well as demarcate the cathartic moment of transformation of negation into affirmation (the eternal Yes to all that is and will be).

This, however, is precisely where Löwith's equation misses a decisive detail. If we agree that Löwith is correct in his assertion that a crucial step is to 'will the dissolution of the will', then I argue that this step reveals an antinomy: the logical completion of the project of negation – the last step of logical world-denial – would also require the negation of the 'will to the dissolution of the will'!

This is the paradoxical historical moment of correspondence between radical negation or scepticism (in the act of willing the eradication of the will) and the radical negation of negation (the last step of logical world-denial is the negation of the will to eradicate the will). It is therefore precisely at the moment in which the philosopher makes the most fundamental existential commitment to 'will the dissolution of its own will' as the necessary task to complete the project of negative philosophy that the antinomy surfaces that this 'will to deny life' itself requires negation.

The implication of this subtle re-articulation of Löwith's point cannot be underestimated for the philosopher of the future: the consequence of the antinomy is an existential transformation, a fundamental shift in the philosopher's own understanding of (its) nature which Müller-Lauter expresses as the necessarily paradoxical – and therefore in his opinion 'unrealizable' – leap towards the 'sublime'.[2] The material experience with this antinomy is, I argue, the experience of the eternal recurrence. As a leap, the experience of the eternal recurrence is not simply a releasing of the 'pleasure principle' but the terrifying transgression of the boundary delimiting a 'normal' state from a pathological one. Bataille calls this antinomic moment the experience of an 'extreme limit' and an 'inner collapse', the moment in which the salvation (qua metaphysical solace) promised by self-sacrifice turns into its opposite, the profound recognition of the absence of salvation. The experience of the emergent antinomy is suffered by the philosopher as a profound and abysmal moment of crisis – perhaps not unlike the unfathomable feeling of abandonment and loneliness expressed through the words of Jesus on the Cross: *Eli Eli, lama sabachthani*? My God, my God, why hast thou forsaken me? Bataille remarks:

> The imitation of Jesus: according to Saint John of the Cross, we must imitate in God (Jesus) the fall from grace, the agony, the moment of 'non-knowledge' of the 'lamma sabachtani'; drunk to the lees,

> Christianity is absence of salvation, the despair of God. It fails, in that it attains its goals out of breath. The agony of God in the person of man is fatal – it is the abyss into which vertigo tempted him to fall. In the agony of a God, the confession of sin is irrelevant. This agony justifies not only heaven (the dark incandescence of the heart), but hell (childishness, flowers, Aphrodite, laughter).[3]

Forsaken by the divine, at this moment Jesus experiences the agony of an existence without God, but what is left is something rather than nothing. His life – Life – nonetheless persists. This is simultaneously the decisive moment in which Jesus experiences existence in its barest, most naked and exposed actuality: in this instant in which knowledge has been arrested, in which he has been forsaken by God, Jesus still exists in the brute occurrence of life itself. As Bataille understands it, this 'agony' is fatal: it signals the 'death' of identity but also the 'inevitability' of life.[4] This experience of the absence of salvation results, for the first time, in a 'justification' that is at once an 'affirmation' of the sacred ('heaven') and the profane ('hell'). What is revealed in this crisis of willing (both the negation and the negation of negation) is that Life is eternally accepting in its infinite endurance: even when one has lost one's 'self' and one's 'God', Life is inexhaustible, it exists, persists. Life 'justifies not only heaven ... but hell' as well. It is in the crisis of the will and the abandonment of the human by the divine that will has been negated and simultaneously affirmed. For Nietzsche, the love of eternity arises from this: Life wills man. The man who experiences the eternal recurrence loves life only because s/he experiences Life's love, love here as the profoundly inexhaustible unified force of nature as *eros*. Here, I invoke Nietzsche's notion of *amor fati*, which I understand not only as 'love of life', but explicitly as the experience of 'Life's love'. Nietzsche's *amor fati* resembles *eros*, but is distinct both from the Platonic Greek triad of love (*eros*, *philia* and *agape*) and from its Latinized Christian counterpart (*amor*, *amicita* and *caritas*).

It is worth briefly justifying my interpretation of love here because it supposes that Nietzschean love more resembles the pre-Socratic conception of *eros* as the all-encompassing unifying creative principle of the cosmos which stood against chaos. In the history of ancient Greek religion, the pre-Socratic dichotomy between Eros and Chaos (characterized, for example, by the Hesiodic, Homeric and Orphic traditions) is transformed by the Socratic and Platonic traditions (and continues in the Latinization of Greek philosophy into Christianity), which as Thucydides remarked developed increasingly with the secularization and democratization of the Greek world. This pre-Socratic *eros* (love) is distinct from both the Platonic Greek triad of love and its Latinized Christian counterpart. Before Plato, the Greek notion of *eros* was not part of a hierarchical ('Olympian') trinity but a unifying principle in itself – indeed, it held a place akin in importance to the Platonic *logos* for the chthonic/pre-Olympian thinkers. *Eros* was the principle of unity set in contradistinction to the chaos that dissolves, dissipates and destroys. In the *Theogony*, Hesiod thus distinguishes Chaos, the 'great void', from Eros, the 'creative force' that brings things together and is the principle of becoming.[5]

Thus I argue that *amor fati* – as the profound love of life and sense of Life's love that results from the antinomic crisis of the will – is held together by a chthonic and mythic understanding of *eros* rather than by the logic qua *logos* of a hierarchical Socratic–Platonic conception of erotic love. In this sense, the eternal recurrence is both a negation and an affirmation of willing, both a denial of life and a love for life. '"Loving" the absolute or fatal necessity is no longer a willing but – judged by willing – a willingness that no longer wills anything, in which willing as such is abolished'.[6]

At the sacrificial altar (which is also a crossroad or crucifix), both Jesus and Zarathustra are engulfed by the terrible truth of the abyss; here, love and death must collide (*eros* and *thanatos*) resulting in the temporary submersion or dissipation of the personal will within the infinite existential facticity of Life as tangible Becoming (the inexhaustible flux of existence-in-the-world). The eternal recurrence occurs in tandem with the negation of life and the realization that the will to power (life) cannot be negated once and for all. What is undergone in the eternal recurrence is a translation back into life. The moment in question is felt as 'sublime' and a 'leap', as Müller-Lauter contends, both a terrifying and cathartic assimilation of the spirit of the highest type with the boundless economy of nature.

Jesus's self-sacrifice and transfiguration on the Cross represents a fundamental core experience for Nietzsche's future philosopher. Nietzsche distinguishes between Jesus and Pauline Christianity; Paul, not Jesus, is considered to be the 'first Christian'.[7] In this sense, Jesus and Zarathustra represent the same type: both teach – 'not to "redeem men" but to show how one must live'.[8] In this respect, both have experienced the eternal inexhaustibility of life – as their darkest and lightest moment. Despair, hope. Melancholy, agony, nausea, lightness, euphoria:

> In truth, the will for an exhausting experience always begins in euphoria. Impossible to grasp what one is engaging oneself in, to

> guess the price that one will pay – but later, one will pay without getting one's fill of paying; no one felt the extent to which he would be ruined nor the shame he would have at not being ruined enough. This said, if I see that one cannot bear to live, that one is suffocating, that in any case one flees from anguish and resorts to projects, my anguish grows from the anguish which turbulence evades.[9]

In the attempt to complete negative philosophy, the philosopher experiences the inexhaustibility of the will to power through the realization that the will to power – life itself – can never be annihilated. Nothingness can never triumph because something will always exist in opposition, and this something (which reveals itself as the negation of willing one's death) is what Nietzsche calls will to power. Willing the dissolution of the will – that is willing death – cannot be the antithesis of Life, for Life has no antithesis. This is the fundamentally new creative moment to emerge in the post-nihilistic history of Western humanity: the overcoming of Christian morality is revealed in the affirmation of a new valuation of sensuous eternally earthly existence. Willing death is revealed, for the first time, as practically and theoretically untenable because death cannot be experienced; it is a cessation of one form of materiality and its return to an aleatory state of becoming. The metaphysics of death is dispelled and reintegrated into a new monadic conception of material existence.

For Nietzsche, this is the consequence of the experience of the eternal recurrence that demarcates the ultimate transformation of the strong into the wise: death is an abstraction because only Life can be experienced. What is revealed in this experience of negating the 'willing of the dissolution of the will' is Nietzsche's most profound faith in and hope for the possibility of affirming existence: nihilism – the belief in the 'nothingness' of existence – is fundamentally and ultimately untenable. In the negation of the highest type's last will to annihilate itself emerges the realization of the eternal inexhaustibility or fatedness of Life as will to power.

Mnemotechnics and the translation into nature

This has serious consequences for Löwith's argument as we shall now consider: the result of this profoundly destabilizing experience – what Klossowski calls 'a sudden unveiling' which has 'the character of a revelation'[10] – is what Nietzsche calls the 'affirmation' of existence, the 'innocence' of 'infancy', the 'translation back into nature' – or simply 'Dionysus'. The experience of the eternal recurrence is felt as a revelation: both a profound crisis of the will in its philosophical and historical manifestations as well as a singular bodily experience. Psycho-physiological existence (both its 'visible' and 'invisible' dimensions) is the chaotic 'ground' or 'groundless ground' (*Abgrund*) of human 'being'. For Nietzsche then, the overcoming of man's decadence requires overcoming the embedded faith in the unity of self-consciousness (self-consciousness that is pitted against its antithesis, the sensuous physical body).

> Against positivism, which halts at the phenomena – 'There are only facts' – I would say: No, facts is precisely what there is not, only interpretations. We cannot establish any fact 'in itself': ... The 'subject' is not something given, it is something added and invented and projected behind what there is ... In so far as the word 'knowledge' has any meaning, the world is knowable; but it is interpretable otherwise, it has no meaning behind it, but countless meanings.[11]

In this regard, nihilism is both a kind of servitude for healthy psycho-physiological existence as well as the mode of its possible affirmation. The 'translation' spurred by eternal recurrence must free the domination of the impulsional body from its bondage to consciousness, which Nietzsche understands to be 'nothing other than a deciphering of the messages transmitted by the impulses ... The notion of the unconscious is here nothing more than an image of forgetfulness'.[12] Kaufmann also notes the importance of 'forgetting' in Nietzsche's account of the historical and unhistorical in his second *Untimely Meditations*: 'in the smallest ... as in the greatest happiness, it is always the same factor that makes happiness happiness; the ability to forget ... to feel unhistorically while it lasts'.[13] Nietzsche writes:

> There could be no judgments at all if a kind of equalization were not practiced within sensations: memory is possible only with a continual emphasizing of what is already familiar, experienced. – Before judgment occurs, the process of assimilation must already have taken place; thus here, too, there is an intellectual activity that does not enter consciousness ... Essential: to start from the body and employ it as guide.[14]

The activity that 'does not enter consciousness' is the primal conflict of the drives – that 'invisible' dimension of the body that is governed by a deep forgetting or *amnesis* (which is also an *an*amnesis, a profounding non-forgetting of the unity of Life and thought). Consciousness and self-consciousness are possible because the cerebral activity or cognition is able to forget its impulsional substratum: 'there is no consciousness without forgetfulness'.[15] As mentioned in the earlier discussion of the mnemotechnics of nihilism, memory makes possible the judgment of the senses by cerebral activity and its translation into the everyday communicable language of experience.

Freedom towards death as the necessary criterion for willing the eternal recurrence is only available to the one who has first travelled the path of negative philosophy, the one who has already destroyed all faith and belief in current human morality. The experience of the eternal recurrence presents itself only when there is no other faith left except the faith in the 'self' that has refuted all other ideals. It is only at the moment that he commits his will to annihilation that the iron grip of self-consciousness, the falsehood of the unified, identical ego that seeks above all security and self-preservation, is loosened. The experience of life's eternality dramatizes (literally by playing out) the displacement of self-consciousness. As Klossowski explains,

> At the moment the Eternal recurrence is revealed to me, I cease to be myself *hic et nunc* and am susceptible to becoming innumerable others, knowing that I shall forget this revelation once I am outside the memory of myself; this forgetting forms the object of my present willing; for such a forgetting would amount to a memory outside my own limits: and my present consciousness will be established only in the forgetting of my other possible identities.[16]

The experience of the eternal recurrence is a material morphosis of the psycho-physiological makeup of the organism. Klossowski describes the organism's experience of morphosis not as a 'thinking' or thought process but as fluctuations of intensity that have no meaning in themselves but only acquire signification through a process of translation by which the affective intensity of impulses becomes culturally and linguistically coded as signs. – 'And this is what we call thought.'[17] It is in this sense and through this experience that the fictionality of the subject is experienced. As the 'most extreme form of nihilism', the eternal recurrence is a pathological state, at once a profound forgetting of the normal limits of the self and a profound un-forgetting of that which was repressed by self-consciousness. This un-forgetting is not cognitive memory in the conventional sense that can be invoked and dispelled by the intellect – rather, it possesses the quality of a phantasm, a terrifying upsurge of the impulses that remained hidden and unknown to consciousness. The experience of eternal recurrence is an *ecstasis* – literally an experience in which something is displaced or 'out' of 'place'. The result, as we have seen, is an abysmal sense of agony and despair, and concomitantly a feeling of euphoria. In this regard, *ecstasis* – the experience of out-of-placed-ness – is accompanied by the 'displacement' of a burden 'well-borne', or the feeling produced by *eu-phorein*.

The thought of the eternal recurrence as communicable teaching requires that the eternal recurrence must be made intelligible through the reconstitutive narrative function of memory and thus rendered infinitely repeatable: it must be a necessity that is willed and re-willed.[18] The eternal recurrence becomes a teaching only when it itself becomes a sign – a memory to which the self (whose identity was dissolved and reconstituted) adheres through language. The teaching of eternal recurrence thus becomes possible as the basis for 'great politics' (the nomothetic re-organization of collective existence) if the organism that undergoes the eternal recurrence can endure, incorporate and translate these various conflicting and overpowering drives, impulses and psychological states into the affirmative language of life which will enable the creation of new values.

It is worth remembering that as early as *The Birth of Tragedy*, Nietzsche characterizes Apollo as the symbol of recollection and Dionysus as that of forgetting. It is in the dialectic between forgetting and remembering that the early Nietzsche advances the dichotomy in ancient tragedy between truth and illusion. The Apollonian is the principle of difference, strength, clarity, of the unambiguous and the typical within the bounds of the law; while the Dionysian expresses the unity, transitoriness, and ecstatic affirmation 'beyond personality, the everyday, society, reality'.[19] 'But the image of Apollo must incorporate that thin line which the dream image may not cross, under penalty of becoming pathological, of imposing itself on us as crass reality; a discreet limitation, a freedom from all extravagant urges ...'.[20]

The Dionysian is the limit or 'thin line' of the Apollonian, says Nietzsche, but this changes with the demise of the Dionysian element in tragedy made by Euripides's conquest of Aeschylus; the Apollonian spirit increasingly usurps the tragic sensibility of the epic rhapsodist such that Apollonian drama forgets Dionysian rhapsody precisely through the disappearing of epic self-forgetfulness. Severed from its dialectical relation to the Dionysian, the Apollonian principle of beauty becomes, in the post-Socratic history of art and existence, the representation of beauty within the limits of reason. All thought about art becomes, with Socrates, *thought* about art – the artistic impulse is severed from its originary well of instinct and becomes a function or handmaid of knowledge.[21]

If the Apollo–Dionysus relationship was 'offensively Hegelian' to Nietzsche's mature sensibility, in *Ecce Homo*, Nietzsche rearticulates this relationship in terms of the problem of negation and affirmation: the psychological problem in the type of Zarathustra is how he that says No and does No to an unheard-of degree, to everything which one has so far said Yes, can nevertheless be the opposite of a No-saying spirit; how the spirit who bears the heaviest fate, a fatality of a task, can nevertheless be the lightest and most transcendent:

> The psychological problem in the type of Zarathustra is how he that says No and does No to an unheard-of degree, to everything which one has so far said Yes, can nevertheless be the opposite of a No-saying spirit; how the spirit who bears the heaviest fate, a fatality of a task, can nevertheless be the lightest and most transcendent – Zarathustra is a dancer – how he that has the hardest, most terrible insight into reality, that has thought the 'most abysmal idea' nevertheless does not consider it an objection to existence, not even to its eternal recurrence – but rather one reason more for being himself the eternal Yes to all things, 'the tremendous, unbounded saying Yes and Amen' – 'Into all abysses I still carry the blessings of my saying Yes'. – But this is the concept of Dionysus once again.[22]

Here, Nietzsche acknowledges the tension regarding the antinomic nature of the philosopher who must both negate and affirm, simultaneously both 'strong' and 'wise'. The transition between the two natures is, as Müller-Lauter rightly notes, not a 'transition' at all, but rather a 'qualitative leap' towards the sublime a metamorphosis that leads to the new creative moment in the post-nihilistic history of Western humanity.

Zarathustra's metamorphoses

The 'Three Metamorphoses' announced at the beginning of *Zarathustra* mark the narrative trajectory of the book, in which Zarathustra will undergo the bodily transformation between camel, lion and finally child. The camel represents the stage of asceticism in which the spirit is sufficiently free to be dissatisfied with the present conditions of the world. The spirit enters the desert to seek truth. Gooding-Williams notes that Zarathustra becomes a camel at the point in which he confronts the possibility that no new values are possible. Man, instead of being a bridge to the Overman, must recur eternally: 'Eternally recurs the man of whom you are weary, the small man'.[23] The soothsayer's prophecy has an effect on Zarathustra's body, which, like the crucified body, is 'dragged', 'croaked', 'gnawed' and 'wailed':

> Zarathustra echoes the prologue's Pauline portrait of his descent, thereby implying that he has failed to recall men to Dionysus and to assign them a feasible purpose. Whereas Zarathustra once claimed that he wanted to become man again, he senses now that he is doomed to suffer man again and again and again ... – without relief – and that the interminable, incessant recurrence of pervasively small and purposeless man is the crucifix to which modern asceticism has eternally bound him.[24]

The first act of *Thus Spoke Zarathustra* sets the stage for the second act in which the transformation between camel and lion occurs. The stage of 'camel-hood' designates a stage in the journey towards overcoming nihilism, but still not free from the burden of nihilism. The transition between camel and lion occurs because Zarathustra realizes that 'the will is still a prisoner. Willing liberates; but what is it that puts even the liberator himself in fetters? "It was"'.[25] If for the camel-Zarathustra, the persistence of Christian morality without exception marks the impossibility of any overcoming of Christian morality, it is because Zarathustra equates this with the will's inability to will backward and therefore to undo the trajectory of Christian nihilism:

> But has [the will] yet spoken thus? And when will that happen? Has the will been unharnessed yet from its own folly? Has the will yet become its own redeemer and joy bringer. Has it unlearned the spirit of revenge and all gnashing of teeth? ... Who could teach it also to will backwards?[26]

What Zarathustra realizes in the third part of the story is that he need not succumb to the spirit of resignation. In his vision of the dwarf (which Gooding-Williams equates with the figure of the eternally recurring 'small man'), Zarathustra relieves himself of his camel-burden by summoning a (leonine) courage to dispel the dwarf's hopelessly nihilistic vision of time. Whereas the dwarf knows nothing of the present moment, Zarathustra repeatedly refers to it to highlight the image of time it affords him. For Zarathustra, the present moment is privileged, in that it enables him to envision the whole of time as an eternal present moment. The dwarf has no place in this moment, for it excludes from time the past per se, and therefore, the Christian-Platonic past, the perpetuation of which the dwarf symbolizes. Zarathustra begins to cope with his abysmal thought. The lion supersedes the Christian God or great dragon by claiming for himself the power and the authority to create values. In 'On the Vision and the Riddle', a leonine Zarathustra supersedes the dwarf by claiming for himself the same power and authority.[27]

But Zarathustra has not yet crossed over to the final stage of infancy because he must now create new values and bring this new teaching to the world. In the fourth and final part, Zarathustra meets the soothsayer who tries to seduce Zarathustra into succumbing to pity, a reaction that would effectively again encumber Zarathustra with the nihilistic burden of the camel. The soothsayer wants to convince Zarathustra that he is still an 'unhappy consciousness' who has not freed himself from the spirit of resignation. Zarathustra counters the gravity of the soothsayer's words with a leonine courage that he transforms into the spirit of lightness, the perspective that the spectacle is 'merely a satyr play, merely an epilogue farce, merely the continued proof that the long real tragedy is at an end'.[28] It is once he envisions the possibility of 'experiencing passional chaos' within modernity that Zarathustra engages in the 'child's game of creation'. Thus, Gooding-Williams summarizes the three metamorphoses:

> It is the camel's thought that involves Zarathustra's belief that the past will repeat itself in the future; his belief, more precisely that the values that have shaped European humanity in the past will shape it in the future. Transforming his thought for the first time, Zarathustra forms the lion's thought of recurrence, which involves his belief that his soul is an omnipresent 'now' ... Transforming his thought a second time, Zarathustra forms the child's thought of recurrence, which involves a belief neither in the repetition of the past, nor in the repetition of the present, but in the repetition of the possibility of a future that interrupts the reproduction and repetition of the past. ... The child's thought of recurrence involves Zarathustra's belief that the possibility of going under to the chaos of the coming god, and thus of making use of uncreated passions to create a future different than the past (to create a future governed by new values), has been returned to some if not to all modern, European bodies.[29]

Eternal recurrence, the overhuman and genesis of novelty

Thomas Altizer's understanding of 'the resurrection of the body' is grasped by Gooding-Williams as the possibility of experiencing passional chaos in an entirely new way. If the completion of nihilism is simultaneously the overcoming of nihilism, it is because, as Altizer argues, the history of nihilism is eschatological rather than teleological:

> The death of God, which brings to an end the transcendence of being, the beyondness of eternity, makes Being manifest in every Now. Being assumes a totally new meaning and identity: no longer is it eternal; rather, it begins or dawns in every actual moment. Here, the verb begins is all important, for it defines or establishes both the subject and the predicate. We might even say that in this affirmation the subject ceases to be, with the result that it is no longer possible to say that being is, or that anything whatsoever is, as everything begins in every Now. Thereby it is revealed that the proposition 'Being is' is a product of the detachment of the speaker from the immediate moment: to be totally immersed in the Now is to be free of a permanent existence of any kind.[30]

What Altizer seems to be expressing herein is what William Planck articulates as a dynamic feature of dissipative systems:

> The Overman is an integral part of the Will to Power which is [...] the Will to Power-as-dissipative-system [...] [I]n the Eternal Recurrence of the Same it is Nature herself which is reborn and reconstituted in all her possible configurations [...] Dionysus means the return of the individual into the universal scheme of things, into the Will to Power in which the Overman takes his place consciously in the Eternal Recurrence, embracing his Amor Fati.[31]

Moreover, as Planck continues,

> The Overman is a potential of the Will to Power (as is the aardvark), when that Will to Power is not frustrated by the static systems of institutionalized pity, religion, nationalism, or feminism (the Overman has no gender) [...] The earth (cosmos) is the Will to Power and to reject the Overman as evolutionary configuration of the Will to Power is to reject the Will to Power and consequently to reject the earth, to reject life as one of those configurations. Thus the

> Overman is an 'earthly' phenomenon, i.e., a phenomenon of the cosmic Will to Power. To teach the Overman is to teach Dionysus; to teach Dionysus is to teach the subsuming of the individual into the tragedy-joy of the undifferentiated in which the individual still remains the individual as the locus, the locally maximized place of change [...] which is necessary [...] To teach the Overman is another way of teaching the Will to Power and the participation in that Will to Power and the love of that participation is called Amor Fati. The Overman is therefore the earth in the most literal, non-metaphorical way.[32]

The experiment and encounter with the eternal recurrence emerge as a consequence of a dynamics of novelty implicit in the historical playing-out of nihilism. The material metamorphosis (in which negation is transformed into affirmation) catalyses a mutation that transmutes the collective field. Moreover, the ability to espouse such a perspective itself distinguishes the highest types. The task and mark of the Overman is this ability to unify the multiplicity of the impulsional body without denying that the 'subject' is fundamentally a 'multiplicity'. 'Great politics' is Nietzsche's term for the political cultivation of the Overhuman as a functional configuration of will to power. It is in this sense that I read the following passage: 'political: the art of enduring the tremendous tension between differing degrees of power'.[33]

The art of politics is intimately tied to the ability of the singular body to endure and organize the contesting disarray of impulses experienced in the 'sudden revelation' of eternal recurrence. The multiplicity of the body is the starting point for the future philosopher (this is what is revealed in the experience of eternal recurrence) who must subsequently strive to achieve a 'semblance of unity'. 'Subject-unity', therefore, can be defined as the 'semblance of unity' that imposes 'upon becoming the character of being – that is the supreme will to power'.[34] Thus, 'great politics' is consonant with Nietzsche's belief that the body is a 'social structure'.[35] The body, both invisible and visible, is an alternator, or conversion mechanism between private and public orders, and between individual and species. The superiority of the highest type, as such, lies in its capacity as a generator that can equate the 'health' and vitality of the species with and in terms of the 'health' and vitality of its own states of becoming.

6
Novum Organum: The Overhuman as the Overmanifold

> [T]he exoteric approach sees things from below, the esoteric looks down from above ... What serves the higher type of men as nourishment or delectation must almost be poison for a very different and inferior type. The virtues of the common man might perhaps signify vices and weaknesses in a philosopher.
>
> *BGE*, 30

For Nietzsche, the encounter with the eternal recurrence separates the merely 'higher' types from the 'highest'. The unfortunate 'patriotism' or 'fatherlandishness' of the higher types of the age is a result of their misdirected belief that the individual is a mere reflection of the relative strength or weakness of the nation; thus, when Nietzsche ponders whether there is anything 'German' about Wagner's art, what he suggests is that it is not the German nation that justifies and gives value to Wagner's art, but rather Wagner's art – which emerges from the rich and manifold 'supra-German' source of Wagner's own physiological and psychological impulses – that justifies and gives value to the German nation.[1]

In his discussion of the historical conditions necessary for the emergence of the philosopher of the future, Nietzsche links the creation of 'new' values to the necessary political order that must accompany it: 'the new philosopher can arise only in conjunction with a ruling caste, as its highest spiritualization'.[2] Stated otherwise, the 'Dionysian' task of translation incorporates an 'Apollonian' or legislative component: the eternal celebration of life must be translated as a political vision for humankind. In this sense, the 'sovereignty' of a 'people' or culture is understood by Nietzsche as an extension and expression of the 'sovereignty' of its highest type. The political order itself is not substantially determinable apart from its 'sacred' (*hieros*) or nomothetic characteristic:

> The order of castes, the supreme, the dominating law, is only the sanctioning of a natural order, a natural law of the first rank over which no arbitrary caprice, no 'modern idea' has any power. In every healthy society, there can be distinguished three types of man of divergent physiological tendency which mutually condition one another and each of which possesses its own hygiene, its own realm of works, its own sort of mastery and feeling of perfection. Nature, not Manu, separates from one another the predominantly spiritual type, the predominantly muscular and temperamental type, and the third ... mediocre type.[3]

This passage from *The Antichrist* reveals something fundamental about Nietzsche's vision of the philosophy of the future: the coming of the highest types occurs in tandem with the rise of a new nomothetic/ political order of which the philosopher is not the executive or ruling element, but its legislator or lawgiver (its spiritual justification). That society should exist for the sake of the highest type is not an arbitrary invention of one man, but rather the very movement, expression and economy of nature. The highest type – the spiritual and strongest type – is not a statesman that administers *nomos*;[4] rather he gives the law to which the rest of society is bound to adhere. It is the muscular type, the second in rank who 'are the executives of the most spiritual order, the closest to them who relieve them of everything coarse in the work of ruling', those who will not (and cannot) command but only follow.

Because the political is an 'art' for Nietzsche rather than a 'truth' or 'true order', the distinction from Plato's analogy between the city and the soul must be made clear: for Plato, the hierarchy of the city should mirror the hierarchy of the soul. The 'myth of the metals' in Book three of *The Republic* clearly establishes the hierarchy of virtues as they determine the organizational hierarchy and division of labour in the ideal city. Book four further solidifies the argument that the right ordering of the soul from the highest to the lowest elements should determine and reflect the right ordering of society. Nietzsche, while in agreement with Plato that the principles governing the ordering of the soul are the same principles governing the ordering of society, does not necessarily extend this argument to the ordering of the philosopher's soul. The philosopher must not strive to reify one configuration of the drives. The highest type must be free to experiment with various 'ruling elements' to the extent that no one drive becomes 'regent' permanently: 'the most spiritual human beings, as the strongest, find their happiness where others would find their destruction: in the labyrinth, in severity towards themselves and others, in attempting ...'.[5] To this extent, Nietzsche's nomothetic order, like Machiavelli's, is 'anti-philosophical' insofar as it depends on the art of well-used 'vice', and also subtly tyrannical insofar as it requires the imposition of a sovereign will that is refined enough to know when to use force and when to use persuasion.

Gooding-William notes that 'as distinct from the ascent Socrates promotes, the movement Zarathustra depicts does not proceed from a world of bodies to a world of ideas. Rather Zarathustra envisions an ascent from one form of embodied, human being to another'.[6] Indeed, Zarathustra's encounter stages the distinction between those 'higher types' and Zarathustra's own philosophical metamorphosis towards the 'highest'. In each encounter, the higher men echo something Zarathustra has previously declared to the degree that Zarathustra must contend with the possibility that those who await him do not yet reflect the Overman but only 'the self he has been in the past'. 'The temptation to succumb to the soothsayer's seduction is, he soon realizes, equally a temptation to identify with the self he once was and to accept as true the soothsayer's assertion that self-overcoming is impossible'.[7] While Zarathustra eventually overcomes the spirit of resignation that the soothsayer's words are intended to invoke, he also does not persuade any of the men he encounters to espouse his own view of eternity. Indeed, Zarathustra tells the kings he encounters,

> You higher men, let me speak to you in plain and clear German. It was not for you that I waited in these mountains ... You may indeed all be higher men ... but for me you are not high and strong enough.[8]

Zarathustra's words are not meant for simply 'higher men' but for those highest types that share Zarathustra's insight. The characters that Zarathustra encounters are 'mere bridges', still camels who carry 'many a burden' who are still threatened by the 'wicked dwarf', that spectre of the 'small man' that haunted Zarathustra earlier. The kings do not want to establish new values but simply want to quell the rising power of the mob through the securing of their own political and military power; so they lament that 'man's fate knows no harsher misfortune than when those who have power on earth are not also the first men'.[9] Zarathustra silently mocks these kings who are mere warmongers and who lust for power and recognition. Like the camel who leaves for the desert, all the higher men – the scientific conscience (leech-man), the magician, the last pope, the ugliest man, the voluntary beggar, and the shadow – have engaged in 'vivisection'[10] – the task of negative philosophy – insofar as each has attempted to criticize and break with the values that surround them. Cognizant of the aristocratic impulse, each seeks to distinguish himself from others (the 'mob'); like the artist, each seeks the power of self-expression; like the saint, each pursues the 'truth'. But for Zarathustra, none of these figures has understood that despite the death of god, 'god is still [their] greatest danger'.[11] None have overcome the death of god – that is none of them are yet capable of divesting themselves of the virtues of their time in order to create new values. As Zarathustra avers, it is not simply a disdain or mistrust for the masses (i.e. a desire for hierarchy or recognition of inequality) that will characterize the highest type – indeed, it is not a concern with man at all that distinguishes the highest from all others: 'I have the Overman at heart, that is my first and only concern – and not man: not the neighbour, not the poorest, not the most ailing, not the best'.[12] The higher men are destined to falter 'like a tiger whose leap has failed' and grow weary of their work because they have misdiagnosed the situation and misrecognized their goals. They are unable to realize that if they are failures, it is because man is a failure; they still long to correct the past with the imposition of their own virtues:

> Thus I have often seen you slink aside, you higher men. A throw had failed you ... You have not learned to gamble and jest as one must gamble and jest ... And if something great has failed you, does it follow that you yourselves are failures? And if you yourselves are failures, does it follow that man is a failure? But if man is a failure – well then! ... Learn to laugh at yourselves as one must laugh! You higher men, how much is still possible![13]

The strength of the higher type does not measure up to Zarathustra's expectations: 'You are not high and strong enough. For me – that means, for the inexorable in me that is silent but will not always remain silent'.[14] More than his expectations, the higher man cannot speak to that which remains yet unspeakable in Zarathustra: the still untranslated epiphany that demands to be proclaimed and taught.

The higher man has not experienced the antinomy of willing that arises out of nihilism and overcomes nihilism, or the enduring implacability of the will to power. Gooding-Williams seems to confirm this in his claim that,

> If the higher man fails to persuade himself that in expressing and striving to distinguish himself he has made good his existence, it is because his will is not inexorable and therefore not capable of sustaining in him the belief that in expressing and striving to distinguish himself he has shown himself to be a truly exceptional and sublime individual.[15]

In *Beyond Good and Evil*, Nietzsche names Napoleon, Goethe, Beethoven, Stendhal, Heine, Schopenhauer, Wagner, Delacroix and Balzac as exemplars of artistic genius who experimented, seduced, allured, compelled, and overthrew; those 'Tantaluses of the will' who were 'born enemies of logic and straight lines, lusting after the foreign, the exotic, the tremendous, the crooked, the self-contradictory'.[16] In other passages, Nietzsche also includes Julius Caesar.[17] The downfall of many of these figures was that they took a wrong turn along the way: instead of continuing to pursue the transitory, limitless and supra-national, they succumbed to the constraints (on their identities, capacities and experimentations) imposed by the requirements of identity, politics and nationalism, much like the higher men in *Thus Spoke Zarathustra*. None but the animals have understood Zarathustra-child's thought of recurrence. And it is to them – the eagle and the serpent – that Zarathustra gives his love.[18]

It is therefore important to distinguish the various types and stages of philosophical development in Nietzsche's work which correspond to the varying degrees of freedom of the spirit that each type of human being has attained. In terms of the three metamorphoses mentioned in *Thus Spoke Zarathustra*, these 'higher' types are arrested in their philosophical development at the stages camel and lion, and lion and child. Save for Nietzsche himself, who proclaimed to have been overtaken by the Zarathustran impulse[19] and perhaps Goethe,[20] all the others 'broke and collapsed in the end before the Christian cross'. Here Nietzsche adds a further comment: 'with right and reason: for who among them would have been profound and original enough for a philosophy of the Antichrist?'[21] Jesus the man (rather than as the Christ), as the representation of the psychological type of redeemer, is ironically enough, like Goethe, one who affirms rather than denies life.[22] Hence, Nietzsche's 'ideal' Zarathustran type is 'the Roman Caesar with Christ's soul'[23] – that is, the one in whom the non-contradiction between strength and wisdom has been revealed.

But even Nietzsche, like Zarathustra, is only a 'herald and precursor', the 'bringer of glad tidings' who announces the coming of a new type that climbs beyond the highest types hitherto. At the end of *Thus Spoke Zarathustra*, we see Zarathustra leave his cave, perhaps ready to descend the mountain, but we are not privy to his actual descent or its consequences. In this sense, Zarathustra's narrative only anticipates Dionysian renewal by staging the various problems associated with communicating the teaching of eternal recurrence, but it does not itself instantiate or inaugurate the dawn of a newly renewed Dionysian culture. Nietzsche himself acknowledges Zarathustra's shortcoming:

> To repeat: how many new gods are still possible! – Zarathustra himself, to be sure, is merely an old atheist: he believes neither in old nor in new gods. Zarathustra says he would; but Zarathustra will not – Do not misunderstand him.[24]

Thus the relationship between the city and the future philosopher – and between the experience and teaching of eternal recurrence – still needs to be qualified. One crucial point to emerge thus far is that the 'strong' type must become 'wise', and this had required that Zarathustra seek solitude away from the distractions of the city and their dwellers. The city must be cut off from the pursuit of philosophy to the extent that the experience of eternal recurrence will necessitate complete solitude and loneliness. But if part of the Dionysian task is to inaugurate a new Dionysian culture, then the 'wise' type must again return to the city in order to become a lawgiver.

The legislator as *polytropos* (manifold)

What is becoming increasingly apparent is that the nomothetic project of future philosophy requires the future philosopher to be as manifold and contradictory as possible: in order to found a new political order that instantiates the creation of new values, the 'wise' must again employ its ability to impose, command and legislate, attributes that were previously associated with the strong type. Whereas the merely strong type wants no contradictions to its own ideals, the wise type is the configuration that is so artful as to be able to channel the ebb and flow of will to power. In other words, the wise type must again affirm resistance as a necessary part of creating new values:

> Legislators of the future. – After having tried in vain for a long time to attach a definite concept to the word 'philosopher' – for I found many contradictory characteristics – I recognized at last that there are two distinct kinds of philosopher:
>
> 1. those who want to ascertain a complex fact of evaluations (logical or moral);
> 2. those who are legislators of such evaluations.
>
> The former try to master the world of the present or the past by concentrating and abridging the multiplicity of events through signs: their aim is to make previous events surveyable, comprehensible, graspable and usable – they assist the task of man to employ all past things for the benefit of his future.
>
> The latter, however, are commanders; they say: 'Thus it shall be!' ... they dispose of the preparatory work of scientific men, and all knowledge is for them only a means for creation.[25]

The merely 'higher' types are 'philosophical labourers'[26] who are unable to transcend their present form; they can engage in the critical project of devaluation but cannot overcome it in order to create new values. The future philosopher, in contrast, is a genuine philosopher[27] who commands and legislates not to 'abridge' multiplicity, but rather in the name of multiplicity, here understood as the precondition for all activity of will to power. Nietzsche's perspective on Socrates seems to bear out my claim that what ultimately distinguishes the 'highest' from the merely higher types is the ability to be transformed from the 'perfect nihilist' to the 'total affirmer of life'. To the extent that Socrates is one who 'is in possession of a pitiless instrument' (the 'hammer' of dialectics), he represents a type of 'conqueror', a 'tyrant', one who masters others.[28] As an exemplum of the perfect negator (qua nihilist), Socrates 'absolutizes' (like the 'strong' types) his ideal even at the risk of his own life. In *The Birth of Tragedy*, Socrates is said to have lacked the artist's 'divine frenzy', but his rationalism nonetheless did prompt a 'regeneration of art'.[29] As a great erotic, Socrates exercised a kind of fascination that attracted the 'agonal instincts of the Hellenes'.[30] Socrates uses philosophy against the conventions of his time: the 'ferocity and anarchy of the instincts',[31] in his case, lead to the regeneration of artistic activity because of the 'anti-scientific spirit' of his entire philosophy (*WP* §441). In his ability to glorify his attributes 'as the highest quality and to represent all other good things as conditioned by it',[32] Socrates's erotic ability is admired by Nietzsche. But his inability and unwillingness to admit his immoralism and self-glorification is ultimately a sign and symptom of his inevitable decadence and baseness. Although he 'absolutizes' his ideal against all counter-ideals, he does so with 'scientific certainty'.[33] Therefore, Nietzsche condemns Socrates of a profound self-deception: even though he makes war on decadence, Socrates fails to admit and therefore overcome his own profound decadence. As such Socrates's vehemence – the tyrannical power that he bestows to reason – turns against his own instincts, and he is ultimately unable to give his instincts the semblance of unity that is the capacity of all higher types.[34] The type 'Socrates' would thus share a rank equal to the scientific consciousness of the 'leech-man' encountered by Zarathustra: he is 'high' insofar as he is able to pit his own ideals against those of his age, but he struggles against his instincts in order to tame and devaluate them:

> Scientific manners: as training or as instinct. – In the Greek philosophers I see a decline of the instincts: otherwise they could not have blundered so far as to posit the conscious state as more valuable. Intensity of consciousness stands in inverse ratio to ease and speed of cerebral transmission. Among Greek philosophers the reverse opinion about instinct prevailed: which is always a sign of weakened instincts.[35]

Socrates, that 'lover of wisdom', ironically enough from a Nietzschean point of view, fails to make the 'sublime leap' towards wisdom. What the Socrates-type lacks, however, is precisely what the future philosopher exudes. The philosopher of the future as a type anticipates a configuration of becoming to which Nietzsche is unable to 'attach a definite concept', but one who must above all be in tune with his contradictoriness and thus self-admittedly 'contradictory'.[36] The manifoldness of the affirmative 'wise' type must include the capacity to employ the 'strength' of previous selves without reifying them. The great mark of the Overman is thus its ability to be *polytropos*, a term Nietzsche uses in *GS* §344 to describe quixotic nature of the highest type (see Kaufmann's footnote to this passage in which he gives the German equivalent of the Greek *polytropos* as *den vielgewandten* or *den vielverschlagenen*). As both 'skilled and dextrous', as well as 'much-traveled' and 'crafty', Nietzsche invokes *polytropos* to describe a type beyond morality and metaphysical faith, a type who affirms life as it is. Kaufmann notes that Nietzsche here refers to Odysseus as a type who reflects the nature of the highest type and who 'owed his survival on many occasions to his virtuosity in deception'.[37] If we do grant that the future philosopher must be *polytropos*, then s/he must be manifold and mutable enough – both adventurous and cunning enough – to assimilate, employ and discard a variety of attributes.

The type that falls under the name of 'Dionysus' thus bears close affinity to two central figures examined thus far: as I argued, the 'psychological type of the redeemer' brings Jesus in close proximity to Nietzsche's depiction of the future philosopher, and as *polytropos*, the future philosopher resembles Homer's intrepid voyager, Odysseus.

Nietzsche asserts that insofar as Jesus fits the psychological type of the redeemer, one could 'call Jesus a "free spirit"' because he is, as a practitioner of life, a total affirmer of life:

> such a symbolist par excellence stands outside of all religion, all conceptions of divine worship, all history, all natural science, all experience of the world, all acquirements, all politics, all psychology, all books, all art – his 'knowledge' is precisely the pure folly of the fact that anything of this kind exists. He has not so much as heard of culture, he does not need to fight against it – he does not deny it … The same applies to the state, to society and the entire civic order, to work, to war – he never had reason to deny 'the world' … Denial is precisely what is totally impossible for him.[38]

This is an incredible description of Jesus, and one would not imagine that it is Nietzsche's own. As argued earlier, the experience of Jesus on the Cross represents a fundamental core experience for Nietzsche's understanding of eternal recurrence. Both Jesus and Zarathustra, as they undergo the metamorphosis from camel to child, experience the eternal recurrence – the eternal inexhaustibility of life – as their darkest and lightest moments. The experience of eternal recurrence transforms the nature of the being that experiences it such that negation (qua resistance and denial) is no longer required in order to achieve a superabundant feeling of power. The wise type is a 'great synthesis' insofar as it does not resist anything. For the wise type, the feeling of active power is a result of the denying of all denials, what I have called the negation of negation.

But Jesus died on the Cross; the history of Christianity after Jesus 'coarsened the type'; as a result, 'the type of the redeemer has been preserved to us only in a very distorted form'.[39] The superiority of the type 'Jesus' is associated with its affinities to Buddhism rather than to Christianity. The Jesus-type, in its complicity with the ascetic impulse, represents 'a new Buddhism' 'for Europeans'.[40] As a 'non-Indian Buddha', Jesus is associated with Buddhist nihilism that is, for all intents and purposes, superior to Christian nihilism for a number of reasons. Buddhist nihilism is constituted by the 'higher and learned classes'; it does not engage in delusions but is 'quite in accordance with actuality'; it is therefore able to overcome a reliance on the concept of sin in order to '[stand] beyond good and evil'. The superiority of Buddhism is demonstrated in its peaceful overcoming of the concept of sin; it focuses on 'the struggle against suffering' and combats suffering by 'directing even the spiritual interests back to the individual person ... the "one thing needful", the question "how can you get rid of suffering" regulates and circumscribes the entire spiritual diet'.[41] Christianity, on the other hand, is made up of the lower types whose suffering is transformed into resentment, into 'an overwhelming desire to do harm, to discharge an inner tension in hostile actions and ideas'.[42] Buddhism is thus superior insofar as it is self-consciously a 'religion for the end and fatigue of a civilization'[43]; its willingness to will nothingness (which, as we recall, is precisely what the Christian cannot do) is a source of its strength as the culmination and threshold of decadence. But this is also the source of its weakness; the Buddhism of the will is a danger for the 'psychological type of redeemer' because here the willingness to will nothingness becomes fixed as a hyper-egoism[44] rather than undergoing the 'sublime leap' into the affirmation of life. Nonetheless, Jesus, is a kind of '"non-Indian Buddha" that "towers over his time'[45].

The second Dionysian model or figure is that of Odysseus as *polytropos,* whom Nietzsche invokes indirectly in the *Gay Science* (§344) and directly in *Beyond Good and Evil.*[46] Odysseus's ability to adapt and use cunning to achieve his task distinguishes him from all others. In addition to his attribute as 'versatile' and 'much-traveled', Homer calls Odysseus *polymetis,* a man of 'many schemes'.[47] This quality is illustrated beautifully in the Cyclops episode of *The Odyssey,* in which Odysseus defeats and overcomes Polyphemus by calling himself 'Outis' – 'ou' being no or none and 'tis' being thing or body. In this passage, Homer poetically links word and act, cunningly intermixing Odysseus's epithet *metis* and his pseudonym *outis*. What's more, here Homer equates the word 'metis' with the word 'outis', having Polyphemus and his neighbours use 'metis' as a word for 'no one' or 'nobody', which of course is the very meaning of 'outis'.[48] As both *polytropos* and *polymetis,* Odysseus is, in *The Odyssey,* both 'much-traveled', 'versatile' and 'deceptive' as well as mutable, multiplicitous, multiple and in consequence 'no one' ('no one' person).[49]

> The 'man of wit' [polymetis] is the Overman, and the 'multiplicity of figures' [polytropos] erupting from the instant of the cogito's splitting (the shattering of the subject as such) is the Überwindung of the Übermensch, the Overman's very overcoming of the manageable whole that is the subject of man.[50]

In *Beyond Good and Evil*, Nietzsche clearly links the Dionysian task of 'translation back into nature' with the attributes of Odysseus (and also of Oedipus):

> To translate man back into nature ... to see to it that man henceforth stands before man as even today, hardened in the discipline of science, he stands before the rest of nature, with intrepid Oedipus eyes and sealed Odysseus ears,[51] deaf to the Siren songs of the old metaphysical bird catchers who have been piping at him all too long, 'you are more, you are higher, you are of a different origin!' – that may be a strange and insane task, but it is a task.[52]

The important thing to notice here is that the superiority of having 'sealed Odysseus ears' is inextricably linked to the 'task' of translation. What makes Odysseus important is that his attributes as *polytropos* and *polymetis* are not aimless, but rather are in the service of his task of returning home. Throughout *The Odyssey*, Odysseus's journey consistently brings him face-to-face with obstacles that he overcomes through his adaptability and cunningness, but that nonetheless pose themselves as temptations that he must choose to overcome. For example, Odysseus hears the song of the Sirens but is able to resist their seduction because he has been bound to the mast of his ship; likewise, Odysseus rejects Calypso's offer of immortality precisely because he refuses to deviate from his task of returning home. 'All this Odysseus rejects, though he knows that the alternative is to entrust himself again, this time alone and on a makeshift craft, to that sea about which he has no illusions'.[53] Against Calypso's divinity, Odysseus is completely and inherently 'worldly', and this, from a Nietzschean perspective, is his great strength and wisdom.

Given that the Dionysian task does involve the instantiation of a new nomothetic order, how will the potential future philosopher translate and make communicable the encounter with eternity? Does the future philosopher become an 'armed prophet' as Machiavelli urged? Or does he use persuasion like a Platonic philosopher-king? The answer must be that the future philosopher, as *polytropos* as well as a *polymetis*, must use both tactics. As a tempter-attempter (*Versucher*), the philosopher experiments with both 'philosophic' and 'anti-philosophic' innovations that may just as likely fail than succeed. Lampert confirms this point: 'the work of the new philosophers would not be a *Versuch* if it were not an experiment risking failure'.[54] Nietzsche names a variety of qualities that the 'free spirit' – the 'herald and precursor' – possesses: malice, gratefulness, curiosity, investigativeness, inhibition, a sense of acuteness, inventiveness, economy in learning and forgetting and solitariness.[55] Although the new philosopher – that 'very free spirit' – may also share these qualities, its goal differs. Nietzsche directly links the 'Dionysus ideal' to the necessarily theatrical qua dissimulative persona:

> Increase in 'dissimulation' proportionate to the rising order of rank of creatures. It seems to be lacking in the inorganic world – power against power, quite crudely – cunning begins in the organic world; plants are already masters of it. The highest human beings, such as Caesar, Napoleon (Stendhal's remark on him), also the higher races (Italians), the Greeks (Odysseus); a thousandfold craftiness belongs to the essence of the enhancement of man – Problem of the actor. My Dionysus ideal – The perspective of all organic functions, all the strongest instincts of life: the force in all life that wills error; error as the precondition even of thought. Before there is 'thought' there must have been 'invention'; the construction of identical cases, of the appearance of sameness, is more primitive than the knowledge of sameness.[56]

The philosopher of the future is, ultimately, not a philosopher, if by 'philosopher' we mean a subject constituted and unified primarily by its 'self-consciousness'. The philosopher in its dramatization as the Overman is a regenerative force that cannot be confined to the model of 'the individual' but rather can be reconceived as the very activity of self-organization of multiplicity out of which individualization occurs.

The implications this has for the political dimension of Nietzsche's thought are both concrete and immanent. By turning the 'topos' of the political from the activity of a subject conducted in objectifiable 'space–time' (the Kantian *Anchauungen*, 'intuition' of 'space–time') to the 'temporalization' (qua organization) of flux within the local context of bodily reality (body as a quantum reality), the political (as will to power) can be understood as 'a plastic force', 'a force of metamorphosis'.[57] Neither a static picture of 'something' nor even a play between 'things' at all (the politics of 'individuality' or of the 'individual' vs. the politics of the 'collective' or 'community'), politics becomes equated firstly as the organizational energy of *polemos*, of 'becoming' itself, and only secondly as institutional arrangements and ideological competitions. Politics becomes understood as the play of forces that, when harnessed, can cross over various ontological and epistemological levels and scales. 'Great politics' must uphold this fundamental principle of Dionysus.

Postface: The Transmigration of *Homo Natura*

> Nothing is more erroneous than to make of psychical and physical phenomena the two faces, the two revelations of one and the same substance. Nothing is explained thereby: the concept 'substance' is perfectly useless as an explanation. Consciousness in a subsidiary role, almost indifferent, superfluous, perhaps destined to vanish and give way to a perfect automatism–
>
> *WP* 523

> Tim said, 'Goethe wrote Part Two [of Faust] just a year before his death. I remember only one German word from that passage: verdienen. Earns. "Earns his freedom." [...] Perhaps it went, "Verdient seine Freiheit –" [...] "Earns his freedom who daily conquers it – them, freedom and existence – anew." The highest point in German Enlightenment. From which they so tragically fell.'
>
> Philip. K. Dick, *The Transmigration of Timothy Archer*

> We are tired of the human ...
>
> *GM* I, 12

For Nietzsche, the problem of nihilism and its overcoming resides in the memory-making or mnemotechnical operation of the organism which corresponds or perhaps even coincides with its psycho-physiological functions of individuation and individualization. The violence of inscribing singular and collective memory into the animal organism proved to be a technical transformation at the level of human consciousness ('bad conscience') and culture ('slave morality'). Although Nietzsche views the mnemotechnics of nihilism as fundamentally degenerate and ultimately degenerative, he knows that this too must be subject to the law of Dionysus, and so it may nonetheless lead to a large-scale material transformation of life. This is one important context in which Nietzsche's 'great politics' as the 'creation of new values' must be read.

In this study, the eternal recurrence is understood to be the catalyst for the breakdown of the engine of mnemotechnics in the singular human animal that has the possibility of having a collective effect (as the teaching of eternal recurrence). The eternal recurrence, in other words, is the cornerstone of Nietzsche's political ontology or, more precisely, his political physiology. Nietzsche's political physiology has been examined as the pathology of 'great politics', 'eternal recurrence' and 'the philosopher of the future', and read in terms of the three stigmata of political, anti-political and over-political that mark the condition of nihilism. Nihilism, Nietzsche says, is a 'pathological transitional stage'.[1]

What we have found in Nietzsche's thought and in the literature of Philip K. Dick is that in the pathological stage of nihilism, ontological instability is the auto-catalyst[2] for the destruction and creation of new cultural formations. The main conceptual problematic at the heart of Nietzsche's political physiology as outlined in this book is the ontological instability between 'real' and 'illusory' that makes the 'self' a process of subjection to aleatory forces beyond the control of human volition and that, instead, both dissolves and transforms the human organism in fundamental ways, translating it anew. In this process of translation which makes up the activity of the highest type, the 'self' is both played out to its finality and overcome, becoming the battleground for the dramatization and exhaustion of the human animal and its ideals. What Nietzsche and Dick show us, above all, is that 'man', the 'individual', as a 'self' and as a 'subject', is a materialization of nihilism (which is why Zarathustra knows that nihilism is overcome only when man itself is overcome).

The Overman is Overhuman, and it will be the aim of this concluding section to suggest that the Overhuman cannot be conceptualized merely, or even chiefly as an 'individual', but equally, as an operative auto-catalytic multiplicity that is over-individual. The Overhuman must have, above all, this power of translatability, which can be understood as the power of trans-mutability, literally the capacity of the organism to be both 'individual' and 'over-individual' simultaneously. In the pathological condition of nihilism that is the context for both Nietzsche's and Dick's political physiologies, the corrosion of Western ontology is operationalized by the dramatic compossibility of the 'human-all-too-human' and the 'Overhuman'. In Dick's oeuvre, this capacity for sporadic auto-organization, this compossibility, is literally depicted as a fungal property: for example, in *The Three Stigmata of Palmer Eldritch*, the new drug Chew-Z brought by Palmer Eldritch is a fungus that turns out to be the very conduit by which the alien Prox civilization, a lichen life form, propagates itself amongst humans, until it is revealed that, in fact, the drug is the life form. So too in *The Transmigration of Timothy Archer*, as we will see in more detail shortly, the conjunction of human and Overhuman which is embodied in the Eucharist is discovered to be the material and mystical experience that results from the ingestion of the anokhi mushroom.

In both Nietzsche's and Dick's thought, this transmigrational capacity becomes palpable only through the breakdown of the 'normal' mnemotechnical functions of the neurophysiological apparatus of the organism. The reformulation of the relationship between remembering, forgetting and time is a chief preoccupation for Nietzsche and Dick, both of whom suffered from mental illness and incorporated their experiences into their literary and philosophical productions. In a 1965 essay called 'Schizophrenia and the Book of Changes', Dick writes:

> What distinguishes schizophrenic existence from that which the rest of us like to imagine we enjoy is the element of time. The schizophrenic is having it all now, whether he wants it or not; the whole can of film has descended on him, whereas we watch it progress frame by frame. So for him, causality does not exist. Instead, the a-causal connective principle which [quantum physicist] Wolfgang Pauli called Synchronicity is operating in all situations – not merely as one factor at work, as with us. Like a person under LSD, the schizophrenic is engulfed in an endless now. It's not too much fun.[3]

For Nietzsche (and taken up by interpreters such as Pierre Klossowski and Alphonso Lingis), the eternal recurrence is the name for 'the liquidation of the concept of "will"'[4] which is experienced as a phantasm or hallucination, and as 'moment' or 'now', because it cannot be assimilated to the necessary mnemotechnical operations of shared reality. This breakdown, however, is a novelty-generating process, a theatre of subjective production (or *subjectivation*[5]) in which synchronicity replaces causality: 'The incessant metamorphosis: in a brief interval of time you must pass through several individual states. Incessant combat is the means'.[6] According to Klossowski, "in this way, Nietzsche introduces a renewed version of metempsychosis [...] It presumes that an individuality's capacity could never exhaust the differentiated richness of single existence, that is to say, its affective potential. Metempsychosis represents the avatars of an immortal soul. Nietzsche himself says, 'If only we could bear our immortality – that would be the supreme thing'".[7]

The present work will thus conclude with the Dionysian principle, which is found to be a root thought in both Nietzsche and Dick: what was once conceptualized within the terms of a specifically human political animal is made politically fungible as Overhuman, that is as a process of material translation and transmigration. The necessary compossibility between human and Overhuman, as such, is embodied chiefly as a fungal capacity for fungibility,[8] that is to say, as the effective interchangeability between individualizing and complexifying functions of organisms.[9]

So what is it that is translated? What is it that transmigrates? The wording of the question itself presupposes the presence of an anterior thing, or form upon which the process of living in the world can be subjectified, and upon which embodied existence can ascribe and assign identifying marks and properties. Nietzsche has already warned us about the dangers of this kind of thinking:

> 'Subject', 'object', 'attribute' – these distinctions are fabricated and are now imposed as a schematism upon all the apparent facts. The fundamental false observation is that I believe it is I who does something, suffer something, 'have' something, 'have' a quality.[10]

The production of knowledge, in the Western tradition at least, has depended on the presence of this substratum, a discrete, inviolable unit, a basic building block either of thought or of matter.[11] Although it was Aristotle who may have first clearly articulated the metaphysics of the human, we see this propensity developing not just in the idealism of Socrates and Plato, but also in the materialist atomism of Democritus and Leucippus. In the speculative tradition that begins with Pythagoras and continues with Socrates and Plato, the metaphysical elements of the individual soul (*logos, thumos, epithumiai*) constitute the hierarchical principle for the organization of civic life. Much later, Hobbes would physicalize this metaphysical substratum by making it subject to the regulatory functions of organic nature. So for example in Hobbes, the functions and distributions of the body politic are modelled along the mechanics of the abstract individual human body. The 'soul' is where the sovereignty of the individual/social body lies, not in metaphysical terms as we see with the Pythagorean thinkers, but in material terms, as an 'engine', 'an artificial soul [...] giving life and motion to the whole body' (*Leviathan*, Introduction). With Locke, the sovereignty that for Hobbes constituted the animating property of the 'artificial animal' or 'automaton' is re-conceptualized in terms of the rational individual's property of self-ownership. And still later with Kant, sovereignty becomes articulated as the basis for the rational and universal legitimacy of the moral individual, as well as the source for cosmopolitan rights.

In Nietzsche's works too, there are innumerable references to the 'individual' and to the significance of 'individual self-expression': take for example the figure of the warrior-hero in *The Greek State* and *Homer's Contest*, the tragic artist in *The Birth of Tragedy*, the cultural genius and educator in *The Untimely Meditations*, the immoralist of *Human-All-to-Human*, the philosopher-legislator of *Beyond Good and Evil* and so on. Does Nietzsche not mean for these 'types' to be 'individuals' in the most common-sensical meaning of the term?

The issue becomes more complex when we bring in Nietzsche's infamous dictum rejecting the presence of such an 'abstract' substratum:

> The subject: this is the term for our belief in a unity underlying all the different impulses of the highest feeling of reality: we understand this belief as the effect of one cause – we believe so firmly in our belief that for its sake we imagine 'truth', 'reality', substantiality in general. – 'The subject' is the fiction that many similar states in us are the effect of one substratum: but it is we who first created the 'similarity' of these states; our adjusting them and making them similar is the fact, not their similarity (–which ought rather to be denied–).[12]

If the 'subject' is indeed a fiction perhaps because effectively it is really a 'multiplicity', then who is this 'we' that creates this fiction? Is there 'something' beneath this Nietzschean 'self' or 'subject'? As Nietzsche has shown, 'subject-unity' is only a shifting amalgamation of multiplicity that organizes spontaneously, akin to the activity of temporary 'regents at the head of a communality':

> The body and physiology are the starting point: why? – We gain the correct idea of the nature of our subject-unity, namely as regents at the head of a communality (not as 'souls' or 'life forces'), also

> of the dependence of these regents upon the ruled and of an order of rank and division of labor as the conditions that make possible the whole and its parts. In the same way, how living unities continually arise and die and how the 'subject' is not eternal; in the same way, that the struggle expresses itself in obeying and commanding, and that a fluctuating assessment of the limits of power is part of life. The relative ignorance in which the regent is kept concerning individual activities and even disturbances within the communality is among the conditions under which rule can be exercised. In short, we also gain a valuation of not-knowing, of seeing things on a broad scale, of simplification and falsification, of perspectivity. The most important thing, however, is: that we understand that the ruler and his subjects are of the same kind, all feeling, willing, thinking – and that, wherever we see or divine movement in a body, we learn to conclude that there is a subjective, invisible life appertaining to it.[13]

In this passage, subject-unity, the 'sovereignty' of the 'self', is not likened to an individual, but rather to the temporary governance of a multitude. The relationship of ruler and ruled is a matter of a division of labour amongst the multitude that permits temporary 'living unities' to 'continuously arise and die'. More significantly still, Nietzsche suggests that subject-unity is guaranteed only if radical instability exists between ruler and ruled[14]: 'the relative ignorance in which the regent is kept concerning individual activities and even disturbances within the communality is among the conditions under which rule can be exercised'. For Nietzsche, this 'not-knowing' is the core of the governing mechanisms of 'perspectivity', which is the engine of difference and novelty at the heart of 'subject-unity'.

If nihilism is a state in which the secure ontological distinction between 'real' and 'illusory' cannot be made, as Nietzsche had surmised, then the distinction between 'ruler' and 'ruled' becomes entirely a matter of ever-shifting power configurations. The question of 'subject-unity' must become the question of a sovereignty in which the 'head' is placed and displaced over and over again.[15] The 'unity' of the subject is one in which the principle of sovereignty is equated with the capacity for ongoing spontaneous self-destruction qua self-organization (this is what Georges Bataille and André Masson had conceptualized in their diagram of the 'headless' body politic, or l'Acéphale). So while sovereignty itself is inviolable, it is so only because it is a multiplicity that reconfigures itself. As Nietzsche might say, it is nothing other than its activity of overcoming. Sovereignty is thus constituted as the ongoing capacity for individuation, rather than as the substance that makes up the constituted individual. The 'self' in other words is not individual, properly speaking, but radically over-individual. And within the context of the pathological condition of nihilism, the 'individuality' of the 'individual' cannot be given ontological priority over its characterization as 'over-individual'.

What Philip K. Dick shows in his last published novel, *The Transmigration of Timothy Archer,* is that the sovereign individual (in the form of the bounded subject) is the fungibility of individual and over-individual processes. It is in this sense that Dick's story can be seen as an exploration of the transmigration of the human into the Overhuman that occurs as a result of the affirmation of nihilism. This transmigration is specifically fungible and fungal, rather than individual and animal.

Timothy Archer is the Archbishop of the Episcopalian Church of California. When Tim is notified of the discovery of scriptures (the 'Zadokite Documents') found in Israel that confirm the teachings of Christ, but which turn out to be written two centuries before the birth of Jesus, his faith is radically de-stabilized by the implications of this discovery. While the title of the novel would lead us to believe that Tim is the protagonist of the story, it is, in reality, Tim's daughter-in-law, Angel Archer, who recounts the events of Tim's life as flashbacks in a day in her own life. For Angel, Tim's credulity is reduced to the choice between 'belief or the falling away of belief. What is at stake here is belief versus nihilism ... for Tim to lose Christ is for Tim to lose everything'.[16]

Characteristic of Dick's use of subjective chimeras and his careful attention to its ontological and epistemological implications, Angel is dramatized as a version and an inversion of Tim, as a consummate critic of all values. Tim, in contrast, is the epitome of the 'polytropic' man insofar as he is described as the opposite of a dogmatist, someone who, despite his ecclesiastical position of power, has the ability to absorb ideals and ideas counter to his own (leading him to seriously incorporate astrology, occultism and other 'heretical' ideas condemned by the Episcopalian Church). 'He was a man, and he thought of himself that way; not a "man" in the sense of a "male person," but a "man" in the sense of human being who lived in many areas and spread out into a variety of vectors'.[17] 'He must live in an endlessly shifting world. Heraclitus' flux world personified'.[18] But as Dick continues to show, belief turns out to be a poor antidote against nihilism. For both Angel and Tim, the distinction between the two cannot be maintained once and for all. Angel's resistance to all beliefs (her self-declared 'nihilism') does not redeem her, just as Tim's propensity for believing everything does not redeem him. Just as Nietzsche had claimed, when nihilism has become a 'normal' (that is to say, 'pathological') condition, the plurality of possible ideals that can be espoused undercuts the ontological stability of all ideals.

But Tim's loss of faith is recovered when he discovers that the Zadokites were a mushroom cult who used the hallucinogenic properties of fungi and encoded this sacred knowledge in their scriptures (which were now suspected of being the original source for Jesus's teachings). For Tim, the entire revelation of the Eucharist becomes trans-substantiated into the fungal mysteries of immortality:

> The anokhi, Angel; the mushroom. It's there somewhere and that mushroom is Christ. The real Christ, whom Jesus spoke for. Jesus was the messenger of the anokhi which is the true holy power, the true source. I want to see it; I want to find it. It grows in the caves. I know it does.[...]
>
> It is there now. Christ is there now. Christ has the power to break the hold of fate. The only way I'm going to survive is if someone breaks the hold of fate and releases me; otherwise, I will follow Jeff and Kirsten. That's what Christ does; he unseats the ancient planetary powers [...] But if I find what I am after, I will change. I will not be as I am. [...] I am taking a risk but it's worth it. I am willing to take the risk because I may find the anokhi and just knowing that makes it worth it.[19]

Tim goes to the desert alone in search of the mushroom caves, without a map, without water, and eventually dies (though his car is found, his body is not). For Angel, Tim Archer is 'human-all-too-human', a living manifestation of what Nietzsche had identified as a danger for the higher types in the 'pathological' stage of nihilism: 'the act is performed with the idea that it will save you, whereas, in point of fact, it delivers you over to the very doom you wish to evade. Tim knew all this. It didn't help him. But he did his best; he tried'.[20]

In the end, Tim does take the risk; he does change, but not as we may have expected. After Tim's death, Angel meets Bill, the schizophrenic son of her best friend, who suffers from hebephrenia, a form of schizophrenic cognitive impairment in which abstract thought cannot be processed by the neurochemistry of the brain. Bill's ratiocination is limited to the concrete. And yet,

> Bill said, 'I came back to this world. From the next world. Out of compassion. That is what I learned out there in the desert, the Dead

> Sea Desert'. His voice was calm; his face showed a deep calm. 'That is what I found'.
>
> I stared at him.
>
> 'I am Tim Archer', Bill said. 'I have come back from the other side. To those I love'. He smiled a vast and secret smile.[21]

Has Bill gone mad? Or has Tim Archer truly come back from the dead? While we, the reader, might simply suspect that Bill has gone insane, as Angel herself supposes, we are forced to consider the possibility that Tim Archer has somehow transmigrated, that Bill is indeed a transmigration of Tim Archer, for Bill is able to demonstrate patterns of abstraction of which he is incapable and that are characteristic of Tim. The compossiblity of Bill and Tim – B/T – is a concrescence of not just two previously incompatible personas, but also of two incompatible existential modalities, human and Overhuman (or 'alien'), co-existing in one physical body. B/T says:

> About a month after his death, Tim came back to me. I didn't understand what was happening; I couldn't figure it out. Lights and colors and then an alien presence in my mind. Another personality much smarter than me, thinking all sorts of things I never thought. And he knows Greek and Latin and Hebrew, and all about theology [...]
>
> I said, 'You speak of Tim in the third person. So, in point of fact, you do not identify yourself with Tim or as Tim; you are Bill Lundborg talking about Tim'.
>
> 'I am Bill Lundborg', he agreed. 'But also I am Tim Archer.'[22]

The co-incidence of the human, Bill, and an alien presence, Tim, is a dramatization of the immanent completion and overcoming of nihilism. The fungibility between the human-all-too-human and the Overhuman is shown to be the material manifestation of what Nietzsche had called 'the eternal law of transformation'.[23] In this dismantling of the conceptual and moral apparatus of the 'individual', the 'subject' and 'subjectivity' consist in nothing other than this activity of transmigration. 'The subject alone is demonstrable; hypothesis that only subjects exist – that "object" is only a kind of effect produced by a subject upon a subject a modus of the subject'.[24]

The status of the 'subject' undergoes a fundamental mutation in Nietzsche's thought: the 'subject-in-itself' which is the necessary corollary of the 'thing-in-itself' is shown to be untenable, and yet in the exhaustion of the classic subject/object dichotomy, the subject is transformed into 'complexes of events apparently durable in comparison with other complexes',[25] which Nietzsche refuses to conceptualize 'as a "being"' but more 'as a process, a becoming [...] as an affect':[26]

> When one has grasped that the 'subject' is not something that creates effects, but only a fiction, much follows.
>
> It is only after the model of the subject that we have invented the reality of things and projected them into the medley of sensations. If we no longer believe in the effective subject, then belief also disappears in effective things, in reciprocation, cause and effect between those phenomena that we call things.
>
> There also disappears, of course, the world of effective atoms: the assumption of which always depended on the supposition that one needed subjects.
>
> At last, the 'thing-in-itself' also disappears, because this is fundamentally the conception of a 'subject-in-itself'. But we have grasped that the subject is a fiction. The antithesis 'thing-in-itself' and 'appearance' is untenable; with that, however, the concept 'appearance' also disappears.[27]

Nietzsche's Overhuman and its corresponding Dionysian collective vision must be a rejection of an objectifiable substratum which constitutes the 'reality' upon which psycho-physiological life forms are constituted. In terms of the philosophy of the future as outlined herein, the Overhuman is understood to be the material expression of the 'eternal law of transformation'. It is not, however, that there is 'nothing' or a vacuum at the most fundamental level of reality, but rather no 'thing' that could act as a stable substratum. Will to power is a dynamic activity, perhaps best articulated in terms of a Heraclitean ontology of 'flux' which, as energetic activity, intensifies, contracts and thus is able to constitute relations that then emerge in various configurations of force (e.g. meta-stabilities).[28]

Will to power, as such, is the Nietzschean conceptualization of Heraclitean *logos*: it is the energetic activity that is ontologically undefinable, but that must enter into relations of order and rank (and thus defined) in order for life to exist at all. Ordering, for both Heraclitus and Nietzsche, is *morphosis*, and not merely the relations of power between pre-constituted objects. This means that for both Heraclitus and Nietzsche, reality cannot be reducible to a 'thing' and thus the world cannot be explained purely by mechanistic laws. The 'individual' becomes articulated as a concrescence, a field or 'system' that has certain configurations that are standardized, the 'fixity' of which is impermanent, but nonetheless produces large-scale systemic effects: 'When one has grasped to what extent the concept "individual" is an error because every single creature constitutes the entire process in its entire course (not merely "inherited" but the process itself –), then the single creature acquires a tremendously great significance'.[29]

Heraclitus said, '*edisesamen emeouton*, I have searched myself',[30] and he is known to have criticized his illustrious predecessor Pythagoras on this point: Pythagoras practiced scientific enquiry beyond all men,[31] but learning alone does not teach understanding[32] until one has the insight to first take one's 'self' as the object of enquiry.[33] For Heraclitus engaging in the task of self-knowledge is the way of both enquiring and experiencing the fundamental *logos* as it emerges (*physis*).[34] But unlike its later Socratic/Platonic variant, the process of Heraclitean self-knowledge aims for an unmasking of the subjective characteristics that make up the 'self'. If indeed 'nature loves to hide', as Heraclitus says, then as a piece of nature, 'my self is somehow absent, hidden or difficult to find',[35] and as such, every 'form' or 'self' encountered must encrypt a more fundamental internal process or play of formation. The 'self' as an 'encryption' or 'mask' is entirely a Heraclitean idea; for Pythagoras the externalities that exhibit form can and must be understood as proportion (*logos*) of number (*geometron*); for Socrates, all external forms are physical representations of metaphysical forms and therefore transcend nature.

Who or what lies beneath the various masks of 'self'? According to one commentator, one's 'self' or character (ethos) is but a façade. In this reading, the Heraclitean process of self-knowledge would be a kind of 'undoing' of the various *ethoi*, a process of 'self-overcoming' according to the eternal law of transformation (fire is the symbol of this destruction/transformation, or *to pyr*[36]:

> One's character (ethos, in Greek) is merely a façade, a mask, a veil, which gives the stamp of being to a more fundamental – and, what's more, ongoing – process of becoming, the nature (phusis) of which is a division or a distribution (daiomai), for instance the division or distribution – the dynamic force – of all things which catch flame, kindle, blaze and burn (the dynamic force of fire, for Heraclitus the exemple par excellence of phusis) ... Heraclitus discovered a dynamism denied by otherwise Apollonian articulations of identity (ipseity). In his search for himself, in undertaking to understand

> his self-individuation, Heraclitus uncovered a Pythian monster: he discovered, as he said, that ethos anthropoi daimon,[37] that man's true character (ethos) is not 'fixed' but fluid, not 'stable' but serpentine, not 'singular' but multiple (divisive, distributive, daiomai, daimonic).[38]

When Nietzsche hypothesizes 'the subject as multiplicity' (*WP* §490), it is in the context of this Heraclitean notion of 'self-undoing' as a process of 'self-overcoming' that we can begin to understand Nietzsche's claim that everything living is 'will to power'. The 'philosopher' is not a fixed 'type' in that it is neither exclusively a thing with properties nor a figment of the mind to which properties can be temporarily attributed; rather, the 'philosopher' as an expression of the strongest 'will to power' is a generative act(ivity), a process of ordering that takes form in direct correspondence with supra-perceptual nature (*physis*). In *Beyond Good and Evil*, Nietzsche associates this 'generative act(ivity)' with the an internal manifoldness[39] that is also a 'tyrannical drive',[40] and a 'commanding and legislating' 'for the future'.[41]

From the perspective of political physiology, what Nietzsche's search for conceptualizing 'the law of becoming' produced was the concept of 'will to power', an engine of *morphosis*. As William Plank has shown, Nietzsche's intuitions regarding will to power are remarkably consistent with the basic premises of 'dissipative systems' (open systems in which the loss of energy is a catalyst for introducing novelty and thus radical reorganization): 'Nietzsche was the first to see, without mathematics, the implications of the flux which results from the rejection of traditional ontology, an ontology which became irrevocably bound to a morality and local reality'.[42]

After his epiphany at Sils-Maria in late summer of 1881, the eternal recurrence became the central preoccupation of Nietzsche's entire thought. From that moment onwards (and arguably even from the beginning), Nietzsche wanted to understand the world insofar as it undergoes the formality of existing. This deceivingly simple statement, I would venture, could encapsulate the entirety of Nietzsche's 'philosophy of the future', the 'prelude' to which was his *Beyond Good and Evil* in 1886. Having devoted his research to developing a political physiology, the late period of Nietzsche's life seemed to focus on the attempt to articulate a materialist account of *morphogenesis*: existence in its generative and formative activity of 'becoming'. At the heart of this experimental ontology was a desire to expose not a hitherto undiscovered and authentic state of anarchy, but rather the 'real' as a complex and conflictual process of continuous ordering. And in this fundamental sense, Nietzsche's re-articulation of the 'political' is expressed as the organizational complexification of materiality (of bodies, knowledges, power). After all, Dionysus – Nietzsche reminds us – is a legislator.

For Nietzsche, Dionysus is the symbolon of eternal recurrence, of the 'dancing' compossibility of the earthly and the divine, the 'human-all-too-human' and the 'Overhuman'. Dancing Dionysus is thus a symbol for thought (just as the dancing Shiva was a symbol of order and disintegration for Aldous Huxley) insofar as dance symbolizes a 'secret virulence' for Nietzsche, not of thought as an externalization (or 'objectification'), but of thought as 'an immanent intensification'.[43] That affect precedes representational intelligibility becomes emblematic of a kind of initiatory 'undergoing', one that is crucial for the task of 'future philosophers' to 'translate' the human 'back into nature'. This task of translation requires the philosophers of the future to be able to decipher eternity in its formation, which is equal to seeing 'culture' as the temporalizing activity of *physis* and the philosopher as 'translator' of the signs, symptoms and signatures of 'that eternal basic text homo natura'.[44] Nietzsche's philosopher is a physician in this sense, marking both Asclepius – symbolized by the serpent coiled around a staff – as well as the alchemical Ouroboros – the snake eating its own tail – as further intensifications (or manifestations) of Dionysus.

The eternal recurrence is the poison (*das Gift*) and the cure (*die Heilung*) for the ailments of a pathological age. Thus spoke Nietzsche.[45]

Notes

Preface: The Three Stigmata

I am grateful to Dan Mellamphy for this title and for the suggestive correlation of Friedrich Wilhelm Nietzsche and Philip Kindred Dick – a correlation first articulated (after Mellamphy 1998) in an undergraduate course he taught at Western: ENG 2071, "Speculative Fiction I – Science Fiction and the 'Modern Prometheus'".

1. As Alain Jugnon has recently claimed of Nietzsche's thought, Nietzsche's philosophy of life is a theatre of material genesis that goes beyond a mere metaphorical description of movements and of the passions of the 'soul'. As a theatre of material genesis, the operation of 'pathos' is itself identified as the fundamental gesture and movement of living matter. Methodologically, according to Jugnon, this theatrical movement announces its own technique:

   In such a staging of life in which matter and movement are interposed, the central question of each and every aim and framework, of every open window on the real becomes: What is underway? (*Que se passe-t-il?*) Like all spectators, philosophy gazes across a scene and manages to construct, by this movement, the mobility of the dramatic matter itself: like all actors, philosophy surveys the scene, mimes the sentiments, is penetrated by pathos, and attempts to establish by these displacements the very direction (*sens*) of drama' (translation mine), see *Nietzsche et Simondon: Le Théâtre du Vivant* (Editions Dittmar 2010, p. 18).

2. For a snapshot of the current debate in Nietzsche scholarship, see the recent volume, *Nietzsche, Power, and Politics,* eds. Herman W. Siemens and Vasti Roodt (Berlin, De Gruyter: 2008).
3. The term 'political physiology' will no doubt bring to mind the work of John Protevi, who has also been working on this concept specifically in relation to the work of Deleuze and Guattari. Protevi has defined 'political physiology' in the following way: 'It is the study of the construction of "bodies politic," that is, the interlocking of emergent processes that link the patterns, thresholds and triggers of affective and cognitive responses of somatic bodies to the patterns, thresholds and triggers of actions of social bodies'. http:/www.protevi.com/john/Geophilosophy.pdf (2005). See also, J. Protevi, *Political Physics: Deleuze, Derrida and the Body Politic* (2001).
4. Siemens and Roodt, 1, 2.
5. *WP* 47.
6. Deleuze (1983) 41.
7. Deleuze (1983) 3.
8. Hayles, 72.
9. Dick, 167–8.
10. *WP* 485.
11. *WP* 676.

12. Klossowski (1997), 32.
13. Thanks to Keith Ansell-Pearson for pointing out that this term also appears in the unpublished notes as early as 1880–1, sometimes as *Wille nach Macht.*
14. *WP* 4.
15. *WP* 5.
16. In the *Nachlass* notes edited by Keith Ansell-Pearson and Duncan Large, these sections constitute sections 1 and 2 of the 'Lenzer heide' notebook on 'European Nihilism', which Kaufmann's edition unnecessarily breaks up into sections 4, 5, 55 and 114 of *Will to Power*. See *The Nietzsche Reader,* especially pages 385–90.
17. *WP*, 2.
18. *WP* Preface: 3.
19. *WP*, 13.
20. *WP*, 14.
21. *BGE* 208.
22. *WP*, 10.
23. Strauss (1983) 194, 195.
24. Löwith, 58.
25. *WP*, 22.
26. See Dan Mellamphy's designation of Nietzsche as a 'compost-modernist' in *The Compostmodern Condition: T.S. Beckett, Samuel Beckett, and the Pre-Platonic Phusio-Logos* (2008) (unpublished manuscript).
27. *WP*, 23.
28. Deleuze (1983) 42.
29. Nietzsche, 'European Nihilism', aphorism 6, *The Nietzsche Reader*, eds. and trans. Keith Ansell-Pearson and Duncan Large (Oxford: Blackwell Publishing, 2006), 386. Also see *WP* 55.
30. *WP*, 47.
31. 'Questions about a General Pharmacology', keynote address, *New French Thought,* conference in the Department of Philosophy, Villonova University, April 3, 2009.
32. Biswas Mellamphy, 'Corporealizing Thought: Retranslating the Eternal Recurrence Back into Politics', *Nietzsche, Power and Politics,* 760.
33. *WP*, 617.
34. *WP*, 37.

Introduction: The Mnemotechnics of Nihilism and the Political Physiology of Eternal Recurrence

1. *GM* III, 27.
2. *GM* I, 6.
3. I am grateful to Bernard Stiegler for this term. Roundtable Discussion with Bernard Stiegler, 'Trans-individuation, Technology, Politics', *New French Thought* conference, Department of Philosophy, Villanova University, April 3–4, 2009.
4. *GM* II, 16.
5. *Ibid.*
6. *GM* II, i.e. §3, 6; *GM* II, i.e. §16, 17.
7. *GM* II, 3.

8. *GM* III, 28.
9. For a more detailed discussion, see Biswas Mellamphy, 'Corporealizing Thought: Retranslating the Eternal Recurrence Back into Politics,' in Siemens and Roodt (2008) 750–7.
10. Evidence exists in Nietzsche's works to support this view: for example see *WP* §1062–7, in which Nietzsche attempts to argue for the non-teleological (§1062), infinite or cyclical (§1066), goal-less, self-creating and self-destroying play of forces (§1067) of the will to power or quanta of forces in contention that underlies all organic life.
11. 'What [Heraclitus] saw, the teaching of *law in becoming* and *play in necessity*, must be seen from now on in all eternity. He raised the curtain on this greatest of all dramas'. *PTA*, 68.
12. For example, see Bernd Magnus, *Nietzsche's Existential Imperative*; Arthur Danto, *Nietzsche as Philosopher*; Stanley Rosen (1995) attempts to draw parallels between Plato's myth of the reversed cosmos in *Timaeus* and Nietzsche's notion of eternal recurrence. Rosen also notes that for Nietzsche, 'nature' is represented by an amalgamation of the pre-Socratic doctrine of *kinesis* and the doctrine of force (*Kraft*) in modern physics, p. 13.
13. *Nietzsche und Schopenhauer: Ein Vortragszyklus* (Leipzig: Duncker & Humblot, 1907), 250–1. For a comprehensive summary of the cosmological view of the eternal recurrence, Schacht (1983), 253–66.
14. Kaufmann, 236–7.
15. Kaufmann, 418.
16. Schacht (1983) 259.
17. Schacht (1983) 266.
18. Kaufmann, 323.
19. Strauss (1973) 55.
20. Ibid.
21. Appel and Abby, 89.
22. Conway (1997a) 8.
23. Conway (1997a) 103.
24. See Leo Strauss (1983), 'Note to the Plan of *Beyond Good and Evil*'; Laurence Lampert, *Leo Strauss and Nietzsche*. Strauss and Lampert offer readings of Nietzsche that are ultimately cosmological. As Thomas Pangle notes, Strauss's understanding of Nietzsche comes by way of his deep commitment to Heidegger's thought: 'Strauss makes clear once again that for him *the* thinker of our age is Heidegger. It is only in Heidegger's writings that one finds the true justification for the fact that "political philosophy has lost its credibility" and has been replaced by "ideology," "value judgments" or "the view according to which all principles of understanding and of action are history" ... It would seem that in this crucial respect, as in so many others, Heidegger embodies the radicalization of his teacher Nietzsche', p. 25.
25. Here I use 'language' in terms of the descriptive and creative terminology used to designate the affects produced on the 'self' by the conflict of bodily drives and states, and 'language' in its broadest sense, as a system of signs codified culturally, socially, politically, etc. primarily for the purposes of creating and fixing values. It is only through language that the body is made into a 'totality' or 'unity' and can be distinguished as a stable or consistent entity.
26. Gooding-Williams, 117.

27. Gooding-Williams, 104.
28. Gooding-Williams, 102.
29. Gooding-Williams, 118, 119.
30. See the third essay of *Genealogy of Morals* for Nietzsche's elaboration of the ascetic impulse as a history of the body: '*the ascetic ideal springs from the protective instinct of a degenerating life* which tries by all means to sustain itself and to fight for existence; it indicates a partial physiological obstruction and exhaustion against which the deepest instincts of life, which have remained intact, continually struggle with new expedients and devices', §13.
31. Gooding-Williams, 119.
32. See Foucault's understanding of the connection between Klossowski and Nietzsche in 'La Prose d'Actéon' (1964) 444–59.
33. Klossowski (1975) 52–3.
34. Klossowski (1985) 115.
35. Klossowski (1985) 111.
36. Klossowski (1985) 111–2.
37. *WP*, 715.
38. Recalling Nietzsche's dichotomy in *The Birth of Tragedy*, it is in this sense that language is the 'Apollonian' form of 'Dionysian' nature: although he eschews this dichotomy in this later works, the Dionysian comes to encompass the Apollonian principle of form. Aphoristic language becomes the 'forms' taken by eternity, see *TI:* Expeditions of an Untimely Man, §51.
39. Klossowski (1997) 3.

1 The Displaced 'Origin' of Political Physiology

1. For example, he notes that 'culture and state – one should not deceive oneself about this – are antagonists: "*Kultur-Staat*" is merely a modern idea. One lives off the other, one thrives at the expense of the other. All great ages of culture are ages of political decline: what is great culturally has always been unpolitical, even *anti-political*', *TI*: What the Germans Lack, §4.
2. See Keith Ansell-Pearson's *Introduction to Nietzsche as a Political Thinker*, especially 72–6, in which Pearson points to Nietzsche's juxtaposition between the ancient Greeks, who were truly political animals, and the modern egoistic individual, for whom the state is only a means to fulfill self-interest. For a comprehensive study of the significance of Hellenism in Nietzsche's early thought, see Quentin Taylor's *The Republic of Genius: A Reconstruction of Nietzsche's Early Thought*, in which he argues that the young Nietzsche's main objective was to refashion and redefine the German spirit (in contrast to the Reich) in the likeness of Greek antiquity: 'Nietzsche's understanding of the significance of Hellenism for contemporary civilization is concisely stated in the following fragment: "Greek antiquity provides the classical set of examples for the interpretation of our entire culture and its development. It is the means for understanding ourselves, a means for regulating our age – and thereby a means for overcoming it"' (Nietzsche, *The Struggle between Science and Wisdom*, 1875), quoted in Taylor, p. 14, footnote 35. See also, Richard J. White's *Nietzsche and the Problem of Sovereignty* for a study of the influence of ancient Greece on Nietzsche's understanding of the 'sovereign individual'.

3. These categories are almost too broad to be able to say much: wide dissent exists even within each category. The following brief selection of examples is therefore neither comprehensive nor exhaustive. For example, the 'political' readings include the following: Ansell-Pearson, *Introduction to Nietzsche as a Political Thinker* (1994); Appel and Abbey, 'Nietzsche and the Will to Politics' (1998); Berkowitz, *Nietzsche: The Ethics of an Immoralist* (1995); Conway, *Nietzsche and the Political* (1997); Detwiler, *Nietzsche and the Politics of Aristocratic Radicalism* (1978); Honig, *Political Theory and the Displacement of Politics* (1993); McIntyre, *The Sovereignty of Joy* (1997); Owen, *Nietzsche, Politics, Modernity* (1995); Warren, *Nietzsche and Political Thought* (1988). The 'a-political' readings include the following: Blondel, *Nietzsche: The Body and Culture* (1991); Kaufmann, *Nietzsche: Philosopher, Psychologist, Antichrist* (1974); Magnus, *Nietzsche's Existential Imperative* (1978); Nehamas, *Nietzsche: Life as Literature* (1985). For a more contemporary treatment of this spectrum, see Siemens and Roodt (2008).
4. Physiology and the body are continuously mentioned as the starting points to understanding the notion of will to power; see for example *WP* §489–92 and *BGE* §19. Richard Schacht (1983) also argues that the primacy of the body is crucial to understanding the task of Nietzsche's philosophical anthropology, that is, of translating man back into nature, 268–71. Robert Gooding-Williams (2001) stresses that the physical body is the central conduit by which a reinvention of Dionysian culture can occur in modernity: 'Nietzsche seeks the advent of Dionysus not in the German nation, but in the healthy human body', 102.
5. *BGE*, 12.
6. The present argument relies heavily on the role of 'drives and affects' in Nietzsche's understanding of will to power and eternal recurrence. Nietzsche's emphasis on 'psychology' is connected to my elaboration of the 'impulsional body' and bears resemblance, albeit superficial, with the Freudian vocabulary of 'conscious' and 'unconscious' drives. It should therefore be noted that by 'affect' Nietzsche seems to mean a variety of things: affect connotes, for example, 'felt emotions' such as contempt and pity (*WP* §56); as 'capacity' such as will to enjoyment and capacity to command (*WP* §98 and *BGE* §19); as an element of the multiplicity that makes up 'subjectivity' (*WP* §556); as the deeper, hidden source of reality (*BGE* §36) that makes up morality (*BGE* §187); as an element that makes up a 'social' tendencies, archetypes, or structures (*WP* §719); and as a quanta of power (*WP* §1024 and *BGE* §117). Nietzsche also uses 'affect' interchangeably with 'drive' (e.g. *BGE* §36) as that which 'compels toward', such as the 'drive to knowledge' (*BGE* §6); as a compulsion for domination and mastery (*BGE* §158); and as 'passion' and 'energy' (*WP* §26). Given the plethora of interchangeable terms and definitions, I equate 'affect', 'drive', 'impulse', etc. with Nietzsche's understanding of 'will to power' as both the unconscious and non-hierarchical quanta of force that compete for conscious expression and the conscious feeling of emotion that results from the competition, conflict, repression and subsequent hierarchy of these unconscious elements.
7. Spinoza, 128.
8. Spinoza, 131.
9. *WP*, 524.

10 *GS*: Preface, 2.
11. *WP*, 524.
12. For a good selection of Nietzsche's letters describing his ailing health, see Klossowski (1997) 16–22.
13. Klossowski (1997) notes that 'the *Selbst*, for Nietzsche has a double meaning: on the one hand, it is, morally speaking, the *Selbstsucht* (the greediness of the self, which is erroneously translated as 'egoism'), and on the other hand, it is force, unconscious to the cerebral consciousness, which obeys a hidden reason', 32.
14. Conway (1997b) 25.
15. Klossowski (1997) 23.
16. *WP*, 785; Müller-Lauter (1999) 12.
17. Klossowski (1997) 38.
18. Klossowski (1997) 23.
19. Nietzsche alludes to this in *GM* III: 27, 'Here I touch once more on my problem, on *our* problem, my unknown friends (for I do not yet know whether I have any friends among you', and in *BGE* §211, 'Are there such philosophers today? Have there been such philosophers yet? *Must* there not be such philosophers?'
20. Müller-Lauter, 13.
21. *WP*, 490.
22. *BGE*, 6.
23. As Greg Whitlock also suggests, Nietzsche names the pre-Platonics as the discoverers of 'the will to power and of the eternal recurrence', (2001) 157. The other 'Pre-Platonic' thinkers in Nietzsche's lecture series are Anaximenes, Parmenides, Xenophanes, Zeno, Anaxagoras, Empedocles, Leucippus, Democritus, the Pythagoreans and Socrates, see Whitlock (2001); also mentioned in *Philosophy in the Tragic Age*.
24. Ahern, 11; Whitlock, xxxvii.
25. Alberto Toscano, 'The Method of Nature, The Crisis of Critique: The Problem of Individuation in Nietzsche's 1867/69 Notebooks', in *Pli* 11 (2001), 36–61. Also see Alberto Toscano, *The Theatre of Production: Philosophy and Individuation Between Kant and Deleuze* (Palgrave Macmillan, 2006).
26. Toscano (2007) 41.
27. Toscano (2007) 60.
28. Whitlock, 178.
29. The word refers to what can loosely be called 'nature', also meaning 'origin' and 'appearance'. Greek Lexicon, *Liddell-Scott*, http://www.perseus.tufts.edu/cgi-bin/ptext?doc=Perseus%3Atext%3A1999.04.0057%3Aentry%3D%23112721.
30. *PP*, 7.
31. *PP*, 62–3.
32. Minar (1942) 116.
33. Wheelwright (1959) 4.
34. Wheelwright (1959) 31.
35. Heraclitus, Diels's translation, 123.
36. *PP*, 8.
37. *PP*, 8.
38. Wheelwright (1959) 33.
39. The source of the principle of *anthropokosmêsis*, or 'man as universe', is not the epistemological analogy of 'city' and 'soul' employed by Plato, for example, in the *Republic* (Book IV), in which soulcraft and statecraft are

juxtaposed. Rather, the source for the principle of *anthropocosmos* has been traced to the Egyptian tradition of 'sacred geometry' (see René Schwaller 1957, 1963) and can also be found in the cosmic architecture of Thales and Anaximander, which is also traced back to Egyptian sources (Hahn 2003, 73). More than merely a form of analogical reasoning, the principle of *anthropocosmos* takes the human to be homologous with (or a living expression of) the whole (not just representing a partial component of the whole). 'Thus the human being is a living whole in which atoms are as alive as he is himself; they form his material substance and his organic components, which in turn reveal and analyze all the functional aspects of the universe', Schwaller (1985) 159–60.

40. This was expressed perhaps most famously in the mathematical philosophy of Pythagoras of Samos (Minar 1942, 123), although we could also consider Anaximander's theory of human generation from primordial moisture (Naddaf, 14) to be another expression of the ancient materialist homology of matter and man, *kosmos* and/as *anthropos*.
41. 'The doctrine of microcosm is the esoteric foundation of all religious and initiatory expressions. It is a doctrine of the principles and functions of life, the abstract character of which is concretized into the functions of physiological economy, into psychic functions of the emotional complex, into mental man's functions of intelligence [...] [B]etween Cosmic Man, who includes the stellar world, and this incarnate human being called microcosm, a harmonic relation must exist', Schwaller (1985) 164. 'The principle of harmonization can be defined as follows: Disharmony is always destructive. It dissociates the constituent elements of a particular state, whereupon there will be a free reassociation into a new harmonious system by the fact of a *natural* affinity between the elements. Selective *affinity* is the source of harmony', Schwaller (1985) p. 164 and fn. 6. This idea corresponds to the Heraclitean notion of *palitropos/palintonos harmonia*, as well as to interpretations of Klossowski (1997) and Deleuze (1983) of the Nietzschean notion of 'Eternal recurrence' as a 'selective thought'.
42. Minar (1942) 116, 122. Minar notes that '"equality" (*isotes*) was the rallying-cry of democracy in Greek cities. Their universal demand was for the equal and indiscriminate admission of all free citizens to the privileges of office. The Pythagorean system endeavored to meet this demand by demonstrating that in the aristocratic society equality – if a particular kind – actually does prevail. This is the so-called 'geometrical equality, which [...] means that the privileges of each man are related to his worth as those of every other citizen. It follows readily that the better man will have more privileges. Geometrical equality is opposed to the arithmetical, which treats all free men as equal irrespective of innate differences, according to the democratic ideal' (1942) 118.
43. Minar (1942) 123.
44. *PP*, 131–41.
45. Diels's translation, fragment 101.
46. *PP*, 145.
47. *PP*, 7–8.
48. *PP*, 4.
49. See *PP*, Whitlock 156–7.

50. *BGE*, 230.
51. *PP*, 3–4.
52. *PP*, 6.
53. Wheelwright (1966) 42.
54. *PP*, Whitlock 179.
55. *PP*, 5.
56. *PP*, 4.
57. Wheelwright (1959) 42.
58. *PP*, 62.
59. *PP*, 4.
60. In *The Pre-Platonic Philosophers,* Nietzsche omits Thales from the list of 'pure' types to name three definitive philosophical types – Pythagoras, Heraclitus and Socrates – all other figures thereafter being some hybrid version of these three, in terms of speculative principles and subjective disposition. Only these three created (whether intentional or not) a 'new image of the wise (*sophos*)'. One reason that Nietzsche may have had for removing Thales that is consistent with Nietzsche's own criteria is that Thales 'still thought in terms of primitive cosmology' and therefore was not truly original in all regards (see Wheelwright 1966, 9). Nietzsche writes, 'We must designate these *three* as the purest paradigms: Pythagoras, Heraclitus, and Socrates – the wise man as religious reformer; the wise man as proud, solitary searcher after truth; and the wise man as the eternal investigator of all things. All other philosophers are, as representatives of a way of life (*bios*), less pure and original' (*PP*, 58).
61. *PP*, 161.
62. Diels's translation, 51. Etymologically, *palintropos harmonia* would translate as 'back turned unity'; Marcovich translates it as 'back-stretched connexion', M27. '(Men) do not understand how what is being brought apart comes together with itself: there is a "back-stretched connexion" like that of the bow or of the lyre'. Among Heraclitus scholars, there is a discussion as to whether this term should read as *palintropos* or *palintonos*. Marcovich favours the latter for a number of reasons, not the least because *palintonos* was a current epithet of 'the bow', 125.
63. Edizesamen emeouton, 'I have searched for myself', Heraclitus Diels 101; or 'I asked myself', Marcovich 15; or 'I went in search of myself', Kahn 28.
64. *PP*, 62.
65. *EH*: Thus Spoke Zarathustra, 8.
66. See Heraclitus, Diels's translation , D 67, 88, 126.
67. Wheelwright (1959) 32. Wheelwright distinguishes between the Heraclitean and the Aristotelian position on alteration: 'Even if we are concerned with change in its directly perceived character – which is to say, as an alteration of quality, not as a conceptualized movement of molecules – it is still an odd thing for us, and a violation of our linguistic and intellectual habits, to speak of the warm becoming cool, the most becoming dry, and so on'. But if we say instead 'What was warm becomes cool', 'we are no longer burdened with the troublesome of idea of something turning into its own opposite; we have substituted for the paradox the more manageable idea of an unspecified something, a 'what', which can successively wear the attributes of warm and cool in somewhat the same way in which a person might successively wear

different suits of clothes. In forming a conception of change, we find ourselves constrained to think, as Aristotle had demonstrated, not dyadically in terms of two opposites alone, but triadically in terms of the pair of opposites and a substance or substratum or subject or thing in which the opposites are conceived successively to inhere' (Wheelwright 1959, 33).

68. Wheelwright (1959) 34.
69. Heraclitus, Diels's translation 10, 50.
70. *PP*, 63.
71. Heraclitus, D 53, 80; M 28, 29.
72. *WP*, 676.
73. *WP*, 635.
74. Deleuze (1983) 80. For Deleuze's discussion of the three misunderstandings of Nietzsche's philosophy of will to power, see 79–82.
75. Patton (2000) 50.
76. Patton (1993) 153.
77. *TSZ* I: On the Afterwordly; also see Part I: On the Despisers of the Body.
78. 'Nature' is a topic that captured Nietzsche's interest right from the beginning. His first large-scale work, *The Birth of Tragedy,* as well as *The Untimely Meditations,* considers the relationship between culture and nature in ancient Greek tragedy and in the new-formed German nation. The theme of 'translation back into nature', however, occurs only explicitly in Nietzsche's 'mature' works, for example, in *Beyond Good and Evil* and in *Twilight of the Idols*. I rely, as such, mostly on these post-Zarathustran works including *Thus Spoke Zarathustra*. I also make use of Nietzsche's unpublished notes that comprise *Will to Power* because it is often in these notes that Nietzsche offers further precision on what he only explains implicitly in his published texts. For example, Nietzsche's elaboration of the central concepts of will to power and eternal recurrence are outlined at length and more systematically in the unpublished notes than anywhere else in Nietzsche's works (for example, Books 3 and 4 of *Will to Power* connect the themes of eternal recurrence found in *Zarathustra* with the notion of will to power outlined in *Beyond Good and Evil*).
79. *WP*, 719.
80. It must be noted that Nietzsche here seems to use the term 'freedom of the will' to mean what he elsewhere calls 'freedom of spirit'. The conventional usage of the term presupposes the metaphysical grammar of 'self-consciousness', and Nietzsche repeatedly asserts throughout his corpus that 'freedom of the will' as 'free will' is an illusion. Amy Mullin (2000) enumerates some of the functions of the illusion of 'free will': 'Nietzsche suggests that belief in freedom of will has many causes: it flatters our vanity and gives us a feeling of power; it subjects us to the power of priests who encourage us in this belief; ... it is the result of our falsely translating a social or political experience into the metaphysical realm such that strength is taken to equate with freedom of will; and it reflects our misleading grammar' (2000) 388–9.
81. *BGE*, 19.
82. *BGE*, 188.
83. I confine my discussion of Nietzsche's references to 'slavery' to Nietzsche's typological framework. Nietzsche, however, claims outrightly that the culture of the future is an aristocracy and makes allusions to the fact that the

religion of the future necessitates a division of labor that enables the practice of slavery (*BGE* §258). But in his order of castes in *AC* §57, Nietzsche *does not* include the practice of slavery in his discussion of the attributes of the 'chandala' or lowest caste. Nietzsche's references to Manu's Laws in *The Antichrist* suggest that the Dionysian culture of the future is not necessarily divided socio-economically between two classes (for example, ancient Athens) but along the lines of a multi-ordered social stratum (for example, ancient India) that reflects a natural order. Louis Dumont defines 'caste system' as a structure that 'divides the whole society into a large number of hereditary groups, distinguished from one another and connected together by three characteristics: separation ... division of labour ... and hierarchy' (p. 21). For instance, social organization in ancient India was constituted by caste stratification understood as the systematic gradation of authority (Dumont, p. 65): Brahman (priests), Kshatriya (military) and Vaishya (mercantile) and Shudra (servants). Economically and socially, one's employment and social rank corresponded to one's caste stratification: 'the lot of the Shudras is to serve, and ... the Vaishyas are the grazers of cattle and the farmers, the 'purveyors' of sacrifice ... who have been given dominion over the animals, whereas the Brahmans-Kshatriyas have been given dominion over 'all creatures' ... the Kshatriya may order a sacrifice as may the Vaishya, but only the Brahman may perform it. The king is thus deprived of any sacerdotal function' (Dumont, 67–8). Nietzsche's description of caste in *AC* §57 preserves the ancient Vedic hierarchy between Brahman and Kshatriya but conflates the last two castes (the Vaishya and Shudra are conjoined under the 'professional-mediocre' caste). More importantly, however, the comparison with the ancient Vedic stratification is consistent with Nietzsche's claim that the executive muscular types who rule do not have ultimate authority (i.e. have no authority with respect to the giving of law and the sacred).

84. *BGE* §211, 260. Nietzsche claims this type is one who would like to be master over all men, and most of all, over God, *WP* §958.
85. *AC*, 57.
86. *BGE*, 51.
87. *BGE*, 260.
88. *AC*, 57.
89. *BGE*, 260
90. *BGE*, 32.
91. *BGE*, 51.
92. *BGE*, 49.
93. *BT*, 7.
94. *BGE*, 61.
95. Burkert (1985) 161. Nietzsche's employment and understanding of 'Dionysus' changes throughout his writings. Specifically, his dichotomy between the force of Dionysus and that of Apollo is eschewed in his mature works in favour of the dichotomy between Dionysus and the 'Crucified'. Kaufmann thus points to the fact that 'the 'Dionysus' in the Dionysus versus Apollo of Nietzsche's first book and the '*Dionysus versus the Crucified*' in the last line of Nietzsche's last book do not mean the same thing' (p. 129). The later Dionysus, suggests Kaufmann, is a synthesis of the two forces illustrated in the *Birth of Tragedy* and represents the ordering and integration of passion

rather than either the formless frenzy of the early tragic Dionysus or the extirpated passion of Christian asceticism. Conway (1995) contends that in the post-Zarathustran works (namely, *Twilight of the Idols*) the function of the Apollonian is incorporated within the economy of the Dionysian (p. 37).

96. *BGE*, 19; cf. *WP*, 492.

2 The Economic Problem of Production: Nature, Culture, Life

1. For an interesting examination of the concept of 'great politics' (*Grossepolitik*), see Herman Siemens, 'Yes, No, Maybe So ... Nietzsche's Equivocation on the Relation between Democracy and "Grosse Politik"', in Siemens and Roodt, 231–68.
2. *GS* Preface, 2.
3. Foucault (1977) 142.
4. Foucault (1977) 148.
5. Foucault (1977) 149, 150.
6. Foucault (1977) 141.
7. Foucault (1977) 142.
8. *UM* III, 7.
9. Ibid.
10. *BGE*, 203.
11. *UM* III, 3.
12. *UM* III, 3;7.
13. *BGE*, 62.
14. *BGE*, 6.
15. *BGE*, 212.
16. *BGE*, 6.
17. *UM* III, 5.
18. Conway (1995) 35–6.
19. Bataille (1985) 117–19; Conway (1995) 37.
20. Conway (1995) 37.
21. Conway (1995) 46.
22. *BGE*, 9.
23. Bataille's definition of *sovereignty* expresses the relationship between the productivity and utility required of the restricted economy and the necessary overcoming of utilitarian concerns present in the general economy: 'The sovereign, if he is not imaginary, truly enjoys the products of this world – beyond his needs. His sovereignty resides in this. Let us say that the sovereign (or sovereign life) begins when, the necessities ensured, the possibility of life opens up without limits. Conversely, we may call sovereign the enjoyment of possibilities that utility doesn't justify (utility being that whose end is productive activity). Life *beyond utility* the domain of the sovereign', see Bataille (1988) 198. This latter Bataille elsewhere calls 'unproductive expenditure', activities which have no end beyond themselves. Unproductive expenditure, which distinguishes the sovereign life, is primarily characterized by 'a *loss* that must be as great as possible in order for that activity to take on its true meaning'. Among activities located within the general boundless economy of

unproductive expenditure, Bataille includes sacrifice and the archaic practice of 'Potlatch', Bataille (1985) 118, 119, 121.

24. Rather, Bataille (1985) argues that general economies have disappeared (p. 124). For Bataille, although energy is available limitlessly on a cosmological or universal scale, on the human scale, we must account for the quantity of energy we have at our disposal. Nonetheless, we have quantities of energy that we must spend, and this expenditure either takes the form of work (which is recuperable within a restricted economy) or leisure (which is essentially the outlet of eroticism, luxuries and amusements), and which exceeds the limits of what is required for basic necessities: 'of course, what we spend in one category is in principle lost for the others ... We need to make a principle of the fact that sooner or later the sum of excess energy that is managed for us by a labor so great that it limits the share available for erotic purposes will be spend in a catastrophic war. Of course, it would be childish to conclude right away that if we relaxed more and gave the erotic game a larger share of energy the danger of war would decrease. It would decrease only if the easing off occurred in such a way that the world did lose an already precarious equilibrium', Bataille (1993) 187–8.
25. `*BGE*, 258.
26. I rely on the Greek etymological roots of *nomothetic*: *nomos* is translatable as 'law', while *thetikos* is from *thetos* as 'placed', or *tithenai* as 'to put or to place'. As an adjective, *nomothetic* has three meanings: the first, of or relating to lawmaking, legislative; the second, as based on a system of law; and the third, of or relating to the philosophy of law. *Nomothetik[os], nomothetik[ê]* or *nomothetik[on]* also refers to first, of or for a lawgiver or legislation; second, of persons fitted for legislation. Most interesting, however, for its Apollonian resonances is *nomos*, or *nemô*, defined as first, that which is in habitual use, practice or possession; second, as melody or strain; third, of course, in architecture, a course of masonry. All these definitions resonate of the *economic* principle underlying the *nomothetic*, namely the nomothetic as a structural economy. All from Henry George Liddell and Robert Scott, *An Intermediate Greek English Lexicon* (1889).
27. *BGE*, 257.
28. *BGE*, 258.
29. *AC*, 3.
30. Rosen (1995) 25.
31. Deleuze (2001) 66.
32. Deleuze (2001) 91.
33. Alain Badiou from *Les Conférences du Perroquet* 37, December (1992): 15, quoted in Zupančič 2003, 9–10.
34. Deleuze (1994) 8.
35. Deleuze (1994) 9–10.
36. Deleuze (2001) 92.
37. Deleuze (1994) 8.
38. Deleuze (2001) 65–6.
39. *BGE*, 19.
40. From the Latin *magnitudo* 'greatness, bulk, size', from *magnus*, 'great'. http://www.etymonline.com/index.php?search=magnitude&searchmode=none
41. *BGE*, 212.
42. *BGE*, 19.

43. *WP*, 983.
44. *BGE*, 207.
45. *TI*: What I Owe to the Ancients, 1.
46. *TI*: What I Owe to the Ancients, 2.
47. *BGE*, 254.
48. D, 202.
49. *BGE*, 2.
50. *BGE*, 4.
51. Nehamas (1986) 96.
52. *WP*, 1041.
53. Ibid.
54. *BGE*, 39.
55. *BGE*, 227.
56. *BGE*, 61.
57. *WP*, 425.
58. *BGE*, 43.
59. *GS*, 382.

3 The Dynamics of Opposition and the Transformation of the Übermensch

1. Yovel (1986) ix.
2. *TI*, Foreword.
3. Müller-Lauter, xi.
4. Müller-Lauter, 62; cf. Nietzsche, *WP*, 567.
5. *WP*, 540.
6. Müller-Lauter, 64–5.
7. *WP*, 862; cf., Müller-Lauter, 64, 65.
8. *WP*, Preface, 3.
9. *WP*, 1020.
10. Müller-Lauter, 73.
11. Ibid.
12. *WP*, 1026; Müller-Lauter, 73.
13. *WP*, 999.
14. Müller-Lauter, 68.
15. *WP*, 1053.
16. *WP*, 259; cf. *WP*, 967.
17. 'Once and for all, there is a great deal I do *not* want to know. – Wisdom sets bounds even to knowledge', *TI*: Maxims and Arrows, §5. Although Nietzsche uses the term 'wisdom' here, Müller-Lauter calls this a 'wisdom of *limiting* knowledge' that is ultimately grounded in aggrandizing a feeling of *strength*. The wise type's wisdom strives for unlimited knowledge of the world and of the self, see Müller-Lauter, 75.
18. *WP*, 996.
19. Müller-Lauter, 75, 77.
20. Müller-Lauter, 70.
21. Müller-Lauter, 78.
22. Müller-Lauter, 86.

23. Müller-Lauter, 121.
24. *TSZ*, Part I: On the Three Metamorphoses.
25. Müller-Lauter, 77.
26. Strauss (1973) 55.
27. Strauss (1983) 185.
28. Strauss (1983) 189.
29. Strauss (1983) 187–8.
30. Strauss will repeat, summoning Aristotle, that 'man is the not yet fixed, not yet established beast (aph. 62): man becomes natural by acquiring his final, fixed character the nature of a being is its end, its completed state, its peak (Aristotle, *Politics* 1252b)', Strauss (1983) 189.
31. Strauss (1983) 189.
32. Nietzsche in *BGE* 207 warns against confusing the 'objective' mind with the 'complementary' nature of the philosopher. While he claims in this aphorism that 'objectivity' is a welcome escape from 'accursed ipsissimosity', objectivity should not be accepted without caution. In a commentary on this passage, Lampert notes that 'gratitude for the welcome flight into objectivity should not lead us to elevate objectivity unduly: such 'de-selfing, depersonalizing of the mind' should not be celebrated 'as an end in itself, as redemption, as transfiguration'. There does exist, however, that which should be celebrated as each of these three things and the section culminates in a description of this individual ... The great failure of objectivity is its loss of aptitude for subjectivity, accursed though it be. "Know thyself" is lost in the subject's turn to the objective, and such a loss is fatal is psychology is the path to the fundamental problems', Lampert (2001) 189.
33. *BGE*, 207.
34. Ibid.
35. Strauss (1983) 189–90.
36. Strauss (1983) 189.
37. Löwith, 37.
38. Strauss (1983) 190.
39. Strauss (1983) 176.
40. Müller-Lauter implicitly recognizes this dialectical characteristic of negative philosophy: 'What he smashes and what he preserves and accumulates are the same thing. It is smashed in its claim to independent validity; it is preserved as that which can serve the possibility of maintaining power. As accumulation it is to be directed toward the goal of having the Overman establish himself', 80. Furthermore, Daniel Conway explicitly addresses the dialectical character of self-overcoming (*qua Selbsaufhebung* rather than as *Selbsüberwindung*): 'Nietzsche customarily treats the logical process of self-overcoming not only as inexorable – thereby raising, once again, an "offensively Hegelian" stench – but also as natural. "Life" (rather than Hegel's *Geist*) as the ultimate subject of self-overcoming, he charts the transformations that ensue when an "great thing" attempts to constitute itself in accordance with its favoured account of its nature and destiny ... . He thus intends the term *self-overcoming*, despite its undeniably destructive connotation, to convey a sense of generative power and promise', Conway (1997a) 66–7.
41. Strauss (1983) 188.
42. Ibid.

43. Strauss (1983) 189.
44. Strauss (1983) 190.
45. Lampert (1996) 56.
46. Strauss (1983) 176.
47. The symbiosis between future philosophy and future religion thus heals the traditional rift between Athens and Jerusalem, philosophy and religion, that Strauss (1953) in his earlier work calls the *fundamental alternative*: 'The fundamental question, therefore, is whether men can acquire that knowledge of the good without which they cannot guide their lives individually or collectively by the unaided efforts of their natural powers, or whether they are dependent for that knowledge on Divine Revelation. No alternative is more fundamental than this: human guidance or divine guidance. The first possibility is characteristic of philosophy or science in the original sense of the term, the second is presented in the Bible. The dilemma cannot be evaded by any harmonization or synthesis. For both philosophy and the Bible proclaim something as the one thing needful, as the only thing that ultimately counts, and the one thing needful proclaimed in the Bible is the opposite of that proclaimed by philosophy: a life of obedient love versus a life of free insight. In every attempt at harmonization, in every synthesis however impressive, one of the two opposed elements is sacrificed, more or less subtly but in any event surely, to the other: philosophy, which means to be the queen, must be made the handmaid of revelation or vice versa', 74–5.
48. Lampert (1996) 53.
49. Strauss (1983) 194.
50. Strauss (1983) 195.
51. *BGE*, 56.
52. Ibid.
53. Löwith, 58.
54. Löwith, 36, 37.
55. Löwith, 67.
56. Löwith, 53.
57. Löwith, 56.
58. Löwith, 53.
59. Müller-Lauter, 78.
60. *TSZ* I: Zarathustra's Prologue, §4.
61. *TSZ* III, The Wanderer.
62. Löwith, 55.

4 Self-Annihilation and the Metamorphosis of Nihilism

1. Müller-Lauter, 73.
2. *WP*, 259; cf. *WP*, 96.
3. Müller-Lauter, 81.
4. *WP*, 2.
5. *WP*, 3, 8.
6. *BGE*, 211.
7. Löwith, 36.
8. *TI:* How the 'Real World' at Last Became a Myth.

9. *WP*, 585.
10. *AC*, 43.
11. *GM* III, §28. I rely here on the Kaufmann and Hollingdale translation of the German '*Lieber will noch der Mensch* das Nichts *wollen, als* nicht *wollen*'. Golffing, for example, translates this passage as 'man would sooner have the void for his purpose than be void of purpose'.
12. Warren (1982) 43.
13. *BGE*, 229.
14. Ansell-Pearson (1993) 267.
15. *GM* II, 16, 17.
16. Freud argues that the possibility of civilization is only guaranteed by the repression of the natural instincts, and this means that there is always an irremediable antagonism between man's nature and man's culture. The boundary between the principle of conscious self-identity, the Ego, and the unconscious Id, is a 'deceptive' one. Freud remarks that the demands of civilization require this boundary to be maintained, p. 12.
17. *BGE*, 242.
18. Also see aphorism 2 of the 'Lenzer Heide' notebook on 'European Nihilism' in Ansell-Pearson and Large, *The Nietzsche Reader*, 386.
19. *WP*, 585.
20. *GM* III, 27.
21. *WP*, 247.
22. *WP*, 916. cf. *WP*, 247; *TI*: Expeditions, 36; *TSZ* I: On Free Death are some examples.
23. 'Did he himself grasp that, this shrewdest of all self-deceivers? Did he at last say that to himself in the wisdom of his courage for death? ... Socrates wanted to die ... "Socrates is no physician," he said softly to himself; "death alone is a physician here ... Socrates himself has only been a long time sick"', (*TI*: The Problem of Socrates, 12).
24. *WP*, 430.
25. *TI*: The Problem of Socrates, 7.
26. *TI*: The Problem of Socrates, 4.
27. *WP*, 429.
28. *TI*: The Problem of Socrates, 7.
29. *TSZ* IV: The Honey Sacrifice.
30. Kaufmann, 403.
31. 'Would that he had remained in the wilderness and far from the good and the just! Perhaps he would have learned to live and to love the earth – and laughter too'. *TSZ* I: On Free Death. Kaufmann contends that Nietzsche's position concerning the distinction between Jesus and Christ 'is so intimately related to the rest of his thought that his philosophy cannot be fully understood apart from it'. (p. 337). It is clear that Jesus, as the historical individual who rebelled against the 'Jewish church' (*AC* §27), is understood by Nietzsche to be proto-typical of the 'psychology of the Redeemer' (*AC* §28). As an example of a strong type, Jesus was a practitioner of 'real life' (*WP* §166); his message was later reversed by Paul (*WP* §167) and annulled by the church (*WP* §167, 168). Christ or the 'Crucified', on the other hand, is representative of Christian morality, resentment and metaphysical faith. For Nietzsche, Jesus is equated with 'practice' while Christ is equated with the otherworldly

idealism of Christianity. Interestingly, it is Paul, not Jesus, that embodies the opposite of the 'psychological type of redeemer' – Paul 'the genius in hatred, in the vision of hatred, in the inexorable logic of hatred' (*AC* §42). For a detailed exposition of Nietzsche's distinction between Christ, Jesus and Paul, see Kaufmann's chapter 'Nietzsche's Repudiation of Christ', 337–90.

32. *AC*, 53.
33. Crawford, 138.
34. *TSZ* I: On Free Death.
35. Lampert (1986) 71–2.
36. *TSZ* I: Zarathustra's Prologue, 4.
37. Löwith (1997) 36.

5 The Pathology of *Amor Fati*: *Eros* and *Eschaton*

1. Müller-Lauter, 78.
2. Ibid.
3. Bataille (1988) 47.
4. In terms of the Bataillean terminology used earlier, this moment of crisis of the will signals the collapse of the restricted economy which opens onto the revelation of the boundless general economy of nature. If the philosopher's activity within the restricted economy – for example the activity of self-overcoming – is necessarily always limited, then the philosopher must also be able to access a boundless general limitless economy which guarantees and regenerates the limitless continuation of his activity of self-overcoming beyond the requirements of utility or social preservation. The eternal recurrence provides the philosopher with the experience of the boundless general economy of nature.
5. See Hesiod's *Theogony* for a description of the Void (*Chaos*) out of which occurs birth of the greatest of the immortal gods *Eros,* Part II, lines 116–53. Also see the account of the Homeric and Orphic creation myths in Robert Graves's *The Greek Myths*.
6. Löwith, 79.
7. *D*, 68; cf. 'In truth, there was only one Christian, and he died on the cross', *AC*, 39.
8. *AC*, 35.
9. Bataille (1988) 48–9.
10. Klossowski (1997) 56.
11. *WP*, 481.
12. Klossowski (1997) 26, 28.
13. *UM* II, 1; Kaufmann, 145.
14. *WP*, 532.
15. Klossowski (1997) 2
16. Klossowski (1997) 58.
17. Klossowski (1985) 111–12.
18. Klossowski (1985) 115.
19. *WP*, 1050.
20. *BT*, 1.
21. It is well known that Nietzsche reconfigures the relationship between Apollo and Dionysus in his mature works. In his early works, Nietzsche argues

that the Dionysian stretches beyond the limits of intelligibility, beyond the realm of the concept to that of the percepts and affects. The Dionysian expresses itself, in contrast to the Socratic, as an experience of the sublime and the mystical, as a deep-rooted *pessimism* concerning man's omnipotence and omniscience (*BT* §18) in the face of the mysteries of nature. This clear 'cosmological' understanding of Dionysian nature is later re-evaluate by Nietzsche within his anthropological conception of will to power. Therefore, while it is convenient to turn to the early works, we must be cautious in making a direct parallel between the Dionysian outlined in the *Birth of Tragedy* and the Dionysus of the Zarathustran and post-Zarathustran works.

22. *EH, Thus Spoke Zarathustra*, 6.
23. *TSZ* III: The Convalescent, 2.
24. Gooding-Williams, 204.
25. *TSZ* II: On Redemption.
26. *TSZ* II: On Redemption.
27. Gooding-Williams, 215.
28. Gooding-Williams, 279.
29. Gooding-Williams, 296, 297.
30. Altizer, 243.
31. Planck, 386–7.
32. Planck, 392–3.
33. *W*, 719.
34. *WP*, 617.
35. *BGE*, 19.

6 Novum Organum: The Overhuman as the Overmanifold

1. *BGE*, 256.
2. *WP*, 978. cf. *BGE*, 262.
3. *AC*, 57.
4. *BGE*, 241.
5. *AC*, 57.
6. Gooding-Williams, 292.
7. Gooding-Williams, 281.
8. *TSZ* IV: The Welcome.
9. *TSZ* IV: Conversation with the Kings, 1.
10. *BGE*, 212.
11. *TSZ* IV: On the Higher Man, 2.
12. *TSZ* IV: On the Higher Man, 3.
13. *TSZ* IV: On the Higher Man, 14, 15.
14. *TSZ* I: The Welcome.
15. Gooding-Williams, 286.
16. *BGE*, 256; cf. *BGE*, 269.
17. *TI*: Expeditions, 38.
18. *TSZ* I: The Song of Melancholy, 1.
19. *EH*: Thus Spoke Zarathustra, 1.
20. *TI*: Expeditions, 49.
21. *BGE*, 256.

22. *AC*, 32.
23. *WP*, 983.
24. *WP*, 1038.
25. *WP*, 972; cf. *BGE*, 211.
26. *BGE*, 211.
27. *BGE*, 211.
28. *TI*: The Problem of Socrates, 7, 9, 10.
29. *BT*, 14, 15.
30. *TI*: The Problem of Socrates, 8.
31. *WP*, 433.
32. *WP*, 441.
33. *BT*, 15.
34. *TI*: The Problem of Socrates, 10, 11.
35. *WP*, 439.
36. *WP*, 972.
37. See footnote 9, *GS*, 344, 282.
38. *AC*, 32.
39. *AC*, 31.
40. *GM* Preface, 5; cf. *WP*, 240; *BGE*, 202.
41. *AC*, 20, 21.
42. *AC*, 22.
43. *AC*, 22.
44. *AC*, 20.
45. Müller-Lauter, 54; cf. *AC*, 29.
46. *BGE*, 230.
47. Knox, 15.
48. Odysseus's 'outis' is thus the ruse (metis) of 'no one' (nobody) and the ruse (metis) as 'no one' (nobody): the hero here becomes his very epithet. When translated into English, the Greek words 'metis' and 'outis' in this passage are both given as 'nobody', 'none' and/or 'no one'. Let us exemplify with two or three well-known translations (one by Fagles, one by Lattimore and one by Knox). In response to his blinded cries, Polyphemus's neighbours exclaim *'e me tis seu mela broton aekontos elaunei/e me tis s'auton kteinei doloi ee biephin'*, to which Polyphemus replies, *'o philoi, Outis me kteinei doloi oude biephin'*. Fagles's translation reads: *'Surely no one's rustling your flocks against your will – Surely no one's trying to kill you now by fraud or force!'*; *'Nobody, friends'*, Polyphemus bellowed back from his cave, *'Nobody's killing me now by fraud and not by force*!' (1996, p. 224). Lattimore's translation, less accurate with respect to the consistency of the *metis* translation (not to mention the translation of *oude*, which should be rendered as 'and not' and not – pardon the redoubling here [*oude*] – as 'or'), reads as follows: *'Surely no mortal against your will can be driving your sheep off? Surely none can be killing you by force or treachery?'* Then from inside the cave strong Polyphemus answered: *'Good friends, Nobody is killing me by force or treachery'* (1967, p. 147). And Knox's translation, which suffers from the same neglect of the *oude* (replacing this *'and not'* by mere punctuation) and adding a silent 'h' to the nominal no(h)body, reads as follows: *'Sure no man's driving off your flock? No man has tricked you, ruined you?'* Out of the cave, the mammoth Polyphemus roared in answer: *'Nohbody, Nohbody's tricked me, Nohbody's ruined me*!' (1993, pp. 138–9). In his commentary on

uncertainty' as 'the realization that the position and velocity of subatomic particles cannot be known precisely but can only be adduced in terms of probabilities', Heisenberg, 86. The innovations in quantum physics have wide-reaching consequences both in the biological sciences and in the study of consciousness. As discoveries of quantum effects at the sub-cellular levels continue to be made, the insight is that matter appears and behaves 'more like a thought than like the cogs of a machine', Satinover, 7. Two basic propositions arise from this: that thought is material, and matter or reality cannot be reduced to its property of quantifiability. The latest research in quantum neuroscience has now scientifically begun to confirm the Dionysian intuitions articulated by Heraclitus and Nietzsche.

3. Dick (1995) 8.
4. Nietzsche quoted in Klossowski (1997) 69.
5. Or as Alain Badiou has claimed, 'the subject *is* subjectivation' (2003) 81.
6. *KSA*, Vol. 9, p. 520, 11[197], Spring-Fall 1881.
7. Klossowski (1997) 70–1.
8. The word 'fungible' comes from the Medieval Latin *fungibilis*, adjective of the verb *fungi*, 'to perform, carry out'. The past participle of this verb, *functus*, underlies the English 'function'. We know that the root of this word originally meant 'enjoy' – probably used in the sense of 'taking advantage of' – for the same root appears in Sanskrit *bhunkte:* 'enjoys', cf. http://www.alphadictionary.com/goodword/word/fungible. One might here discern the 'joy' ('joyful wisdom') of 'fungi' as a functional (if not fungal) 'interchangeability'. The *synchronicity* (the 'meaningful coincidence') of two different etymologies, that of *fungi* in the sense of *fungibilis* and of *fungi* in the sense of *spongos*, lies at the root (or rather, is the 'spore') of this concluding chapter.
9. From etymonline http://www.etymonline.com/index.php?search=transmigration&searchmode=none.

   1297, from L.L. transmigrationem (nom. transmigratio) 'change of country', noun of action from L. transmigrare 'to wander, to migrate', from trans- 'over' + migrare 'to migrate'. Originally literal, in reference to the removal of the Jews into the Babylonian captivity; general sense of 'passage from one place to another' is attested from 1382; sense of 'passage of the soul after death into another body' first recorded in 1594.
10. *WP*, 549.
11. In the twentieth and twenty-first centuries, the radical questioning of concept of the 'individual' or the 'self' as necessary for the production of knowledge converged around those who were studying the nature of consciousness in relation to the development of intelligent machines. This encompassed those such as Norbert Wiener working under the aegis of 'Cybernetics' and its most successful offshoot 'cognitive neuroscience' (of which the most well-known proponent today is the German philosopher Thomas Metzinger), as well as critics of Cybernetics such as Georges Canguilhem and Gilbert Simondon, whose concepts of 'organology' and 'individuation' revolved around articulating a 'general phenomenology of machines' (under the aegis of which we now have the works of contemporary theorists such as Gilles Deleuze, Bernard Stiegler and Bruno Latour, to name a few).
12. *WP*, 485.
13. *WP*, 492.

14. See Jorge-Luis Borges's 'Lottery in Babylon' as an illustration of this Nietzschean idea.
15. Italo Calvino's short story 'Beheading the Heads' is an illustration of this idea.
16. Dick (1990) 145.
17. Dick (1990) 189.
18. Dick (1990) 204.
19. Dick (1990) 206–7, 209.
20. Dick (1990) 192.
21. Dick (1990) 229.
22. Dick (1990) 232, 233.
23. Nietzsche, *PP*, 62–3.
24. *WP*, 569.
25. *WP*, 552.
26. *WP*, 556.
27. *WP*, 552.
28. *Panta rhei. Everything flows* (H. Kahn 50, 21, D 12, 91; M 40a, 40c). *Reality* is flux and all form is an impermanent auto-organization or auto-configuration of flux (by 'auto-organization', I mean that it is self-mapping but not because it is purely deterministic but rather because indeterminacy itself becomes the generative principle of ordering). Randomness, not organization, is the principle of diversity, differentiation or heterogeneity in the mechanics of a system. Perhaps this is best articulated in Prigogine (Nobel Prize in 1977) and Stengers's definition of systems 'far-from-equilibrium', which was the basis for their revolutionary reinterpretation of the Second Law of Thermodynamics: 'entropy is not merely a downward slide toward disorganization. Under certain conditions, entropy itself becomes the progenitor of order' (*Order Out of Chaos,* xxi). cf. *WP*, 1064; *KSA* 11:35[54], 11:35[55]). 'That a state of equilibrium is never reached proves that it is not possible ... The measure of force (as magnitude) is fixed, but its essence in flux'. 'The ordering, the same for all, no god nor man has made, but it ever was and is and will be: fire everliving, kindled in measures and measures going out' (H. Kahn 37, Diels's translation 30, Marcovich 51).
29. *WP*, 785.
30. Diels's translation, 101.
31. Heraclitus, Diels's translation, 129.
32. Diels, 40.
33. Diels's translation, 116.
34. Kahn's translation, 116.
35. Kahn, 116.
36. Nietzsche, *PP*, 63.
37. Heraclitus, B121, D119, K114, M97, S57, W69.
38. Dan Mellamphy (2008, unpublished manuscript) 4, 5.
39. *BGE*, 19.
40. *BGE*, 12.
41. *BGE*, 211.
42. Plank, xxii.
43. Badiou (2005) 59.
44. *BGE*, 230.
45. *And* Palmer Eldritch ('That's my gift to you', spoke Eldritch – 'and remember: in German, *Gift* means *poison*'; Dick (1975) 171).

Bibliography

I Nietzsche's Works and Key to Abbreviations

PTA (trans. Marianne Cowan), *Philosophy in the Tragic Age of the Greeks* (Chicago: Henry Regnery Company, 1962).
BT (trans. Walter Francis Golffing), *The Birth of Tragedy* (New York: Doubleday Books, 1956).
UM (trans. R. J. Hollingdale), *Untimely Meditations* (Cambridge: Cambridge University Press, 1983).
GS (trans. Walter Kaufmann), *The Gay Science* (New York: Random House, 1974).
TSZ (trans. Walter Kaufmann), *Thus Spoke Zarathustra in The Portable Nietzsche* (New York: Penguin Books, 1982).
BGE (trans. Walter Kaufmann), *Beyond Good and Evil* (New York: Random House, 1966).
GM (trans. Walter Kaufmann), *On the Genealogy of Morals* (New York: Random House, 1967).
TI (trans. R. J. Hollingdale), *Twilight of the Idols* (New York: Penguin Books, 1990).
AC (trans. R. J. Hollingdale), *The Antichrist* (New York: Penguin Books, 1990).
EH (trans. Walter Kaufmann), *Ecce Homo* (New York: Random House, 1967).
PP (trans. Greg Whitlock), *The Pre-Platonic Philosophers* (Chicago: University of Illinois Press, 2001).

II Collected Works

WP (trans. Walter Kaufmann) *The Will to Power* (New York: Random House, 1967).
KSA Nietzsche (eds Giorgio Colli and Mazzino Montinari), *Sämtliche Werke: Kritische Studienausgabe* (Berlin: Walter de Gruyter, 1980), vol. 10.
The Nietzsche Reader, ed. and trans. Keith Ansell-Pearson and Duncan Large (Oxford: Blackwell Publishing, 2006).

III Other Works

Abbey, Ruth and Frederick Appel, 'Nietzsche and the Will to Politics' in *Review of Politics* (Notre Dame: Winter, 1998), volume 60, 83–114.
Altizer, Thomas J. J., 'Eternal Recurrence and Kingdom of God' in *The New Nietzsche*, ed. David B. Allison (Cambridge: MIT Press, 1985), 232–46.
Andrew, Edward G., *The Genealogy of Values: The Aesthetic Economy of Nietzsche and Proust* (Lanham: Rowman and Littlefield Publishers, 1995).
Ansell-Pearson, Keith, Introduction to *Nietzsche as a Political Thinker: The Perfect Nihilist* (Cambridge: Cambridge University Press, 1994).
—— 'The Significance of Michel Foucault's Reading of Nietzsche: *Power, the Subject and Political Theory*', in *Nietzsche: A Critical Reader*, ed. Peter Sedgwick (Oxford: Basil Blackwell, 1995), 13–30.

—— 'Toward the Comedy of Existence: On Nietzsche's New Justice' in *The Fate of the New Nietzsche*, ed. Keith Ansell-Pearson and Howard Caygill (Aldershot: Avebury, 1993), 265–82.

—— *Viroid Life: Perspectives on Nietzsche and the Transhuman Condition* (New York: Routledge, 1997).

Babich, Babette, *Nietzsche's Philosophy of Science: Reflecting Science on the Ground of Art and Life* (Albany: State University of New York Press, 1994).

Badiou, Alain, *St. Paul: The Foundation of Universalism*, trans. Ray Brassier (Stanford: Stanford University Press, 2003).

Badiou, Alain and Alberto Toscano, 'Dance as a Metaphor for Thought' in *Handbook of Inaesthetics* (Stanford: Stanford University Press, 2005), 57–71.

Bataille, Georges, *The Accursed Share*, trans. Robert Hurley (New York: Zone Books, 1988).

—— *Inner Experience*, trans. Leslie Anne Boldt (Albany: SUNY Press, 1988).

—— "The Notion of Expenditure" in *Visions of Excess*, trans. Allan Stoekl (Minneapolis: University of Minnesota Press, 1985), 116–29.

Benjamin, Walter, *The Arcades Project*, trans. Howard Eiland and Kevin McLaughlin (Cambridge: Belknap Press, 1999).

—— 'Theses on the History of Philosophy', in *Illuminations*, trans. Harry Zohn (New York: Schocken Books, 1968).

Berkowitz, Peter, *Nietzsche: The Ethics of an Immoralist* (Cambridge: Harvard University Press, 1995).

Biswas Mellamphy, Nandita, '*Corporealizing Thought:* Retranslating the Eternal recurrence Back Into Politics' in Herman W. Siemans and Vasti Roodt (eds), *Nietzsche, Power, and Politics* (Berlin, De Gruyter: 2008), 741–63.

Blondel, Eric, Nietzsche, *The Body and Culture: Philosophy as a Philological Genealogy*, trans. Sean Hand (Stanford: Stanford University Press, 1991).

Borges, Jorge-Luis, 'The Lottery in Babylon' in *Labyrinths: Selected Stories and Other Writings* (New York: New Directions, 1962), 30–5.

Burkert, Walter, *Greek Religion* (Cambridge: Harvard University Press, 1985).

—— *Lore and Science in Ancient Pythagoreanism* (Cambridge: Harvard University Press, 1972).

Calvino, Italo, 'Beheading the Heads' in *Numbers in the Dark* (New York: Pantheon Books, 1995).

Conway, Daniel, *Nietzsche and the Political* (New York: Routledge, 1997)

—— *Nietzsche's Dangerous Game: Philosophy in the Twilight of the Idols* (New York: Cambridge University Press, 1997).

——'Nietzsche's Götterdämmerung' in *Nietzsche: A Critical Reader*, ed. Peter Sedgwick (Oxford: Basil Blackwell, 1995), 31–52.

Crawford, Claudia, *To Nietzsche: Dionysus, I love you!, Ariadne* (Albany: State University of New York Press, 1995).

Dallmayr, Fred, *Margins of Political Discourse* (New York: SUNY Press, 1989).

Danto, Arthur, *Nietzsche as Philosopher* (New York: Columbia University Press, 1980).

Deleuze, Gilles, *Nietzsche and Philosophy*, trans. Hugh Tomlinson (Chicago: Athlone Press, 1983).

—— *Difference and Repetition*, trans. Paul Patton (New York: Columbia University Press, 1994).

—— *Pure Immanence* (New York: Urzone, 2001).

Détienne, Marcel, and Jean-Pierre Vernant, *Les ruses de l'intelligence: La metis des Grecs* (Paris: Champs Flammarion, 1974).

Derrida, Jacques, *Mémoires d'aveugle: L'autoportrait et autres ruines* (Paris: Éditions de la Réunion des musées nationaux, 1990).

Detwiler, Bruce, *Nietzsche and the Politics of Aristocratic Radicalism* (Chicago: Chicago University Press, 1990).

Dick, Philip K., *The Three Stigmata of Palmer Eldritch* (New York: Manor Books, 1975).

—— 'The Transmigration of Timothy Archer' in *The Valis Trilogy* (New York: The Schaffner Agency, 1990), 6–253.

—— *The Shifting Realities of Philip K. Dick: Selected Literary and Philosophical Writings by Philip K. Dick*, ed. Lawrence Sutin (New York: Vintage Books, 1995).

Dodds, Eric Robertson, *The Greeks and the Irrational* (Berkeley: University of California Press, 1951).

Dombowsky, Don, *Nietzsche's Machiavellian Politics* (London: Palgrave Macmillan, 2004).

Dreyfus, Hubert, 'Heidegger on the Connection Between Art, Technology and Politics' in *The Cambridge Companion to Heidegger*, ed. Charles Guignon (Cambridge: Cambridge University Press, 1993), 289–316.

Dumont, Louis, *Homo Hierarchicus*, trans. Mark Sainsbury, Louis Dumont and Basia Gulati (Chicago: University of Chicago Press, 1980).

Euripides, *Hecuba in Euripides: The Bacchae and Other Plays*, trans. Philip Vellacott (London: Penguin Classics, 1954).

Foucault, Michel, 'La Prose D'Actéon' in *La Nouvelle Revue Française*, March 1964, number 135, 444–59.

—— 'Nietzsche, Genealogy, History' in *Language, Counter-Memory, Practice: Selected Essays and Interviews by Michel Foucault*, ed. Donald F. Bouchard (Ithaca: Cornell University Press, 1977), 139–164.

Freud, Sigmund, *Civilization and Its Discontents*, trans. and ed. James Strachey (New York: W. W. Norton & Company, 1961).

Fulcanelli, *Le Mystère des Cathédrales*, trans. Mary Sworder (Albuquerque: Brotherhood of Life, 1984).

Gooding-Williams, Robert, *Zarathustra's Dionysian Modernism* (Stanford: Stanford University Press, 2001).

Graves, Robert, *The Greek Myths* (London: Penguin Books, 1979).

Guattari, Felix, 'Machine and Structure', in *Molecular Revolution*, trans. R. Sheed and D. Cooper (New York: Penguin 1984).

Hahn, Robert, 'Proportions and Numbers in Anaximander and Early Greek Thought,' in Dirk Couprie, Robert Hahn, Gerard Naddaf (eds), *Anaximander In Context : New Studies In The Origins Of Greek Philosophy* (Albany: SUNY Press, 2003), 78–130.

Han-Pile, Béatrice, 'Nietzsche and Amor Fati', *European Journal of Philosophy*, no.doi:10.1111/j.1468-0378.2009.00380.x (Oxford: Blackwell, 2009), 1–38.

Hayles, N. Katherine, *My Mother was a Computer: Digital Subjects and Literary Texts* (Chicago: University of Chicago Press, 2005).

Heidegger, Martin, *Being and Time*, trans. John Macquarrie and Edward Robinson (New York: Harper and Row, 1962).

—— 'The Question Concerning Technology' in *The Question Concerning Technology and Other Essays*, trans. William Lovitt (New York: Harper, 1977), 3–35.

—— 'The Word of Nietzsche: God is Dead' in *The Question Concerning Technology and Other Essays*, trans. William Lovitt (New York: Harper, 1977), 53–112.

—— *Nietzsche*, ed. David Farrell Krell (New York: Harper & Row, 1987), volume III.

Heisenberg, Werner, 'The Copenhagen Interpretation of Quantum Theory' in *The World Treasury of Physics, Astronomy and Mathematics*, ed. Timothy Ferris (New York: Little, Brown and Company, 1991), 86–96.

Hesiod, *Theogony*, trans. Norman O. Brown (New York: Macmillan, 1953).

Hobbes, Thomas, *Leviathan*, ed. R. Tuck (Cambridge: Cambridge University Press, 1991).

Holy Bible, Revised Standard Edition, ed. Herbert G. May and Bruce M. Metzger (New York: Oxford University Press, 1962).

Homer, *The Odyssey*, trans. Robert Fagles (New York: Viking, 1996).

Homer, *The Odyssey of Homer*, trans. Richmond Lattimore (New York: Harper and Row, 1965).

Honig, Bonnie, *Political Theory and the Displacement of Politics* (New York: Cornell University Press, 1993).

Horkheimer, Max; and Theodor W. Adorno, 'Excursus I: Odysseus or Myth and Enlightenment' in *Dialectic of Enlightenment*, trans. John Cumming (New York: Continuum, 1993), 43–80.

Hutter, Horst, *Shaping the Future: Nietzsche's New Regime of the Soul and its Ascetic Practices* (Maryland: Lexington Books, 2006).

James, Ian, *Pierre Klossowski: The Persistence of a Name* (Oxford: Legenda, 2000).

Jugnon, Alain, *Nietzsche et Simondon: Le théâtre du vivant* (Paris: Editions Dittmar, 2010).

Kafka, Franz, 'The Silence of the Sirens' in *Franz Kafka: The Complete Stories*, ed. Nahum N. Glatzer (New York: Schocken, 1971).

Kahn, Charles, *The Art and Thought of Heraclitus* (Cambridge: Cambridge University Press, 1979).

Kaufmann, Walter, *Nietzsche: Philosopher, Psychologist, Antichrist* (Princeton: Princeton University Press, 1974).

Kerslake, Christian, 'Felix Guattari's Desiring Machines' unpublished manuscript.

Klossowski, Pierre, *Nietzsche et le cercle vicieux* (Paris: Mercure de France, 1975).

—— *Nietzsche and the Vicious Circle*, trans. Daniel W. Smith (Chicago: Chicago University Press, 1997).

—— 'Nietzsche's Experience of the Eternal recurrence' in *The New Nietzsche*, ed. David B. Allison (Cambridge: MIT Press, 1985), 107–20.

Knox, Bernard, 'Introduction' in Homer, *The Odyssey*, trans. Robert Fagles (New York: Viking, 1996).

—— 'The Odyssey' in *The Norton Anthology of Classical Literature*, ed. and trans. Bernard Knox (New York: Norton Books, 1993), 127–43.

Lampert, Laurence, *Leo Strauss and Nietzsche* (Chicago: Chicago University Press, 1996).

—— *Nietzsche's Task: An Interpretation of Beyond Good and Evil* (New Haven: Yale University Press, 2001).

—— *Nietzsche's Teaching* (New Haven: Yale University Press, 1986).

Laruelle, François, *Nietzsche contra Heidegger. Thèses pour une politique nietzschéenne* [Paris: Payot, 1977).

Lemm, Vanessa, *Nietzsche's Animal Philosophy: Culture, Politics and the Animality of the Human Being* (New York: Fordham University Press, 2009).

Lincoln, Bruce, 'Competing Discourses: Rethinking the Prehistory of Mythos and Logos' in *Arethusa* (Baltimore: The Johns Hopkins University Press, 1997), vol. 30, 34167.

Lomax, J. Harvey, *The Paradox of Philosophical Education: Nietzsche's New Nobility and the Eternal Recurrence in Beyond Good and Evil* (Lanham: Lexington Books, 2003).

Löwith, Karl, *Nietzsche's Philosophy of the Eternal Recurrence of the Same*, trans. Harvey Lomax (Berkeley: University of California Press, 1997).

Machiavelli, Niccolo, *Discourses on the First Ten Books of Titus Livius*, ed. and trans. Peter Bondanella and Mark Musa, *The Portable Machiavelli* (New York: Penguin, 1979).

Magnus, Bernd, *Nietzsche's Existential Imperative* (Bloomington: Indiana University Press, 1978).

Marcovich, M, *Heraclitus: Greek Text with a Short Commentary* (Venezuela: The Los Andes University Press, 1967).

Marx, Karl, 'On the Jewish Question' in *The Marx-Engels Reader*, ed. Robert C. Tucker (New York: Norton, 1978), 26–52.

Mauss, Marcel, *The Gift: The Form and Reason for Exchange in Archaic Societies*, trans. W. D. Halls (New York: Routledge, 1990).

McIntyre, Alex, *The Sovereignty of Joy* (Toronto: University of Toronto Press, 1997).

McKenna, Terence, 'Eros and the Eschaton' (lecture, transcribed by Dan Mellamphy), presented June 17–19, 1994 at the *Rim Institute*, Phoenix Arizona.

Mellamphy, Dan, *The Compostmodern Condition: T. S. Eliot, Samuel Beckett, and the Pre-Platonic Phusio-Logos*, unpublished manuscript 2008.

—— '*Fragmentality:* Thinking the Fragment' in *Dalhousie French Studies* (Halifax: Dalhousie University Press, 1998), volume 45, 83–98.

—— 'YOU, the U-Bomb, or *"YOU-Bomb Goes Kabloom"*': An Essay on Anonymity, Risibility and Quantum Subjectivity" in *The Canadian Review of Comparative Literature* (1996), Volume xxiii, 427–55.

—— and Nandita Biswas Mellamphy, 'What's the "Matter" with Materialism?" in *Janus Head: Journal of Interdisciplinary Studies in Literature, Continental Philosophy, Phenomenological Psychology, and the Arts* (Summer 2009), volume 11 number 1, 162–82.

—— and Nandita Biswas Mellamphy, 'PAULITICS' in *Symposium: The Canadian Journal of Continental Philosophy* (Winter 2008), volume 12 number 2, 127–46.

—— and Nandita Biswas Mellamphy, '*In "Descent" Proposal:* Pathologies of Embodiment in Nietzsche, Kafka, and Foucault' in *Foucault Studies* (November 2005), volume 1 number 3, 27–48.

Mellamphy, Ninian, '*Macbeth's Visionary Dagger:* Hallucination or Revelation?' in *English Studies in Canada*, 1978, volume IV, number 4, 379–392.

Minar, Edwin, *Early Pythagorean Politics In Practice And Theory* (Baltimore: Waverley Press, 1942).

Müller-Lauter, Wolfgang, *Nietzsche: His Philosophy of Contradictions and the Contradictions of His Philosophy*, trans. David J. Parent (Chicago: University of Illinois Press, 1999).

Mullin, Amy, 'Nietzsche's Free Spirit', in *Journal of the History of Philosophy* (Berkeley: July 2000), volume 38.3, 383–405.

Nehamas, Alexander, *Nietzsche: Life as Literature* (Cambridge: Harvard University Press, 1985).

—— 'Will to Knowledge, Will to Ignorance, Will to Power in Beyond Good and Evil', in *Nietzsche as Affirmative Thinker: Papers Presented at the Fifth Jerusalem Philosophical Encounter*, ed. Yirmiyahu, Yovel (Dordrecht: Martinus Nijhoff, 1986), 90–108.

Owen, David, *Nietzsche, Politics, Modernity: A Critique of Liberal Reason* (London: Sage Publications, 1995).

Pangle, Thomas L. 'Introduction' in *Leo Strauss, Studies In Platonic Political Philosophy* (Chicago: Chicago University Press, 1983), 1–26.

Patton, Paul, *Deleuze and the Political* (London: Routledge, 2000).

—— 'Politics and the Concept of Power in Hobbes and Nietzsche' in *Nietzsche, Feminism and Political Theory*, ed. Paul Patton (New York: Routledge, 1993), 144–61.

Planck, William, *The Quantum Nietzsche: The Will to Power and the Nature of Dissipative Systems* (Lincoln: Writer's Club Press, 1998).

Plato, *The Republic*, trans. W. H. D. Rouse, in *Great Dialogues of Plato* (New York: New American Library, 1984).

—— *The Apology*, trans. Hugh Tredennick, in *Plato: The Collected Dialogues*, ed. Edith Hamilton and Huntington Cairns (Princeton: Princeton University Press, 1961).

Prigogine, Ilya and Stengers, Isabelle, *Order out of Chaos* (New York: Bantam, 1984).

Protevi, John. *Political Physics: Deleuze, Derrida and the Body Politic* (London: Athlone, 2001).

—— 'Geophilosophy and Political Physiology' (2005), *protevi.com/john/Geophilosophy.pdf.*

Rosen, Stanley, *Masks of Enlightenment* (Cambridge: Cambridge University Press, 1995).

Rousseau, Jean-Jacques, *The Social Contract*, trans. Lowell Blair, in *The Essential Rousseau* (New York: Penguin, 1975).

Satinover, Jeffrey, *The Quantum Brain: The Search for Freedom and the Next Generation of Man* (New York: John Wiley & Sons, 2001).

Schacht, Richard, *Nietzsche* (London: Routledge and Kegan Paul, 1983).

—— 'Nietzsche on Philosophy, Interpretation and Truth', in *Nietzsche as Affirmative Thinker: Papers Presented at the Fifth Jerusalem Philosophical Encounter*, ed. Yovel Yirmiyahu (Dordrecht: Martinus Nijhoff, 1986), 1–19.

Schwaller de Lubicz, R. A. (René Schwaller), *The Temple of Man* (Inner Traditions, 1957).

—— *The Egyptian Miracle* (Inner Traditions, 1985).

Sedgwick, Peter, 'Nietzsche's Institutions' in *Nietzsche: A Critical Reader*, ed. Peter Sedgwick (Oxford: Basil Blackwell, 1995), 1–11.

—— 'Violence, Economy, Temporality', *Nietzsche Studien* (Berlin: Walter de Gruyter, 2005), 163–85.

—— *Nietzsche's Economy* (London: Palgrave Macmillan, 2007).

Shapiro, Gary, *Nietzschean Narratives* (Indiana: Indiana University Press, 1989).

Siemans, Herman W. and Vasti Roodt (eds), *Nietzsche, Power, and Politics* (Berlin, De Gruyter: 2008).

Siemens, Herman, 'Yes, No, Maybe So ... Nietzsche's Equivocation on the Relation Between Democracy and "Grosse Politik"' in Siemens and Roodt (eds), *Nietzsche, Power, and Politics* (Berlin, De Gruyter: 2008), 231–68.

Silk, M. S. and J. P. Stern, *Nietzsche on Tragedy* (Cambridge: Cambridge University Press, 1981).

Spinoza, Benedict, *Ethics*, trans. R. H. M. Elwes (New York: Prometheus Books, 1989).
Stiegler, Barbara, *Nietzsche et la critique de la chair: Dionysos, Ariane, le Christ* (Paris: PUF, 2005).
Stiegler, Bernard, 'Questions About a General Pharmacology', *New French Thought*, keynote speech at Villanova University, April 3–4, 2009.
Strauss, Leo, *Natural Right and History* (Chicago: University of Chicago Press, 1953).
—— 'Note on the Plan of Beyond Good and Evil' in *Studies in Platonic Political Philosophy* (Chicago: University of Chicago Press, 1983), 174–191.
—— *What is Political Philosophy?* (Connecticut: Greenwood Press, 1973).
Strong, Tracy, *Friedrich Nietzsche and the Politics of Transfiguration* (Berkeley: University of California Press, 1975).
Taylor, Quentin, *The Republic of Genius* (New York: University of Rochester Press, 1997).
Toscano, Alberto, "The Method of Nature, The Crisis of Critique" in *Pli* 11 (2001), 36–61.
—— *The Theatre of Production: Philosophy and Individuation Between Kant and Deleuze* (Palgrave Macmillan, 2006).
Warren, Mark, *Nietzsche on Nihilism and Power* (Ph.D dissertation, University of Toronto, 1982), 90–111.
—— *Nietzsche and Political Thought* (Cambridge: MIT Press, 1988).
—— 'Political Readings of Nietzsche' in *Political Theory* (February, 1998), volume 26.1, 90–111.
Wheelwright, Philip, *Heraclitus* (New Jersey: Princeton University Press, 1959).
—— *The Presocratics* (New York: Odyssey Press, 1966).
White, Richard, J., *Nietzsche and the Problem of Sovereignty* (Urbana: University of Illinois Press, 1997).
Yovel, Yirmiyahu, 'Preface' in *Nietzsche as Affirmative Thinker: Papers Presented at the Fifth Jerusalem Philosophical Encounter*, ed. Yovel Yirmiyahu (Dordrecht: Martinus Nijhoff, 1986).
Zupančič, Alenka, *The Shortest Shadow: Nietzsche's Philosophy of the Two* (Cambridge: The MIT Press, 2003).

Index